201123)

From Courtroom to Clinic

Why do present-day mental health professionals practice the way we do? Over the past 50 years, a number of landmark court rulings have changed such basic principles as what material is confidential, how civil commitment and involuntary treatment are conducted, and when a therapist has a duty to protect the public from a dangerous patient. Unlike most legal texts, this volume explores these complex principles through the human stories of the litigants involved.

Peter Ash, MD, is a forensic child and adolescent psychiatrist and a professor of psychiatry at Emory University, where he directs the Psychiatry and Law Service. He is also a past president of the American Academy of Psychiatry and the Law and of the Georgia Psychiatric Physicians Association.

From Courtroom to Clinic

Legal Cases That Changed Mental Health Treatment

Edited by

Peter Ash, MD

Emory University

Group for the Advancement of Psychiatry
Committee on Psychiatry and the Law

CAMBRIDGE
UNIVERSITY PRESS

CAMBRIDGE
UNIVERSITY PRESS

University Printing House, Cambridge CB2 8BS, United Kingdom

One Liberty Plaza, 20th Floor, New York, NY 10006, USA

477 Williamstown Road, Port Melbourne, VIC 3207, Australia

314–321, 3rd Floor, Plot 3, Splendor Forum, Jasola District Centre,
New Delhi – 110025, India

79 Anson Road, #06-04/06, Singapore 079906

Cambridge University Press is part of the University of Cambridge.

It furthers the University's mission by disseminating knowledge in the pursuit of
education, learning, and research at the highest international levels of excellence.

www.cambridge.org
Information on this title: www.cambridge.org/9781108421515
DOI: 10.1017/9781108377171

First published 2019

Printed in the United States of America by Sheridan Books, Inc.

A catalogue record for this publication is available from the British Library.

ISBN 978-1-108-42151-5 Hardback
ISBN 978-1-108-43265-8 Paperback

To our families and colleagues.

Contents

Contributors

Jacob M. Appel, MD, JD
Assistant Professor of Psychiatry, Mount Sinai School of Medicine, New York, NY

Peter Ash, MD
Professor, Department of Psychiatry and Behavioral Sciences; Director, Psychiatry and Law Service, Emory University, Atlanta, GA

Alec Buchanan, PhD, MD, FRCPsych
Associate Professor, Department of Psychiatry, Yale School of Medicine, New Haven, CT

Susan Hatters Friedman, MD
Associate Professor, Departments of Psychiatry and Pediatrics, Case Western Reserve University School of Medicine, Cleveland, OH; Associate Professor of Psychological Medicine, University of Auckland, New Zealand

Deborah Giorgi-Guarnieri, MD
Lead Adult Psychiatrist, Colonial Psychiatric Association; President and Director of Clinical Research, DGG Medical, Inc.; Partner, Forensic Entertainment Productions, Williamsburg, VA

Richard Martinez, MD, MH
Robert D. Miller Professor of Forensic Psychiatry, University of Colorado Denver Medical School, Denver, CO

Alan W. Newman, MD
Chair, Department of Psychiatry, California Pacific Medical Center, San Francisco, CA

Debra A. Pinals, M.D.
Clinical Professor of Psychiatry; Director, Program in Psychiatry, Law, and Ethics, Department of Psychiatry, University of Michigan, Ann Arbor, MI

Phillip J. Resnick, MD
Professor of Psychiatry, Case Western Reserve University; Director, Division of Forensic Psychiatry, University Hospitals of Cleveland, Cleveland, OH

Megan Testa, MD
Assistant Professor, Case Western Reserve University, Cleveland, OH

Preface

When a new court opinion is reported in the news, the focus is on the principle the case establishes. But the court ruling comes in the middle of a story, a story that begins with the individual experiences of the litigants that gave rise to the case, and a story that continues after the holding as the new principle affects others in comparable situations. This book tries to illuminate these richer stories of how eleven landmark court cases in mental health law have affected mental health treatment.

Clinicians trained today may take as givens such principles as confidentiality, informed consent, and the right to refuse treatment, without realizing how these principles developed. Forensic psychiatrists and psychologists – those mental health professionals who testify on mental health issues that come before the courts – and attorneys who work on cases involving mental health issues study the opinions in these cases to learn the principles they establish. But that study is often limited to the principles embodied in the court holdings.

This book arose out of the interest of a group of forensic psychiatrists to learn the stories behind the cases. That group is the Committee on Psychiatry and the Law of the Group for the Advancement of Psychiatry (GAP). Where possible in researching the chapters, the authors spoke with those who were involved in the case: the attorneys, the litigants, and the families who were directly involved.

GAP was founded in 1947 as a think tank for psychiatry. Part of its mission is to "offer an objective, critical perspective on current issues facing psychiatry" and to "shape psychiatric thinking, clinical practice, and mental health programs."[1,2] GAP has approximately 300 members and is organized into working committees tasked with considering particular areas of psychiatry.

The Committee on Psychiatry and the Law is a group of GAP members with a special interest in forensic psychiatry. Each chapter of this book was initially written by a member of the committee, and was then reviewed and discussed by the committee. Finally, each chapter was critically reviewed by the members of the GAP Publication Board. So although each chapter has a listed primary author, each has had extensive input by more than a dozen GAP members.

REFERENCES

1. Group for the Advancement of Psychiatry. Available at: www.ourgap.org Accessed Oct. 4, 2017.
2. Deutsch, A: *The Story of GAP*. New York: *Group for the Advancement of Psychiatry*, 1959, also available at http://gap-dev.s3.amazonaws.com/documents/assets/000/000/292/original/story_of_gap_by_albert_deutsch.pdf?1429593382 Accessed Oct. 4, 2017.

Acknowledgments

We would like to acknowledge the contributions of those lawyers and others who participated in the cases and who shared with us their perspectives on how the cases developed. They added unique perspectives to our work. We also very much appreciate the support of our families through the lengthy process of writing and revising our chapters. Damian Love did an excellent job of preparing the index. Finally, we would like to thank those at Cambridge University Press, especially Sapphire Duveau, David Repetto, Meera Smith, and Isabel Stein for shepherding our work through the publication process.

1   Introduction

Jacob M. Appel

In 1962, the Association of the Bar of the City of New York commissioned a panel of 13 experts – 3 physicians and 10 attorneys – to assess the civil liberties of psychiatric patients in New York State.[1] The committee's more than 300-page assessment is most memorable for one of its conclusions, which it specifically applied to the hospitalization process, but which pertained as well to many aspects of its findings regarding mental health care: "No one represents the patient."[2] That bleak judgment summed up the legal protections afforded to psychiatric patients across the nation. As recently as the early 1960s, most states guaranteed few if any rights to patients with mental disorders. Large state institutions like Bryce Hospital in Tuscaloosa, Alabama, and Central State Hospital in Milledgeville, Georgia, became holding pens of last resort for society's most vulnerable members. Writing of the Alabama facility, where three psychiatrists served 15,000 residents, former United States Attorney Ira Dent wrote:

Anybody who was unwanted was put in Bryce. They had a geriatric ward where people like your and my parents and grandparents were just warehoused because their children did not care to take care of them in the outside world, and probate judges would admit them and commit them to Bryce on a phone call, on a letter from a physician saying that they could not take care of themselves … Bryce had become a mere dumping ground for socially undesirables, for severely mentally ill, profoundly mentally ill people, and for geriatrics.[3]

In many jurisdictions, patients could be committed for indefinite periods of time – without any independent review – on the authority of one psychiatrist. Rules applied to mental patients often stood unchanged from those of an earlier era when "lunatics" and "madmen" were thought to deserve few if any legal rights. At best, caring psychiatrists provided treatment that nearly always valued beneficence and the patient's welfare over autonomy and the patient's wishes. At worst, the system offered no opportunity for patients to challenge significant limitations to their freedom and impositions on their bodily integrity – conditions captured for the public imagination in Ken Kesey's 1962 novel, *One Flew Over the Cuckoo's Nest*.

A similar attitude of benevolent paternalism – "Doctor knows best" – pervaded much of medicine in the middle decades of the 20th century. Many physicians routinely withheld pertinent information regarding diagnosis and treatment from patients. As late as 1961, a survey of Chicago physicians found that only 10% would tell a patient of a terminal cancer diagnosis.[4] When Tennessee Williams depicted this phenomenon in his Pulitzer Prize–winning drama *Cat on a Hot Tin Roof*, the decision to keep a fatal diagnosis secret from the main character and his wife reflected routine medical practice. Patients and their family members often received broad and blanket reassurances designed to garner blind compliance and "spare" the patient further suffering. In a landmark case discussed in Chapter 7 of this book, *Canterbury v. Spence*, a surgeon responded to specific questions about a dangerous procedure with the dismissive remark that the operation was "no more serious than any other operation."[5] One of the authors of this book relates a similar episode: When his wife asked a physician for details about the nature and side effects of a medication in 1960, the provider responded, "I'm the doctor. Just take it."[6] By today's norms, such a response seems both callous and grossly incompatible with informed medical decision-making. At the time, it passed as the standard of care.

Over the next three decades, both medicine and psychiatry changed radically. A generation of young attorneys, veterans of the campaign for African American liberties that culminated in the passage of the Civil Rights Act of 1965, pursued justice for other disenfranchised populations, including the mentally ill. A liberal-minded Supreme Court under Chief Justice Earl Warren, and progressive federal judges like Alabama's Frank Johnson and Spottswood Robinson of the United States Court of Appeals of the D.C. Circuit, approached the authority of institutions and of medical professionals with skeptical eyes, often imposing new and radical doctrines whole-cloth. Most important, individual patients suffering from mental illness courageously sought to make their voices heard and to press from below for systematic reforms. After 15 years confined against his will to a hospital in Florida, Kenneth Donaldson managed to persuade a series of judges, including a unanimous Supreme Court, that his indefinite hospitalization defied the Constitution. In Massachusetts, Ruby Rogers won her fight to require physicians to obtain judicial approval before forcing psychotropic medications on objecting patients. The family of Nancy Cruzan waged a seven-year legal battle to remove her from life support, paving the way for the relatives of other incompetent patients to resist unwanted care. What follows are the stories of these people – the lawyers, judges, and individual litigants who transformed medicine and psychiatry over the past five decades.

This volume has three distinct goals. First, the authors hope that by exploring the origins of contemporary rules and standards through land-mark cases, readers will gain an understanding of why we present-day psychiatrists practice the way we do. Each of these cases is designed to answer specific questions regarding contemporary practice. Five of these cases helped reshape inpatient psychiatric practice. In *Wyatt v. Stickney*, the federal courts laid out minimum standards of care for patients in state-run institutions. Five years later, in *O'Connor v. Donaldson*, the Supreme Court established principles regarding when patients could be retained in such institutions. *Olmstead v. L. C.* clarified when institu-tionalized patients had a right to placement in the community. *Rogers v. Commissioner of Mental Health*, a Massachusetts case that drew national attention, secured judicial review for involuntary treatment decisions. *Parham v. J. R.* addressed aspects of the commitment process unique to children. Four other cases have significant implications for those practicing in both inpatient and outpatient settings. *Tarasoff v. Regents of the University of California* established rules governing a psychiatrist's duty to protect the interests of third parties. *Jaffee v. Redmond* for the first time established a testimonial privilege that ensures the confidentiality of psychotherapy against court interference. *Roy v. Hartogs* publicly confronted the sexual exploitation of the psychiatrist–patient relation-ship by rogue practitioners and led to increased awareness regarding therapeutic boundaries.

We have also included four cases from general medical and pedi-atric practice that have a significant bearing on psychiatric practice. In *Canterbury v. Spence*, a federal appeals court established principles for informed consent that have gained widespread acceptance across the mental health professions. *Cruzan v. Director, Missouri Department of Health*, a high-profile case regarding the right to terminate care, led to the widespread acceptance of advance directives and health care proxies in medical decision-making. Finally, *United States v. Hinckley*, arguably the most widely known of these cases, reshaped public attitudes toward the insanity defense and led to considerable change in laws regarding the criminal responsibility of those with psychiatric illness.

A second purpose of this volume is to explain how these landmark cases shaped the day-to-day practice of psychiatry. The authors make no claim that these are the only important cases shaping current psychiatric practice, or even that they are the most important. Any such determi-nation will prove inherently subjective. However, the authors do believe that these cases have demonstrated a widespread and lasting impact. For example, if you are a second-year resident wondering why you write treatment plans, *Wyatt v. Stickney* offers the answer. If you are a therapist in a private office wondering how to answer a federal subpoena for your process notes, *Jaffee v. Redmond* provides essential guidance regarding your duties and prerogatives. And if you are a psychiatric nurse completing a health care proxy form with a patient, you are likely charged with this responsibility as a result of the Nancy Cruzan case. This is, at its core, a book of questions and answers: How did it happen that we as mental health professionals need to acquire informed consent? Why is civil commitment limited to certain circumstances? When and why do psychiatrists have a duty to protect third parties from danger? Only by studying landmark cases can a provider come to understand the reasons mental health professionals do what we do.

The third purpose of this volume is to share the stories of the men and women behind these landmark cases. Every legal case is also a human story, a deeply personal drama shaped by history, social context, and individual personalities. Unlike law textbooks, which often confine themselves to "the facts of the case," this book strives to explore the distinctive human factors that ultimately shaped the law. Whenever possible, we also follow the lives of the litigants after their encounters with the legal system: Many mental health practitioners, at some point in their careers, wonder what happened to Ricky Wyatt and Kenneth Donaldson and Mary Lu Redmond. We have made every effort to find out.

The authors hope you find these stories informative and inspiring. We also hope you find them as compelling as we have.

REFERENCES

1. Davidson, HA. Review: *Mental Illness and Due Process*. Association of the Bar of the City of New York, *Am J Psychiatry.* 120: 202–3, 1963
2. Association of the Bar of the City of New York with Cornell University Law School. *Mental Illness and Due Process*. Ithaca, NY: Cornell University Press, 1962, p. 20
3. *Wyatt v. Stickney*: A landmark decision. *Alabama Disabilities Advocacy Program Newsletter,* July 2004. Available at: www.adap.net/Wyatt/landmark .pdf Accessed Apr. 30, 2017
4. Oken, D. What to tell cancer patients. A study of medical attitudes. *JAMA.* 175: 1120–8, 1961
5. *Canterbury v. Spence*, 464 F.2d 772 (D.C. Cir. 1972) p. 62
6. Phillip Resnick. Personal communication, Nov. 17, 2012

Raising American Standards in the
       Treatment of Persons with Mental Illness
       Wyatt v. Stickney (1972)

Susan Hatters Friedman

What services do psychiatric inpatients have the right to receive? Why do mental health professionals have to write treatment plans for their patients? Should patients have a right to meet members of the opposite sex? Make telephone calls?

A city in the western central region of Alabama, Tuscaloosa is home of the University of Alabama and is currently the state's fifth-largest city. In the early 1900s, Tuscaloosa grew because of both the university and its mental health facilities. Manufacturing plants arrived in the second half of the 20th century. Tuscaloosa is now a regional center for healthcare, industry, commerce, and education.

Now known as Bryce Hospital, the oldest and largest psychiatric facility in Alabama opened in Tuscaloosa in 1861. Over time, its formal names included Alabama State Hospital for the Insane and the Alabama Insane Hospital. It was designed using the Kirkbride model of "moral architecture" concept,[1] an idea that the building structures themselves can be curative. The hospital was the first building in the city with gas lighting and central heating. The hospital was renamed for Dr. Peter Bryce, its first superintendent. Bryce, then age 27, was originally from South Carolina, but had trained in Europe. He demanded that patients be treated with respect; in fact by 1882, the use of restraints had been abandoned at Bryce. In the late 19th century, Bryce's commitment to scientific treatments was recognized throughout the United States. Little distinction was made between the mentally retarded and the mentally ill.[1] Patients were engaged in farm work as part of their therapy, work that paid most of the expenses of the institution.

During the 1930s, standards of care fell abysmally,[1] not just not in Alabama, but throughout the nation. In a 1958 address to the American Psychiatric Association (APA), its president, Harry Solomon, noted that 545,000 people were institutionalized in nonfederal public mental institutions when there was a capacity of only 520,000 beds. Of these, 85,000 beds were considered unacceptable on the basis of fire and health hazards.[2] Solomon admonished that state mental hospitals were "bank-rupt beyond remedy."[3]

In 1970, Alabama had the lowest per capita spending for mental health of any state.[4] In that year, a cigarette tax was cut, proceeds of which had been allocated to mental health treatment. Because of the budget cuts, 100 Bryce hospital employees were let go, including 20 professionals.[5] For the 5,000 patients, there were 17 physicians, 12 psychologists, 12 nurses, 13 social workers, 12 activity workers, and 900 aides.[6] Only 3 physicians, 1 psychologist and 2 social workers were involved in direct care.[6] Subsequently, there was 1 physician for each 350 patients, 1 nurse for every 250 patients, and 1 psychiatrist per 1,700 patients.[5] Psychologists from the University of Alabama had attempted to file suit on behalf of workers, but were denied.[5] At least 5,000 patients were living in inhumane conditions, which the editor of the *Montgomery Adviser* had likened to a concentration camp.[5]

A former U.S. attorney who worked on the *Wyatt* case, Ira DeMent, who later became a judge, observed:

Anybody who was unwanted was put in Bryce. They had a geriatric ward where people like your and my parents and grandparents were just warehoused because their children did not care to take care of them in the outside world, and pro-bate judges would admit them and commit them to Bryce on a phone call, on a letter from a physician saying that they could not take care of themselves. They were not mentally ill. Bryce had become a mere dumping ground for socially undesirables, for severely mentally ill, profoundly mentally ill people, and for geriatrics ... There was one ward with nothing on it but old people. Beds were touching one another and they were simply warehoused. There was a cemetery in the back, but no records. Someone would die – they would merely dump them in an unmarked grave and that was the end of it and no accountability, supervision, no investigation to determine the cause of death – nothing. (Ref. 5, p. 2)

In 1960, Morton Birnbaum, himself both an attorney and a physi-cian, published a seminal article that called for "the recognition and enforcement of the legal right of a mentally ill inmate of a public mental institution to adequate medical treatment for his mental illness" (Ref. 7, p. 499) and for courts to query whether "the institutionalized men-tally ill person receives adequate medical treatment so that he may regain his health, and therefore his liberty, as soon as possible" (Ref. 7, p. 502). Birnbaum's right-to-treatment argument was constitu-tional: "Substantive due process of law does not allow a mentally ill person who has committed no crime to be deprived of his liberty by indef-initely institutionalizing him in a mental prison" (Ref. 7, pp. 502–503).

Birnbaum argued that involuntarily committed psychiatric patients were essentially prisoners in the state psychiatric hospitals. Yet they were not receiving even adequate psychiatric treatment and were often held for years with minimal hope of recovery.[7] He argued that courts should recognize a right to treatment so that the loss of liberty due to mental illness requiring hospitalization would entitle treatment.[7] Dr. Birnbaum wrote that civilly committed patients had a legal right to treatment that would give "a realistic opportunity to be cured or improve [their] mental condition." Otherwise, they should be able to "obtain [their] release at will in spite of the existence or severity of [their] mental illness" (Ref. 7, p. 503). Of note, 50 journals refused to publish Birnbaum's article prior to its acceptance by the American Bar Association.[2]

The Boy before the Case

Ricky Wyatt was born in Tuscaloosa in 1954 and was 15 years old when the case was filed.[8] He was delivered by Dr. Partlow, the doctor who, he said, "delivered our family" (Ref. 8, p. 25). He was raised by his great-grandmother. He explained that his mother "was unable to take care of me because she got in trouble. We have always been close and we still are, but she just couldn't be here for me when I was young" (Ref. 8, p. 25). When his great-grandmother became too elderly to care for him, his aunt Mildred Rawlins became his guardian.

Ricky often played on the Bryce Hospital grounds as a child; his aunt was an employee there. In fact, over 50 members of his family worked at Bryce between 1927 and 1982. As he observed: "I have more memories of family members coming here to pick up paychecks than I do of my time here as a patient."[8] His great-great-grandfather made ice at Bryce in its first ice house. His grandmother worked there as a dietician. His aunt Mildred (who helped him file the lawsuit) was a nurse's aide. His cousin Jackie worked in the psychiatric department. Other aunts worked as nurses or in food services.[8] As he later put it: "It's like my whole family history is tied up here. I just never knew how tied up I myself would become with this place."[8]

In his later childhood, Wyatt was sent to the Industrial School in Birmingham because of conduct issues. He recalled, "Eventually they sent me back to Tuscaloosa, but I stayed in trouble and got sent away again. Nothing real bad, I was just a hell-raiser like a lot of young boys. I mean, I broke some windows or something" (Ref. 8, p. 25). He was subsequently sent to Selma to live in the Methodist Children's Home. While there, he excelled at basketball and was mentored by boys from the local high school. In 2009, Wyatt reflected: "That Methodist Home was a great place, looking back on it. I just didn't realize it at the time. Unfortunately, I kept getting in trouble and they decided to let the state take me so I came back to Tuscaloosa. My Aunt Mildred already had her hands full so she decided the best thing she could do was to put me into Bryce" (Ref. 8, p. 25).

At age 14, Ricky was committed to Bryce Hospital, 1 of 5,000 patients. He recalled that within two hours of meeting up with Mr. Upchurch, his probation officer, he was committed.[8] Reflecting on his hospitalization decades later, Ricky Wyatt explained that he was the youngest patient at Bryce "by far … I'd say the next person was maybe ten years older than I was. I never had a diagnosis or anything. I didn't have mental illness. I was even a pretty good student. I was just a little wild and didn't have much supervision."[8]

Initially, he recalled being "scared to death."[8] He was admitted to a ward where many other patients were "very delusional … They didn't know who they were and they weren't getting any care. They were basically being fed and medicated. That's about it."[8] He was treated with the first-generation antipsychotic agent chlorpromazine. He believed that this was "because it was simple and easy … That was the easiest way to take care of all those people, just zone them out on meds. But I was really young, and I didn't even have a diagnosis. I knew what was happening, and I at least had my family around. They would come see me and I always said the same thing to every one of them: 'Get me out of here!'"[8]

Wyatt stated that the hospital employees on his ward were often cruel. Patients would be locked up so that staff could play card games uninterrupted. In order to wake the patients, they would throw hot water on them or poke them with brooms. Staff would "make people fight so they could bet on the winners."[8]

What Led to the Case

Ricky Wyatt's aunt Mildred, his guardian, who was working on the hospital's geriatric unit, came to visit him one night.[8] He made a plea for her to help him get off the ward. His aunt returned with her daughter (his cousin Jackie) and Dr. Walpole. Ricky told Dr. Walpole about the intolerable conditions on his ward. As Wyatt recalled decades later: "I told him I had no reason to lie to him.… He just told me to try and remember what all was going on back here, and he would see what he could do."[8]

A month later, Ricky was called to Dr. Walpole's office, where his cousin and an attorney were also present. It was decided that a lawsuit would be filed about the conditions at Bryce hospital. Mr. Wyatt recalled that his attorney "asked me if I knew what I was doing to file such a complaint that could lead to a large lawsuit. And I told him I did know what I was doing. That was the end of that as far as I knew."[8]

Bringing the case was contextually related to massive hospital layoffs after the loss of cigarette tax money. The Bryce psychology department initially organized the lawsuit under another name, so that jobs might be reinstated, with Ricky Wyatt involved so that the point could be made that treatment of patients was poor as a result of the layoffs. As Carol Stickney noted, "The suit by the psychologists was lost at the federal level, but rumor has it that as they were leaving the courtroom that Frank Johnson [the judge] mused that they were missing the big picture; that being incarcerated against their will, the patients had the right to adequate care."[9]

Is there a constitutional minimum requirement for adequate treatment of involuntarily committed patients? Two overarching themes of the lawsuit are: (1) the right to treatment; and (2) deinstitutionalization of the mentally ill into the least restrictive treatment option.

Legal Course

On October 23, 1970, a class action lawsuit was filed in federal court,[4] alleging that involuntarily committed patients hospitalized at Bryce were being denied treatment, in violation of their civil rights. This was related to the recent layoff of staff at the state-run facility.[4] The defendants in the lawsuit were the Alabama Department of Mental Health and Commissioner Dr. Stonewall Stickney, who himself agreed that patients were not receiving adequate care.[9]

During the trial, Ricky Wyatt and his aunt both testified. Ricky explained that he slept on wet floors and was locked in a room with the only light coming from slats in the door. He was threatened with electroconvulsive therapy (ECT). His aunt spoke of how heavily Ricky was medicated. She would not consent to him receiving ECT.[5]

Uniquely in the *Wyatt* case, the hospital staff agreed that patients should have the requested rights.[2,9] There were extreme examples of abysmal conditions presented at trial. For example, there was no fire safety equipment; a patient had been restrained in a straitjacket for nine years in order to prevent thumb sucking; and a third patient had ingested the contents of 40 unlocked medication bottles and died. Another had had a garden hose inserted into his rectum, which ruptured his spleen and caused death when it was turned on. Yet another had been scalded to death.[5,10]

In congressional hearings, Albert Deutsch, an American journalist, testified about his investigations of state hospitals:

Some physicians I interviewed frankly admitted that the animals of nearby piggeries were better housed, fed and treated than many of the patients on their wards. I saw hundreds of sick people shackled, strapped, straitjacketed, and bound to their beds. I saw mental patients forced to eat meals with their hands because there were not enough spoons and other tableware to go around – not because they couldn't be trusted to eat like humans … I found evidence of physical brutality, but that paled into insignificance when compared with the excruciating suffering stemming from prolonged, enforced idleness, herd-like crowding, lack of privacy, depersonalization, and the overall atmosphere of neglect. The fault lay … with the general community that not only tolerated but enforced these subhuman conditions through financial penury, ignorance, fear and indifference. (Constitutional Rights of the Mentally Ill, Hearings Before the Senate Subcommittee on Constitutional Rights of the Judiciary on 87th Cong., 2nd Sess. [1961], as cited in Ref. 11)

George Dean and Jack Drake, the Alabama attorneys representing Wyatt, based their argument on Birnbaum's "right to treatment" concept.[6,12] Birnbaum himself was both original plaintiff co-counsel and helped coordinate the *amicus curiae* (literally "friend of the court") parties.[2] Birnbaum was an advocate for services for the mentally ill. Civil libertarians who sought to eliminate state hospitals were also involved in the case. Bruce Ennis, who worked at the New York American Civil Liberties Union as Director of the Mental Patients Rights Project,[13] became plaintiff co-counsel. Initially, he had not wanted the right to treatment to be the central issue.[12] Ennis is quoted in a 1974 interview as saying: "I was afraid if they [lawsuits based on the right to treatment] were successful … it would become a legitimizing stamp on involuntary confinement, another basis for depriving people of their liberty."[12] An obvious conflict in strategy occurred because of a concern that improvements in hospitals could make further involuntary commitments more justifiable. A compromise was reached when the civil libertarians realized that civil commitment was unlikely to be abandoned, but that requiring the state to provide more services to civilly committed patients would be tantamount to discouraging unneeded commitments.[2] Thus Ennis noted that if the standards were set so high as to make them difficult to meet, then the right to treatment would act "as the best method for deinstitutionalizing thousands of persons."[12]

Amicus curiae briefs entered by the American Orthopsychiatric Association, the American Psychological Association, the American Civil Liberties Union, and the American Association of Mental Deficiency offered proposed standards for treatment to help guide the court's decision-making. The court held formal hearings and invited comment by a broad array of professional organizations. Expert testimony was presented in support of these proposals.[11] Several top experts in mental health testified, including Dr. Karl Menninger,[9] who had co-founded the renowned Menninger Clinic. Of note, the American Psychiatric Association did not enter an *amicus* brief in the district court case. Standards were set that would not be to the liking of psychiatry.

Federal District Court Judge Frank Minis Johnson, Jr., was serving by appointment of President Eisenhower and had the distinction of being the youngest federal judge in the country.[14] He has been described as a judge's judge, who was known to speak his mind from the federal bench. An Alabama native and decorated World War II veteran who had practiced as an attorney in Montgomery, Johnson had made landmark rulings in the American Civil Rights movement to end Southern segregation of schools, buses, and libraries and to enforce voting rights. He was "the most hated man in Alabama" to the Ku Klux Klan, according to his obituary in 1999.

On March 12, 1971, Judge Johnson ruled that Wyatt and other involuntarily committed patients had the constitutional right to receive individual treatment that would give them a realistic opportunity of improving their condition. He reasoned:

The purpose of involuntary hospitalization for treatment purposes is treatment and not mere custodial care or punishment. This is the only justification from a constitutional standpoint, that allows civil commitments to [a state hospital] ... There can be no legal (or moral) justification for the State of Alabama's failing to afford treatment – and adequate treatment from a medical standpoint – to the several thousand patients who have been civilly committed to Bryce for treatment purposes. To deprive any citizen of his or her liberty upon the altruistic theory that the confinement is for humane therapeutic reasons and then fail to provide adequate treatment violates the very fundamentals of due process. [Ref. 10, pp. 784–785]

(Due process of law is required by the Fourteenth Amendment to the U.S. Constitution.) The state of Alabama were given six months to implement a new treatment program to fulfill appropriate standards.

On August 22, 1971, mentally retarded patients were also added to the suit, as were two other inpatient treatment facilities.[5] Thus the hearings expanded to include not only Bryce patients, but all patients in state mental institutions in Alabama. On December 10, 1971, after further expert testimony, Judge Johnson found that the treatment program at Bryce Hospital was lacking in a humane environment, sufficient numbers of qualified staff, and individualized treatment plans.[5] Meetings were held in Atlanta in January 1972, with both parties to define standards for minimally adequate mental health treatment.[5]

On April 13, 1972, Judge Johnson made his historic ruling that established minimal constitutional standards for treatment of the mentally ill and mentally retarded in Alabama. Subsequently, the court ordered "medical and constitutional minimums ... mandatory for a constitutionally acceptable minimum treatment program" [Ref. 10, p. 376]. Importantly, a failure to comply with these minimums could not be justified by lack of funding. A human rights committee would oversee the changes in Alabama.

These minimum standards included: (1) humane physical and psychological environments under the least restrictive conditions necessary; (2) qualified staff in numbers sufficient to administer treatment; and (3) individualized treatment plans. The thirty-five minimum standards included not only psychiatric/medical treatment and staffing, but also numbers of chaplains, dieticians, and maintenance workers, as well as nutrition, safety code, and environmental standards.

Included in the requirement for a humane environment were the patient's right to dignity and privacy, visitation, telephone use, sending and receiving mail, and opportunities for interaction with members of the opposite sex. The rights to religious worship, to exercise, and to be outdoors daily were accorded patients. They required one toilet and lavatory for each six residents which, they specified, "shall be clean and free of odor." The hospital day rooms were to be over 40 square feet per patient and "shall be attractive and adequately furnished with reading lamps, tables, chairs, television, radio and other recreational facilities ... [and] shall have outside windows." Showers (one per each eight patients), heating, air conditioning (with permissible indoor temperatures from 68 to 83 degrees Fahrenheit only), and dishwashing (at 180 degrees) were laid out. Even what information would be included in the medical record was spelled out. Patients had a right to be free from excessive or unnecessary medications, and from restraint or seclusion except in emergencies, which could only be declared by psychiatrists, psychologists, social workers or experienced nurses. "Electric shock" (a reference to ECT) was "considered a research technique" and was not to be used except in "extraordinary circumstances" under the direct order of the superintendent. Patients also had a right to not be subjected to experimental research without informed consent.

Dr. Birnbaum noted that the decision would lead to the discharge of many patients because of the state's overwhelming financial problems. He realized that if state hospital patients were eligible for Medicaid benefits, then Alabama would have four times the money it currently had available to spend on mental health.[12] The other attorneys did not participate in challenging the constitutionality of Medicaid legislation excluding mental hospital patients from benefits because of the attorneys' competing interests in deinstitutionalization. Birnbaum therefore left the *Wyatt* case in order to challenge the Medicaid exclusion, but was unsuccessful in this.[12]

In *Wyatt v. Stickney*, the court took on a recalcitrant state government. Though Governor George Wallace and the Alabama Mental Health Board appealed Judge Johnson's ruling, the fifth U.S. Circuit Court of Appeals upheld the decision.[4,6] Birnbaum noted that although the court accepted standards from the *amici curiae*, it rejected a higher set of standards recommended by Dr. Jack Ewalt, Chairman of the Department of Psychiatry of Harvard Medical School.[2] However, the Alabama mental health department did not have sufficient funds to improve the facilities and was unable to attract more physicians.[6]

In 1974, Dr. Stickney published an article describing the attempts of the mental health department to meet standards set by the court.[15] In addition to the standards at Bryce being nearly impossible to meet, Dr. Stickney suggested that these standards were too restrictive to serve the patients' best interests.[15] In 1977, Dr. Philip Leaf from Yale published an article that examined the extent to which the standards had been achieved at Bryce Hospital and described issues arising from attempting to meet them.[16] Of patients released from Bryce in 1972–1973, most lived with family members and the majority had not been readmitted to a state psychiatric hospital by 1975–1976.

By June 1977, a federal court office began to monitor compliance with the standards.[4] This was related to information from two sources: Paul Davis, a journalist who reported on physical abuse, and patient rights committees.[6] By 1980, the Department of Mental Health and the Department of Mental Retardation of the State of Alabama were placed in receivership under Governor Forrest James.[4,6] A decade after the initial decision by Judge Johnson in 1972, the case was scheduled for a hearing in 1983. Between 1972 and 1983, substantial changes had occurred at both the state and national levels. At that time, issues again being considered included financial and care issues.[17]

In 1986, a consent decree was reached that all state facilities should be required to achieve Joint Commission on the Accreditation of Healthcare Organizations (JCAHO) accreditation and Medicaid certification. The decree also required that there be progress in discharging patients, a consumer advocacy system, and quality assurance with outside agents.[4,6]

In 1995, another lengthy trial was held, with Judge Myron Thompson presiding. The department was found to be compliant with only one-third of the standards.[4] By 1999, the consent decree was dissolved, and in 2000, a new three-year settlement agreement began.[6] In Alabama, the mental health commissioner created work groups to develop compliance plans whose goals included decreasing the institutionalized hospital population, expanding community services, and improving placement of special groups in the community.[4]

On Friday December 5, 2003, the Wyatt case was finally dismissed by Judge Myron Thompson after a fairness hearing at which Governor Bob Riley and mental health commissioner Kathy Sawyer both testified.[1,4] During the hearing, presentations were given regarding a joint motion from plaintiff and defense indicating compliance. Several mental health consumers objected in the hearing.[4]

In giving his verdict, Judge Thompson stated: "The principles of humane treatment embodied in the *Wyatt* settlement are not only a part of the fabric of the law in this state but in the nation. No one judge can terminate *Wyatt*. I can enter an order terminating the litigation. But I can't enter an order terminating *Wyatt*. That is beyond my power."[4] He added: "The enormity of what this case has accomplished cannot be overstated. The principles of humane treatment of people with mental illness and mental retardation embodied in this litigation have become part of the fabric of law in this country, and indeed, international law."[1] On this historic day, the governor of Alabama observed that "we do not look at the end of the case as a diminishment of our responsibilities, but as more responsibility we have to shoulder ourselves."[4] Alabama's mental health commissioner Kathy Sawyer said, "*Wyatt* has brought about many positive reforms in the public mental health system. Over 95% of Alabama citizens with mental illness and mental retardation are now served in community settings rather than in state institutions. Because of *Wyatt*, people with mental disabilities now have the right to personally prescribed health care plans and the dignity and freedom to experience recovery through community-based services."[4]

Impact on Practice

The *Wyatt v. Stickney* case was in litigation from 1970 to 2003, the longest-running mental health lawsuit in America's history.[4] Those 33 years included the terms of nine governors and fourteen different mental health commissioners in Alabama.[4] An estimated $15 million was spent on its litigation.[4]

When *Wyatt v. Stickney* was filed in Alabama in 1970, 8,000 people lived in mental health hospitals and 2,200 in mental retardation facilities, and under 15,000 received community-based treatment.[4] At the time, Alabama was ranked last in the nation in per capita expenditures for mental health and mental retardation.[5] Inpatient expenditure was only 50 cents per patient per day for food, and $6 total per day, compared with the $15 national average.[6] By 2003, fewer than 1,500 patients were in state institutions, with 110,000 receiving community-based care.[4] There were fewer than 400 patients at Bryce in 2004.[1]

One unintended outcome of *Wyatt* was budgetary waste. In an attempt to follow the order, improvements were done on many old buildings, which were subsequently abandoned as patients were deinstitutionalized.[12] Those who remained as inpatients found improved staff-to-patient ratios and hospital facilities.[12] However, it has been argued that staffing ratios were more about the reputation of the professions rather than about patients' needs.[12] The decision led to new barriers to the use of ECT and a ban on nontherapeutic patient labor.[12] A subsequent case, *Wyatt v. Hardin* (1974, revised 1992) set standards regarding the use of ECT as well as requirements before an inpatient could be sterilized in Alabama.[1] Alabama was under federal monitoring from 1979 through 2003.

Rouse v. Cameron, 373 F.2d 451 (1966), has been described as "the spiritual predecessor of *Wyatt*."[11] In *Rouse*, the United States Court of Appeals District of Columbia Circuit (headed by Judge Bazelon) recognized a statutory right to treatment under the D.C. mental health act after a patient from St. Elizabeth's Hospital who had been adjudicated insane for a crime brought a *habeas corpus* petition. This was the first appellate court recognition of a right to treatment. The court reasoned that "the purpose of involuntary hospitalization is treatment, not punishment." When a person was deprived of liberty because of needing treatment, but not provided with treatment such deprivation was "tantamount to a denial of due process."[11] The hospital needed to show a "*bona fide* effort" to "cure or improve" insanity acquittees. Furthermore, programming needed to suit the individual patient's needs. Though the findings of *Rouse* may seem like common sense now, they were nonetheless criticized sharply by the American Psychiatric Association for interfering with medical practice, which noted: "The definition of treatment and the appraisal of its adequacy are matters for medical determination" (Ref. 11, p. 240).

Wyatt v. Stickney and *Jackson v. Indiana* were cases that spurred the new area of "mental disability law."[11] In *Jackson v. Indiana*, the Supreme Court found that the State could not constitutionally indefinitely commit a pretrial defendant who was incompetent to stand trial; the nature and duration of the commitment must be reasonably related to the rationale for the commitment. Because *Wyatt* was a district court decision rather than a decision of an appellate court or the Supreme Court, it did not set a legal precedent. Similar cases were litigated elsewhere including in Ohio (*Davis v. Watkins*).[18] However, *Wyatt v. Stickney* had a significant impact on mental health law because many state legislatures adopted its requirements, which had been previously unheard of from a legal perspective. The minimum standards for the treatment of individuals with mental illness and mental retardation described in the case have been emulated throughout the nation. Unable to meet the standards, many states have released psychiatric patients.

Many forces led to deinstitutionalization, among them legal cases such as *Wyatt*, newer antipsychotic medications, and financial issues. Custodial care was no longer considered adequate.[19] Across the United States, many states had difficulty meeting the inpatient standards articulated in *Wyatt*, including individualized treatment and increased staffing. States felt pressure to decrease the number of state hospital beds.[19]

Aftermath

Judge Frank M. Johnson, Jr., died in 1999 at the age of 80, before the *Wyatt* case finally concluded. Former Alabama Governor George Wallace made a number of verbal attacks on the judge, calling him a "scalawagging ... integrating liar."[20] In his obituary in *Time*, Johnson was described as an "uncompromising federal judge from Alabama whose rulings invigorated the civil rights movement." The magazine noted that "Johnson always insisted he was simply upholding 'the supremacy of the law.'"[20] The Montgomery, Alabama, Federal Courthouse is named in his honor.

Bruce Ennis and other attorneys working on the case, including Charles Halpern, Paul Friedman, and Margaret Ewing, formed the Mental Health Law Project, which later became known as the Bazelon Center in Washington, D.C. Ennis served as chairman of the board for many years.[12,13] He went on to work on the *O'Connor v. Donaldson* treatment case reviewed elsewhere in this volume and was involved in 250 U.S. Supreme Court cases, including mental health rights and freedom of expression cases. Ennis died of leukemia in 2000.[13]

Morton Birnbaum, the scholar who first suggested a "right to treatment," went on to work on the *Donaldson* case, which ran from the early 1960s until it reached the Supreme Court in 1975.[2,13] He died of a stroke in 2005 at age 79. In his obituary, the *New York Times* called him a "champion of the mentally ill."[21]

Dr. Stonewall Stickney died in Mobile Infirmary in 1996 after suffering a stroke at the age of 72. He has been referred to as "the defendant who got famous for siding with the plaintiff" for his contributions to this mental health rights case.[22] Dr. Stickney had written a column entitled "Ask Dr. Salvoin" in the Mobile *Harbinger* for almost a decade prior to his death. The *Harbinger* noted that he had "entertained us with his wonderful story-telling ... [and his] sage analyses of the human condition ... proffered with humor and humility."[23]

Ricky Wyatt narrated that "as a result [of the lawsuit], I got moved into the Token Economy Ward, where you were rewarded with tokens for good behavior."[8] His probation officer and mentor Mr. Upchurch alerted Bryce staff that Ricky was supposed to be receiving an education while at the hospital. Although he did not attend school, he was assigned a new counselor[8] and was eventually moved from the Token Ward to an open ward, where he had freedom to come and go. He received his GED (General Equivalency Degree for completing the equivalent of high school work) at age 16, and subsequently progressed to attending rehabilitation for seven hours a day before advancing to a halfway house. However, he explained that, "I wanted to go to mechanic school and they wanted me to become a janitor, so I just said forget it. For that I got sent back to Bryce."[8] Ricky was placed on a substance abuse ward where his cousin worked, though he did not drink or use drugs. He has said that while there he focused on anger management.[8]

Wyatt entered rehabilitation in Montgomery. Compared to Bryce Hospital, he noted: "That place was nice. To me it seemed like a resort."[8] While in Montgomery, he worked various jobs, primarily as a motel desk clerk. He briefly "ran off with a girl" who was also a patient there. After the relationship ended, he returned to Tuscaloosa. Thereafter, he remained out of the state mental health hospital system.[8] He also found work in Florida. After falling from a ladder on a painting job, he required a walker.[24]

Reflecting on the landmark case in 2009, Wyatt observed: "I had a genuine feeling that these people, these patients who were basically helpless, were tortured in their minds and they still had to put up with these horrible conditions. I didn't know of course that it would turn into such a big thing. I just wanted relief for myself and for all these people I saw who needed relief."[8] He continued to have a working relationship with attorney James Tucker, who worked with him on the settlement of his landmark case.[8]

With a plan of completion by 2020, Alabama is working on building a new hospital at Bryce. As Wyatt explained, "Bryce Hospital and the preservation of its grounds and buildings are important to me. ... This has all been a big part of my life. I grew up here. It hasn't all been good. Being a patient here certainly wasn't. But it's my family heritage. It's part of who I am."[8] He added: "I want Bryce preserved and remembered for the patients who spent their lives here and all the people who worked their whole lives and retired here." In commenting on the restoration of the old hospital, he said: "But if we build a museum don't let it look like a fancy spa. Show the different treatments that have been used, good and bad. Show how the patients really lived in the tough times. And they were tough. But show the good side, too. The people who worked hard and tried to do good. There are lots of them."[8]

Ricky Wyatt died in 2011 at the age of 57. His *New York Times* obituary indicated that he lived his final years in a trailer next to his mother's home in Alabama.[24] The Tuscaloosa newspaper's tribute quoted Alabama Disabilities Advocacy Program's attorney James Tucker, who said: "Ricky Wyatt will be remembered because people who never knew his name lived better lives because he stood up for what's right so many years ago."[25]

In sum, Wyatt's lawsuit changed the face of institutionalization of the mentally ill in America forever. Referred to by Perlin as "the most important case finding a constitutional right to treatment ... without doubt,"[11] the 1971 landmark case ultimately helped lead to deinstitutionalization of millions of Americans who were either mentally ill or intellectually disabled, leading the nation from warehousing the mentally ill to more community-based outpatient treatment programs.

NOTE

I wish to thank Mrs. Carol Stickney; Frank Hickman, Esq.; Judge Steve Leifman; and Rebecca Birnbaum, MD, for their insights on this chapter.

REFERENCES

1. Alabama Department of Mental Health & Mental Retardation: The Legacy of Wyatt: The road to self-determination—the past, the present and the future. Dec. 5, 2003. Available at: www.mnddc.org/parallels2/one/video/Legacy_of_Wyatt_Transcript.pdf Accessed Jan. 29, 2018

2. Birnbaum R: My father's advocacy for a right to treatment. *J Am Acad Psychiatry Law.* 38: 115–23, 2010

3. Solomon H: Presidential Address: the American Psychiatric Association in relation to American psychiatry. *Am J Psychiatry.* 115: 1–9, 1958 as cited in: Perlin ML. "May you stay forever young": Robert Sadoff and the history of mental disability law. *J Am Acad Psychiatry Law.* 33: 236–44, 2005

4. Ziegler JC: Historic Wyatt case ends. MDMR. Press release. Dec. 8, 2003. Retrieved from: www.mh.state.al.us/admin/downloads/MediaCenter Documents/PR_31208_HistoricWyattCaseEnds.asp Accessed Oct. 31, 2010

5. Carr LW: Wyatt v. Stickney: A landmark decision. *Alabama Disabilities Advocacy Program Newsletter.* July 2004, 1–3

6. Belcher DJ: Wyatt v. Stickney. *Encyclopedia of Alabama.* 2010. Available at: www.encyclopediaofalabama.org/face/Article.jsp?id=h-2375 Accessed Jan. 29, 2018
7. Birnbaum M: The right to treatment. *ABAJ.* 46: 499–505, 1960
8. Davis S, Alabama Department of Mental Health Office of Consumer Relations: Ricky Wyatt. *Listen.* 14 (3): 25–7. Winter 2009. Available at: www .mh.alabama.gov/brycehospitalproject/History/RickyWyatt.pdf and also at www.mnddc.org/parallels2/pdf/00s/09-listen-bryce.pdf Accessed Jan. 28, 2018
9. Stickney C: Wyatt v. Stickney: 'Let's go mama, there's nothing but a bunch of damn fools in here.' *The Harbinger,* Apr. 10, 2001. Available at: www .theharbinger.org/xix/010410/stickney.html Accessed Jan. 29, 2018
10. *Wyatt v. Stickney,* 325 F. Supp. 781,785 (M.D. Ala. 1971), Suppl., 334 F. Supp. 1341 (M.D., Ala. 1972), 344 F. Supp. 373 (M.D. Ala. 1972), 344 F. Supp. 387 (M.D. Ala. 1972)
11. Perlin ML: "May you stay forever young": Robert Sadoff and the history of mental disability law. *J Am Acad Psychiatry Law.* 33:236–44, 2005
12. Treatment Advocacy Center: Wyatt v. Stickney. 2009. Retrieved from: www.treatmentadvocacycenter.org/index.php?option=com_content& task=view&id=345. Accessed Oct. 31, 2010. [no longer available.]
13. Bersoff DN: Bruce J. Ennis: A remembrance. *Law & Human Behavior.* 25(6): 663–65, 2001
14. Peltason JW: *Fifty-eight Lonely Men: Southern Federal Judges and School Desegregation.* Urbana, IL: University of Illinois Press, 1971
15. Stickney S: Problems in implementing the right to treatment in Alabama: The Wyatt v. Stickney case. *Hosp Community Psychiatry.* 25: 453–60, 1974
16. Leaf P: Wyatt v. Stickney: Assessing the impact in Alabama. *Hosp Community Psychiatry.* 28: 351–6, 1977
17. Marchetti AG: Wyatt v. Stickney: a historical perspective. *Appl Res Ment Retard.* 4(3): 189–206, 1983
18. *Davis v. Watkins.* 384 F. Supp. 1196 (1974) United States District Court, N. D. Ohio 1974, W. D.
19. Cautilli J: Behavior analysis and the treatment of schizophrenia: an alternative to Wong's (2006) view of the political economy. *Behavior and Social Issues,* 16: 221–25, 2007
20. August M, Barovick H, DeLeon A, et al.: Milestones. *Time Magazine,* Aug. 2, 1999. Available at: www.time.com/time/magazine/article/0,9171,991651,00 .html Accessed Oct. 31, 2010
21. Potts M: Morton Birnbaum, 79, Champion of the mentally ill dies. *New York Times,* Dec. 14, 2005 Available at: www.nytimes.com/2005/12/14/nyregion/ 14birnbaum.html Accessed Jan. 30, 2018
22. Personal communication with Carol Stickney, Oct. 29, 2011
23. Tsang E: Farewell, Dr. Stonewall B. Stickney. *The Harbinger,* Mar. 26, 1996. Available at: www.theharbinger.org/salvo/960326.html Accessed Jan. 29, 2018

24. Martin D: Ricky J. Wyatt, 57, dies: led mental care suit. *New York Times*, Nov. 4, 2011, p. A21. Available at: www.nytimes.com/2011/11/04/health/ ricky-wyatt-57-dies-plaintiff-in-landmark-mental-care-suit.html   Accessed Apr. 11, 2017

25. Beyerle D: Tuscaloosa man whose case changed mental health care in the US dies. *Tuscaloosa News*, Nov. 3, 2011. Available at: www .tuscaloosanews .com/article/20111103/NEWS/111109961 Accessed Jan. 29, 2018

3   The Limits of Hospitalization after Commitment

O'Connor v. Donaldson (1975)

Deborah Giorgi-Guarnieri

When can a mentally ill person be confined against his will? Does the Due Process Clause guarantee a right to treatment for the mentally ill? What treatment is due to the involuntarily committed patient?

On October 12, 1773, the first patient was admitted to the Public Hospital for Persons of Insane and Disordered Minds in Williamsburg, Virginia.[1] The hospital was the first North American public building dedicated to the treatment of the mentally ill. Treatment of the mentally ill and hospitals for the mentally ill preceded the adoption of the United States Constitution on September 17, 1787.[2] Physicians practiced admission and treatment before commitment and post-commitment laws existed.

In the late 1960s and early 1970s the trend to end indefinite and inappropriate civil commitment of persons suffering with mental illness and/or substance abuse emerged in the United States. The Lanterman-Petris-Short Act[3] of 1967, passed in California, set the precedent for modern involuntary commitment procedures. In 1975, 202 years after the first patient was admitted to a public mental hospital, 188 years after the Constitution was adopted, and three years after the Lanterman-Petris-Short Act went into effect in California, the U.S. Supreme Court faced constitutional questions concerning the confinement of the mentally ill. The landmark case was *O'Connor v. Donaldson.*[4]

The facts of the case began one day in 1943 when William Kenneth Donaldson overheard his coworkers whispering their plans to attack him after work.[5] He blacked out on the way home from work. The police took him to the local court to decide his disposition. Donaldson and the judge agreed that he had suffered a nervous breakdown and/or exhaustion. Given the choices of joining the military, going back to work and getting beaten up, or going to a mental hospital, Donaldson elected to go to Marcy State Hospital in New York. His treatment consisted of medication and up to 23 electroconvulsive therapy (ECT) treatments, according to the records. After a four-month hospitalization, he returned home to his wife and three children.

In 1953 William Kenneth Donaldson changed his name to Kenneth McCullough.[6] In 1955 he changed his name from Kenneth McCullough to Kenneth Donaldson. Both name changes were attempts to escape the threats. He divorced. He moved from place to place. He held numerous different jobs. He started his own business.[5] Donaldson often blamed the ECT treatments for his inability to use his mind during his work. In 1956 he found himself in Philadelphia General Hospital for treatment of paranoid schizophrenia.

In December 1956, shortly after his release from Philadelphia General Hospital, Kenneth Donaldson traveled to Florida to visit his parents. During his visit, Donaldson told his parents that his neighbor in Philadelphia was poisoning his food.[7] Donaldson's father petitioned the court for a sanity hearing (the term used for a civil commitment hearing in Florida in 1956), as he thought that Donaldson suffered from paranoid delusions.

In January 1957 the county judge committed Donaldson (who had no lawyer) to the Florida State Hospital in Chattahoochee with the diagnosis of paranoid schizophrenia.[5] The judge predicted that Donaldson should be in the hospital for a few weeks while they tried some new medications.[8]

Donaldson was admitted to Department A, with over 1,000 other patients. He recounted that some of the other patients were dangerous criminals (forensic patients). No psychiatrists or counselors ran the ward.[5] Nurses kept the day-to-day activities going. One physician, J. B. O'Connor, maintained responsibility for all 1,000 patients. Dr. O'Connor, who trained to be an OB-GYN, served as Donaldson's doctor and as acting clinical director from January 1957 until mid 1959. Donaldson and O'Connor developed a contentious relationship. In mid 1959, Dr. O'Connor became clinical director. Then Dr. John Gumanis became Donaldson's physician in the fall of 1959 and continued to treat him until the spring of 1967. Donaldson and Gumanis had a less contentious, but strained relationship. In 1967 Donaldson was transferred to Department C. Drs. Israel Hanenson and Jesus Rodriguez consecutively served as Donaldson's attending physicians from 1967 until 1971, when Donaldson was released. Donaldson's 14-year stay far exceeded the county judge's prediction of a few weeks.

There are always two sides to every landmark legal case. In this case, Donaldson narrated one side and the hospital recounted the other side. Donaldson claimed that during his hospitalization his doctors provided very little psychiatric treatment.[4] The hospital explained that Donaldson refused both medications and ECT throughout his hospitalization because he was a Christian Scientist. Donaldson also claimed that the hospital offered no other treatment. The hospital noted three types of therapy: recreational, religious, and milieu.[8] Recreational therapy included outdoor breaks and sports. Religious therapy consisted of going to church. Milieu therapy conceptually embraced the benefits of being in an environment with social interactions that help the person's emotional and individual needs. Donaldson felt it was the type of custodial care that criminals received.

Donaldson made requests for grounds privileges and occupational therapy. O'Connor and his staff denied both. Donaldson also made requests to speak with his attending physician. Donaldson surmised that he spent a total of one hour discussing his case with Dr. O'Connor in the 18 months O'Connor treated him. Similarly Donaldson deduced that he met with Dr. Gumanis not more than two hours in 8½ years.

Donaldson planned his own discharge. He involved Helping Hands, Inc. (a halfway house for persons with mental illness), and a friend from college, John Lembcke.[4] In 1963 Helping Hands offered housing to Donaldson in a house in which a housemother and the president of Helping Hands, Inc., resided. They would sign Donaldson out of the hospital and make him a resident in the house. The hospital's response stated that Donaldson would need strict supervision upon release. The hospital added that only Donaldson's parents would be capable of such supervision.[5]

John Lembcke, a friend of Donaldson's from college, attempted to help Donaldson obtain release four times. First, in July 1964, Lembcke sent an inquiry to the hospital. He basically asked the conditions of release for Donaldson to come to New York under his supervision. The hospital's response simply explained that Donaldson remained the same mentally and required complete supervision. In November 1964 Lembcke made a second attempt. In a note, O'Connor gave three reasons to Gumanis for refusing to release Donaldson to New York. He wrote that parental consent would be required, the hospital was not familiar with John Lembcke, and Donaldson would not likely remain with Lembcke. Gumanis wrote a letter to Lembcke stating that Donaldson needed further hospitalization.

Lembcke tried again through a third letter in December 1965. This time the hospital answered with two conditions. The hospital required Lembcke to provide adequate supervision and obtain the parents' consent. Accordingly, Lembcke traveled to Florida in May 1966. He saw Donaldson. He obtained the parents' consent. He met with O'Connor and Gumanis. Nothing happened.

Lembcke began his final attempt in March 1968. After the general staff of Department C recommended release, Lembcke wrote another letter, offering to take Donaldson to New York. The hospital imposed three conditions. The hospital wanted Lembcke to pick up Donaldson, supervise him, and take Donaldson to a psychiatrist if he needed treatment. Lembcke agreed in a letter. In April 1968 the hospital added two more conditions. The hospital asked Lembcke to provide written details of the supervision and written consent for release from the parents. Lembcke sent a letter outlining the supervision. In September 1968 Lembcke sent the written authorization of the parents, which had been notarized in May 1968. Later that month the hospital responded with the opinion that such a release would be unfair to both Donaldson and Lembcke. The hospital also noted that the parents gave consent in May and Lembcke had forwarded it in September so the hospital would need a more recent consent. Lembcke ended his efforts for his friend's release.

In addition to requesting privileges and making his own discharge plans, Donaldson employed legal means for release from nearly the beginning of his commitment.[8] He filed many petitions for a writ of habeas corpus (a petition for a court to review the legality of a detention). He asked to speak to a lawyer and have his commitment case reheard. He argued that he was not dangerous. He asserted that he was not mentally ill. He added that if he were mentally ill, he was not given treatment. He complained that his release was denied unjustly. The hospital countered that he was not suitable for release and that his plans for release were inadequate. Finally the New York Civil Liberties Union became involved.[9] Their involvement sent the message that Donaldson's case was to be about the individual's constitutional right to treatment.

On February 1, 1971 O'Connor retired as superintendent. In late February 1971, Donaldson, along with all the other patients on his ward, filed a class action lawsuit. The lawsuit would be restructured several times. On July 31, 1971 Donaldson achieved release.[8] His greatest day in court, however, was yet to come.

Legal Course

The Probate Court (January 15, 1957): Donaldson's journey to the U.S. Supreme Court began in probate court. On December 10, 1956, police showed up at the Donaldson home with a *Writ of Inquisition of Incompetency* for Kenneth Donaldson. Donaldson's father had petitioned the probate court for civil commitment of his son.[11] The police took Kenneth Donaldson to the Pinellas County jail. On January 15, 1957, the judge in the county court located in the city of Clearwater, in the County of Pinellas, Florida, committed Donaldson for "care, maintenance, and treatment," with a preliminary diagnosis of schizophrenic reaction, paranoid type.[8] According to §394.22[11] of the State Public

Health Code: "Whenever any person who has been adjudged mentally incompetent requires confinement or restraint *to prevent self-injury or violence to others*, the said judge shall direct that such person be forthwith delivered to a superintendent of a Florida state hospital, for the mentally ill, ... *for care, maintenance, and treatment.*"[12]

When the court involuntarily committed Kenneth Donaldson to Florida State Hospital at Chattahoochee in 1957, the standard was "for care, maintenance, and treatment." States had developed their own standards for commitment, and commitment standards varied throughout the United States. The standards typically balanced the individual's civil rights to live free of commitment against society's rights to protect itself against dangerous persons. Some states, like Florida, had expanded the "dangerous" standard into a "need for treatment" standard.[11]

New ideas about civil commitment emerged in the late 1960s and early 1970s. The trend to end indefinite and inappropriate civil commitment of persons suffering with mental illness and/or substance abuse permeated the United States. The Lanterman-Petris-Short Act[3] of 1967 of California set the precedent for modern involuntary commitment procedures. The Act enumerated seven intents: end indefinite commitment, provide prompt evaluation and treatment, ensure public safety, protect individual rights, focus on individualized treatment, utilize placement services, and safeguard the mentally ill from criminal acts.[3]

Donaldson used all these arguments in hopes of discharge from the hospital through numerous petitions and self-initiated release plans. After 14 years of persistence, Donaldson was not released by the probate court, but was discharged by the hospital superintendent. The new superintendant, Dr. Milton Hirshberg, granted Donaldson a competency discharge on July 31, 1971.[5] The legal inquiries and proceedings, however, did not end.

The Trial Court (November 28, 1972): Throughout his 14-year hospitalization, Donaldson always felt that his commitment was unfair.[5] He unsuccessfully brought complaints in the county and state courts. He wrote to the New York Civil Liberties Union and reached out to Morton Birnbaum during his hospitalization. Just prior to Donaldson's discharge, Birnbaum, an advocate for the constitutional right to treatment for the mentally ill, agreed to represent Donaldson. Birnbaum, both an attorney and internist, introduced the concept of a right to treatment in 1960 in an article, "The Right to Treatment," published in the *American Bar Association Journal*.[13] He advocated for people with mental illness and proposed that the United States Constitution could be interpreted to provide a right to treatment. He also asserted that the medical treatment should meet an establishment standard of care. Birnbaum agreed to represent Donaldson in one of several cases he planned to use to convince federal judges to acknowledge a constitutional right to treatment for the mentally ill.

Donaldson, with Birnbaum's representation, filed a class action lawsuit in the United States District Court for the Northern District of Florida Federal District Court.[5] The class of plaintiffs was all patients in Department C. Donaldson sought release of all patients through a writ of habeas corpus. He also sought injunctive and declarative relief for lack of psychiatric treatment. The court dismissed the class action lawsuit and Donaldson amended the complaint as an individual. He was the sole plaintiff when his case reached the federal trial court.[8]

In Federal District Court, the facts were established in a colorfully written decision. Donaldson alleged that O'Connor and his staff had intentionally and maliciously robbed him of his constitutional right to liberty. Donaldson testified about his many efforts at release, his lack of treatment, his persistent nondangerous status, and his lack of mental illness. Gumanis and O'Connor's defenses consisted of their good faith and adherence to state law.

Donaldson, Gumanis, and O'Connor spouted eyebrow-raising statements in their testimonies. Donaldson stated: "Yes, padlocks on each window" ... "Some of the beds were touching" ... "The entire operation of the ward was geared to criminal patients," and "I was treated worse than the criminal patients." Gumanis stated that he recommended "recreational" and "religious" therapy, he could not explain why he denied grounds privileges or occupational therapy, and denied saying that he only talked to patients that he liked. O'Connor stated that Donaldson could not make "a successful adjustment outside the institution," but admitted he had no knowledge that Donaldson had ever acted dangerously toward himself or others. Lembcke testified about several of O'Connor's handwritten notes, indicating O'Connor had no intention of releasing Donaldson. The testimony played out the years of contention and opposition.

Donaldson won at the trial level (Federal District Court) after a jury trial lasting four days. The jury awarded compensatory (actual) and punitive damages (damages in the form of punishment) against O'Connor and Gumanis. The issue at the trial court level was the right to treatment for an involuntarily committed mentally ill individual. The trial court focused on the hospital's lack of treatment and on the treatment that should follow a commitment. The court did not focus on the definition of mental illness, the commitment standard, or on a constitutional right to treatment.

The Appellate Court (April 26, 1974): Both parties argued misapplication of law in this appeal. In Federal Circuit Court, *O'Connor and Gumanis v. Donaldson,* Donaldson asserted that he had a constitutional right to receive treatment or to be released from the state hospital. O'Connor and Gumanis claimed that mentally ill patients who were civilly committed involuntarily do not have a right to treatment under the U.S. Constitution.[8] These claims opened the door for the Federal Circuit Court to address the constitutional right to treatment issue that Birnbaum was pushing.

O'Connor and Gumanis also stated that the evidence did not support the jury's verdict or their punitive damages. Donaldson had brought his action under 42 U.S.C. §1983.[14] Section 1983 of Title 42 allows an individual to seek damages against persons acting under color of state law for deprivation of federal constitutional and/or federal statutory rights. The District Court's instructions were based on §1983.[8] The circuit court focused on two of the instructions:

You are instructed that a person who is involuntarily civilly committed to a mental hospital does have a constitutional right to receive such individual treatment as will give him a realistic opportunity to be cured or to improve his mental condition.

And

The purpose of involuntary hospitalization is treatment and not mere custodial care or punishment if a patient is not dangerous to himself or others. Without such treatment there is no justification, from a constitutional standpoint, for continued confinement. (Ref. 8, p. 519)

The circuit court boldly walked through the opened door on the issue of whether patients hospitalized through an involuntary civil commitment had a constitutional right to treatment. This was the opportunity Birnbaum and the ACLU had anticipated when they took Donaldson's case. The court reviewed four prior district court holdings and one circuit court holding on this issue. The court then held that "a person involuntarily civilly committed to a state mental hospital has a constitutional right to receive such individual treatment as will give him a reasonable opportunity to be cured or to improve his mental condition" (Ref. 8, p. 520).

The court noted the severe restrictions on liberty and the stigma associated with civil commitment. The court climbed two steps to reach the holding. The first step, *substantive due process,* requires an acceptable governmental goal. The second step, the *governmental interests,* must justify the restrictions on the individual's liberty. The three basics of civil commitment are danger to self, danger to others, and need for treatment.

The rationale for government intrusion usually comes from either the police powers or the *parens patriae* principle. *Police powers* means the capacity of states to regulate individuals' behaviors. The *parens patriae* principle argues that if a court confines an individual because he is in need of treatment, then the hospital must provide treatment. Therefore, the hospital must provide something more than custodial care to continue confinement. The court concluded that "where a nondangerous patient is involuntarily civilly committed to a state mental hospital, the only constitutionally permissible purpose of confinement is to provide treatment," and said that "such a patient has a constitutional right to such treatment as will help him to be cured or to improve his mental condition" (Ref. 8, p. 527). This holding shocked both the legal and medical professions.

The U.S. Supreme Court (June 26, 1975): O'Connor filed a petition for certiorari (a request for review), asking the U.S. Supreme Court to rule on the Fifth Circuit's recognition of a constitutional right to treatment.[4] The Supreme Court granted the petition based on the important constitutional question.

Woodward and Armstrong chronicled the Supreme Court debates about *Donaldson* in their book *The Brethren: Inside the Supreme Court*.[15] Chief Justice Warren Berger considered the case the most important of the term as well as an opportunity for revenge. He maintained a long-standing legal disagreement with David Bazelon concerning persons with mental illness and criminal law. The Fifth Circuit Court quoted Bazelon extensively. Berger also viewed a right to treatment for patients with mental illness to be nonsense. Joel Klein, Justice Lewis Powell's clerk, surfaced as the chief justice's major opponent. The justices' opinions varied from deciding the right to treatment question, to acknowledging the violation of Donaldson's basic right to liberty, to defining treatment, to the award of damages. The chief justice's law clerk drafted the first opinion, deciding the question of the right to treatment. The first opinion had minimal backing. Justice Potter Stewart's clerks circulated a dissenting opinion, focusing on the deprivation of an individual's liberty. The minimal impact of Stewart's opinion on novel legal ground appealed to the majority of the justices. Berger eventually yielded to Stewart's draft and gave the opinion to Stewart to write.

In the opinion, the Supreme Court noted that the commitment proceedings were not at issue. The issues centered on Donaldson's long confinement. The Court also noted that the circuit court took on the question of whether "the Fourteenth Amendment guarantees a right to treatment to persons involuntarily civilly committed to state mental hospitals" (493 F.2d, at 509).

The Supreme Court disagreed with the circuit court's framing of the issue: the Supreme Court opined that a Fourteenth Amendment right to treatment was not the issue.[4] The Court wrote:

A finding of "mental illness" alone cannot justify a State's locking a person up against his will and keeping him indefinitely in simple custodial confinement. Assuming that that term can be given a reasonably precise content and that the "mentally ill" can be identified with reasonable accuracy, there is still no constitutional basis for confining such persons involuntarily if they are dangerous to no one and can live safely in freedom. (p. 575)

The Supreme Court held that for involuntarily civilly committed patients who were not a danger to themselves or others:

In short, a State cannot constitutionally confine without more a nondangerous individual who is capable of surviving safely in freedom by himself or with the help of willing and responsible family members or friends. (p. 576)

The decision was a non-decision, important mostly for its lack of legal decision. It buffered the shock of the circuit court's decision by negating it. The case gained its notoriety through subsequent interpretations of the words "without more."

In summary, when Kenneth Donaldson's case made its way into federal court, he was the sole plaintiff alleging violation of his constitutional rights.[9] O'Connor v. Donaldson raised constitutional issues dealing with right to treatment (Fifth Amendment Substantive Due Process clause). The Fifth Amendment protects individuals from abuse by governmental authority in legal proceedings. The Fourteenth Amendment selectively applies this protection of the individual against state governments. Some argued that substantive due process for the civilly committed mentally ill patient could be satisfied only with a right to treatment. The circuit court took on this argument and found a constitutional right to treatment for the confined mentally ill.[8] The Supreme Court did not think the case presented the right to treatment issue and decided the case based on liberty interests.[4] The holding focused on the "nondangerous" individual and left the words "without more" undefined.

This holding communicated several important decisions.[16] First, the Supreme Court did not recognize a constitutional right to treatment for a civilly committed individual with mental illness. Second, the Court emphasized that an individual must be dangerous to self or others to be "confined for treatment." Third, the Court upheld individual rights for persons with mental illness. Finally, the Court found that hospital officials could incur damages for malicious or oppressive actions that violate individual rights.

Readers of this decision interpret this holding into many and few directives.[17] Many believe that the Court upheld post-confinement rights without finding a constitutional right to treatment. Many believe that "without more" means without treatment. Many believe that courts still rubber-stamp the opinions of psychiatrists concerning dangerousness. Few believe that dangerousness is clearly defined or clearly definable. Few believe that the dangerousness standard encompasses the essence of when a person with mental illness should be confined. Few believe that state doctors should incur punitive damages for their treatment decisions.

The press reported that the Supreme Court found a constitutional right to treatment, that the end of long-term institutionalization was near, and that psychiatrists would have to treat or release mental patients. Law review articles discussed the many misinterpretations of the Supreme Court's holding.[18] In the end *O'Connor v. Donaldson*, saying very little in a calculated and vague manner, changed the practice of post-commitment treatment.

Impact on Practice

Not surprisingly, mental illness and hospitals for the mentally ill survived this legal intrusion. Conversely, civil commitment is alive and well in all 50 states. A common interpretation of *O'Connor v. Donaldson* is that commitment exists for treatment of the individual who is imminently dangerous, the individual whose life is in immediate danger, and the individual who is not considered "capable of surviving safely in freedom."[11] The holding impacted civil commitment laws as well as procedures in the practice of psychiatry. State laws had already begun to change to include the dangerousness standard and to exclude language that would lead to the confinement of a nondangerous individual. *O'Connor v. Donaldson* furthered the change. Most states instituted procedures to guarantee due process. Everyday hospital treatment heeded the Supreme Court language. Even progress notes began to reflect the dicta of the Supreme Court. Every patient in the hospital expected treatment or release. But did anything really change?

Maybe *O'Connor v. Donaldson* improved patients' liberties. Improvement of patients' liberties means due process restrictions on civil commitment, stricter legal proceeding standards, shorter commitment times, rights against forced treatment, more liberties in the hospital, and maybe even termination of involuntary treatment. After *O'Connor v. Donaldson*, many states amended their statutes. In a number of states, the commitment laws that had been broadened to include some variation of a "need for treatment" standard were narrowed in language or in application.[11] The states that continued to implement the law insisted that the individual meet the "dangerousness" standard and that the testimony reflect the "dangerousness" language.[17] Interpretations of dangerousness flowed from the pens of justices to the mouths of psychiatrists. Most states required a hearing within three to five days of emergency confinement to ensure that such confinement met constitutional requirements. States also adjudicated definite periods of confinement with periodic reviews of the commitment.

Hospital admissions and discharges focused on treatment and "dangerousness," however vague the definition might have been. In the spirit of *Wyatt v. Stickney* (1971) and *Lake v. Cameron* (1966), inpatient psychiatrists embraced the treat-and-release concept. The court of *Wyatt v. Stickney* taught that "[Patients] unquestionably have a constitutional right to receive such individual treatment as will give each of them a realistic opportunity to be cured or to improve his or her mental condition."[19] In *Lake v. Cameron*, the D.C. Court of Appeals explained that the system should employ the least restrictive alternative when a patient is not dangerous.[20] Physician and hospital efforts concentrated on maximizing inpatients' therapeutic benefits, and hospitalization restrained the individual's liberties as little as possible. Patients participated in their commitment hearings. Patients took a more active role in deciding their medications and treatment. Length of stay decreased drastically. Many insurance companies required daily proof of dangerousness to justify further coverage. Certainly deinstitutionalization moved forward rapidly.

Maybe it made things worse for patients. The interpretation of *O'Connor v. Donaldson* that a nondangerous individual must be incapable of surviving safely opened the door to commitment for severe mental and physical decompensation before an individual became dangerous.[17] Some commitment hearings just gave lip service to the standard, but still found some way to care for nondangerous individuals who could not care for themselves. Some patients learned what to say to remain in the hospital. Doctors documented the dangerousness language in daily progress notes, but it was a legally chosen word with little clinically accepted meaning.

Without these crafted improvements, the holding left the mentally ill without treatment longer than professionals deem healthy. Some physicians and lawyers think that the "need for treatment" standard more accurately reflects the goal of inpatient treatment. After all, many nondangerous mentally ill persons end up in jails and prisons, where the standard of treatment certainly is less than what the dangerous mentally ill receive in the hospital.

Ironically, the undefined "without more" language affected treatment. Whether the court meant without treatment or not, the medical professional interpreted this language as a warning to improve treatment.

Where Are They Now?

What happened to the Supreme Court opinion? The U.S. Supreme Court issued its opinion, vacated the judgment of the Court of Appeals, and remanded the case. The Federal Circuit Court ruled:

[T]he district court's instructions were insufficient in defining the scope of the qualified immunity possessed by state officials under 42 U.S.C. §1983. Moreover, since the case was tried before the Supreme Court decided *Wood v. Strickland,* the interests of justice require that the plaintiff and both defendants, Dr. J. B. O'Connor and Dr. John Gumanis, have an opportunity to present evidence and to articulate their arguments on the issue of official immunity. (Ref. 21, p. 59)

The remanded case ended in a $27,000 out-of-court settlement.[10]

O'Connor v. Donaldson is the most cited Supreme Court case about involuntary treatment and substantive due process. Twenty-six Supreme Court cases and innumerable federal and state lower court cases cited *Donaldson.* Cases citing *Donaldson* address a range of direct and ancillary issues: the burden of proof in civil commitment proceedings, periodic review of commitment, mental health professionals' liability for bad-faith actions, the least restrictive alternative principle, commitment of sexual predators, treatment of prisoners, and commitment and duration of commitment for persons found "not guilty by reason of insanity." *Donaldson* is a landmark case.

Prior to the Supreme Court's decision in *Donaldson,* the Federal District Court in *Lessard v. Schmidt* (1972) marked the most restrictive commitment standard.[22] The court found the Wisconsin commitment statute unconstitutional and went on to establish a new commitment standard: "there is an extreme likelihood that if the person is not confined he will do immediate harm to himself or others." Other courts have not implemented all the restrictions of the *Lessard* court.

In contrast, *O'Connor v. Donaldson* has been interpreted and used in ancillary decisions extensively. For example in *Jones v. United States* (1983), the Supreme Court upheld legislation that permitted insanity acquittees to be involuntarily committed and hospitalized indefinitely beyond the original term of imprisonment.[23] Similarly, in *Kansas v. Hendricks* (1997), the Supreme Court upheld a Kansas state law that established involuntary civil commitment procedures for mentally ill offenders classified as sexually violent predators.[24] In *Youngberg v. Romeo*

(1982), the U.S. Supreme Court recognized an involuntarily hospitalized patient's constitutional right to "minimally adequate" rehabilitation, training, and treatment; freedom from undue restraint; and the basic necessities of life.[25] *O'Connor v. Donaldson* has not been overturned.

Most recently, a law review article[26] and a Low Income Housing Coalition article[27] cited *O'Connor v. Donaldson* for its consequences of deinstitutionalization and the increased need for community services. Both articles related the case's individual-liberties language to current efforts to provide more access to mental health care under the Mental Health Parity and Addictions Equity Act of 2008 and the Patient Protection and Affordable Care Act of 2010. Neither article mentioned the Supreme Court's refusal to acknowledge a constitutional right to treatment (healthcare).

What happened to Kenneth Donaldson? After 12 state and federal claims and four Supreme Court claims, the hospital granted Donaldson his release in 1971. He was 62 years old. He returned to his hometown of Syracuse, New York. He obtained employment as a hotel night clerk. He wrote and published *Insanity Inside Out*,[5] a book about his plight. He and his book toured the United States during the late 1970s. Kenneth Donaldson died on January 5, 1995, in Sierra Vista, Arizona.

What happened to O'Connor? J. B. O'Connor died on November 21, 1975.

What happened to Gumanis? Dr. Gumanis continued to work at the Florida State Hospital in Chattahoochee until his retirement. He died on March 5, 1986.

REFERENCES

1. Eastern State Hospital website: The History of Eastern State. Available at: www.esh.dmhmrsas.virginia.gov/history.html Accessed Mar. 17, 2013
2. About.com website: Constitution Day. Available at: http://usgovinfo.about .com/blconstday.htm Accessed Mar. 17, 2013
3. The Lanterman–Petris–Short (LPS) Act (Cal. Welf & Inst. Code, sec. 5000 et seq.)
4. *O'Connor v. Donaldson*, 422 U.S. 563 (95 S.Ct. 2486, 45 L.Ed.2d 396) 1975
5. Donaldson K: *Insanity Inside Out*. New York: Crown Publishing Group, 1976
6. Kenneth Donaldson Papers. Manuscripts and Archives, Yale University Library. Also available at http://drs.library.yale.edu:8083/fedora/get/mssa: ms.1677/PDF. Accessed Mar. 23, 2013
7. eNotes, O'Connor v. Donaldson. Available at: www.enotes.com/oconnor-v-donaldson-reference/oconnor-v-donaldson. Accessed Mar. 23, 2013
8. *Donaldson v. O'Connor*, 493 F.2d 507 (5th Cir. 1974)
9. Birnbaum R.: My father's advocacy for a right to treatment. *J Am Acad Psychiatry Law*. 38: 115–23, March 2010. Available at: www.jaapl.org/ content/38/1/115.full Accessed Mar. 17, 2013

10. *Donaldson v. O'Connor*, 454 F. Supp. 311 (Dist. Court, N.D. Florida 1978)
11. Treatment Advocacy Center, O'Connor v. Donaldson. Available at: www .treatmentadvocacycenter.org/component/content/article/341. Accessed Mar. 23, 2013
12. Fla.Laws 1955—1956 Extra. Sess., c. 31403, § 1, p. 62
13. Birnbaum M: The right to treatment. *Am Bar Assoc J.* 46: 499–505, 1960
14. *42 U.S.C. §1983*
15. Woodward B, Armstrong S: *The Brethren: Inside the Supreme Court.* New York: Simon & Schuster, 2005
16. Hartz F: Health science librarians and mental health laws. *Bull Med Libr Assoc.* 66(4), October 1978
17. Szasz T: *The Myth of Mental Illness: Foundations of a Theory of Personal Conduct.* New York: Harper Perennial, 2010. Available at: www.scribd.com/doc/21198016/Szasz-Thomas-Psychiatric-Slavery Accessed Mar. 23, 2013
18. Stanton R: Involuntary civil commitment proceedings: Some further thoughts, *New Jersey Law J.* 98: 1&10–11, Sept. 11, 1975 p. 1
19. *Wyatt v. Stickney*, 325 F. Supp. 781 (M.D. Ala. 1971)
20. *Lake v. Cameron*, 364 F.2d 657 (1966)
21. *Donaldson v. O'Connor*, 519 F.2d 59 (1975)
22. *Lessard v. Schmidt*, 349 F. Supp. 1078 (E.D. Wis. 1972), Vacated and Remanded, 414 U.S. 473, On Remand, 379 F. Supp. 1376 (E.D. Wis. 1974), Vacated and Remanded, 421 U.S. 957 (1975), Reinstated, 413 F. Supp. 1318 (E.D. Wis. 1976)
23. *Jones v. U.S.*, 463 U.S. 354, 103 S.Ct. 3043 (1983)
24. *Kansas v. Hendricks*, 521 U.S. 346 (1997)
25. *Youngberg v. Romeo*, 457 U.S. 307, 102 S.Ct. 2452 (1982)
26. Bianchi C: America's mental health system: Closing the revolving door between hospitals, correctional facilities, & the streets. *St. Thomas Law Rev.* 28: 99–120, 2015
27. National Low Income Housing Coalition: 40 years ago: Study simulates move toward community-based mental health model, *Memo to Members.* 19(40), Oct. 20, 2014.

4   Who Speaks for the Children?
Parham v. J. R. (1979)

Peter Ash

Who decides what mental health treatment a child receives? A competent adult can refuse treatment, but do children have any rights to refuse?

Although there are exceptions such as cases of emancipated minors (minors who are either married or living apart from parents and are self-supporting), children are usually treated as incompetent under the law and cannot make legal decisions for themselves. Should a parent always be allowed to decide for a child? And what should happen when the state has custody? Overworked child protection workers have competing interests between their desire to do the best for a child and the day-to-day necessity of managing a large caseload of children who are competing for scarce treatment resources. Historically, in most states, child protection workers have given consent for medical treatment, including decisions about admission to a mental hospital. Do children have any rights to protest or to have their care reviewed?

J. L., later identified publicly as Joey Lister, was adopted shortly after birth. His adoptive father, a dentist, had arranged to adopt the out-of-wedlock boy without consulting his wife.[1] When Joey was three, his parents divorced and he went to live with his adoptive mother, who later remarried. Janet Scott, a social worker at Central State Hospital in Milledgeville, Georgia, saw Joey as an outpatient for about two months prior to his admission and thought that he was being scapegoated in the home and might benefit from placement in a different family, although she did not think he needed to be hospitalized. Nevertheless, on May 15, 1970, at the age of 6½, Joey was admitted by his parents to Central State Hospital after being diagnosed with hyperkinetic reaction of childhood (what we now call attention deficit hyperactivity disorder or ADHD). After a stay of 2½ years, he went home, but 10 days later, his mother brought him back and had him readmitted. After several months, hospital personnel told the Georgia child protective services agency (the Department of Family and Children Services, or DFACS) that Joey did not need hospitalization but should be placed in specialized foster care. However, DFACS said that they could not pay for such care unless Joey was eligible for federal funds from Aid to Families with Dependent Children (AFDC) or Social Security. Since Joey was not eligible, he remained at Central State Hospital for the next several years. In 1974, when he was 10, his parents relinquished their parental rights, and Joey became a ward of the state.

J. R., who was never publicly identified, was removed from his parents because of neglect and placed in a succession of foster homes. In 1970, when he was almost eight, he was admitted to Central State Hospital, diagnosed with borderline mental retardation and "unsocialized aggressive reaction of childhood." In 1973, hospital personnel began asking that he be placed in long-term foster or adoptive home care because they felt that he "will only regress if he does not get a suitable home placement, and as soon as possible."[2] Two years later, at age 13, when his attorneys sued to have him released, he remained in the hospital with nowhere else to go.

Background to the Case

In the spring of 1964, Robert Kennedy, then United States attorney general, delivered an address at the University of Chicago Law School in which he chastised the audience for failure to serve the poor. Several months later, as part of President Lyndon B. Johnson's War on Poverty, Congress passed the Economic Opportunity Act, which led to the establishment of the Legal Services Program, a federal program that funded poverty lawyers. The Legal Services Program attracted bright, young, idealistic lawyers, including women and African Americans who had difficulty getting into private firms. These attorneys began representing the poor in an array of cases involving public assistance programs, consumer relationships, and landlord–tenant arrangements.

The Georgia Legal Services Program (GLSP) was one of these programs. Since the poor often did not know that they now had access to legal services, legal services programs went out looking for clients. Initially, GLSP took on a large number of divorces,[3] later shifting to domestic violence cases. David Goren, a young GLSP lawyer, was assigned to represent patients at Central State Hospital, a huge complex, even a town within a town, which held about 9,000 inpatients at its height in the 1960s, making it one of the largest mental hospitals in the country. Many of the staff were sympathetic to the plight of patients at Central State and helped Goren locate patients in need of legal assistance. Thus, although Central State staff was employed by the state, many were sympathetic to supporting lawsuits to help force changes they thought would be in patients' best interests.

On the child service, some staff thought some of the children did not need to be hospitalized but would be better served in outpatient placements. Goren and the GLSP began thinking about how the law could be used to help those children. Goren took a personal interest in his clients. Over the course of the case, Joey (J. L.) made numerous visits to his home and became quite attached to him.[4]

In the courts, children had been slowly achieving more rights. The Supreme Court had been expanding minors' rights: in 1967, the Court gave juvenile defendants many more rights in juvenile court.[5] Two years later, it allowed increased freedom of political expression in public schools.[6] As the Parham case worked its way through the lower courts, the Supreme Court would go on to expand minors' privacy rights to abortion[7] and contraception.[8] The time seemed right for trying to achieve rights for children with regard to mental health treatment.

Legal Course

J. L. and J. R.'s predicament raised several legal questions. First, was a child entitled to have a review of his admission to a mental hospital? Although the child's admission was formally considered a voluntary admission in that consent had been obtained from a parent, it was involuntary from the child's point of view. Second, was there a difference between when a parent admitted his or her child and when a state agent authorized admission for a child in state custody? It seems more likely that a parent would have the child's best interest at heart than an overworked state case worker would. Third, once the child was in the hospital, should there be some sort of impartial periodic review to see if continued hospitalization was appropriate? And finally, if the only reason that the child was in the hospital was that certain outpatient placements or services were hard to come by, did the state have an obligation to fund and provide those services? Put another way, did the state have the obligation to provide the least restrictive environment for services to youth in state custody?

Trial Court Case

On October 24, 1975, GLSP filed a class action suit in federal district court in Georgia on behalf of J. L., J. R., and the class of 200 children committed to Central State Hospital. They sued the state and James Parham, then commissioner of the Georgia Department of Human Resources, alleging that the children had been deprived of their liberty without having had a meaningful opportunity to be heard and without periodic review of consideration of placement in "the least drastic environment."[9] Since the suit attacked the constitutionality of a state statute, the district court convened a three-judge panel. One of the judges, Griffin Bell, was then a sitting judge on the U.S. Court of Appeals for the Fifth Circuit. Two years later, Judge Bell became attorney general under President Jimmy Carter while the case was still before the Supreme Court.

The district court and the parties conducted extensive fact finding regarding inpatient and outpatient state mental health services afforded to children in Georgia. The judges visited Central State Hospital and were not pleased with what they saw. The adolescent unit, in particular, through which the judges passed on their way to the child unit, was old, crowded, and decrepit. Over 20 expert depositions were taken regarding the discrepancies between the care being provided to children and the care they needed.

In the district court opinion,[10] the court noted that a state commission and hospital personnel had found that "more than half of the hospitalized children and youth would not need hospitalization if other forms of care were available in communities" (Ref. 10, p. 25). The court went on to observe, "The hospitalization of children for whom a county Department of Family and Children Services is custodian generally results from a determination that foster parental care is unavailable or has been tried and found to be unworkable, leaving hospitalization as the only available alternative" (p. 60). The court drew a parallel to *In re Gault*,[5] a 1967 landmark decision about minors' rights in juvenile court:

To paraphrase what the [*Gault*] Court there said: Ultimately, however, we confront the reality of that portion of the mental health process with which we deal in this case. A child is alleged to be emotionally disturbed. The child is admitted to a mental hospital where he may be detained and restrained of liberty for years. It is of no constitutional consequence – and of limited practical meaning – that the institution to which he is admitted and in which he is detained is called a hospital. The fact of the matter is that however euphemistic the title, a regional hospital named Central State Hospital or Georgia Mental Health Institution is an institution known by all as one for the confinement of mentally ill children and adults, in which the child is confined for a greater or lesser time. His world becomes a building with locked doors and windows, regimented routine and institutional hours. Instead of mother and father and sisters and brothers and friends and classmates, his world is peopled by psychiatrists, psychologists, social workers, state employees and children who are to a greater or lesser extent, also emotionally disturbed.

In view of this, it would be extraordinary if our Constitution did not require the procedural regularity and the exercise of care implied in the phrase 'due process,' [*citation omitted*], for children to be confined and detained under Georgia's voluntary admissions statute. (Ref. 10, p. 69)

The district court found portions of Georgia's admission statute unconstitutional and ordered the state to provide necessary outpatient resources to treat those children who did not need to be hospitalized. It was a clear victory for the plaintiff children. The state appealed directly to the Supreme Court.

U.S. Supreme Court

Since several justices were absent at the first hearing, the Supreme Court heard oral arguments twice in the Parham case.[11] Feelings ran strong: two of the justices had family members who had been committed to mental hospitals as children, and the justices peppered the attorneys with questions. John Cromartie, Jr., the director of the GLSP, who argued the case before the Court, spoke with a southern drawl and later said that he had to push himself to talk much faster than usual to get his points in.[12] In the period before the Court issued its opinion, Joey Lister was released from the hospital to the custody of his adoptive father. Tragically, their relationship did not flourish, and Joey committed suicide prior to the Court's decision.

The American Psychiatric Association (APA) filed an *amicus* brief in the case. The organization generally supported the proposition that parents should decide for their children, but proposed limiting admissions without the possibility of judicial review to "those cases in which (1) parents in an intact family wish to admit (2) a pre-adolescent child (3) to an accredited institution (4) for a short-term period (*e.g.*, less than 45 days)."[13] Chief Justice Warren Burger delivered the opinion of the Court on June 20, 1979, 18 months after first hearing oral argument. The Supreme Court reversed the district court and upheld Georgia's procedures.[14] The justices were unanimous in thinking that it was constitutional for a parent or a state custodian to admit a child, subject only to approval by an evaluating physician. The Court weighed the liberty interest of the child, the interest of the parent, and the interest of the state, giving the most weight to the parent's interest and asserting that there was a strong presumption that parents acted in their children's best interest. They were confident that a psychiatrist who conducted a thorough evaluation would be able to ferret out those few cases where the parents did not have the child's interest in mind, and in any event would be better at that task than a judge. They were also concerned that a more formal hearing would take clinicians' time and energy away from the business of treating patients. They believed that a hearing was unlikely to be thorough, citing three studies indicating that the average commitment hearing took less than ten minutes. While the Court noted that for youth in state custody, the social worker might be less invested than a parent, it nevertheless concluded that review by a physician of the medical indications for admission was a sufficient protection for the child. In a dissent, three justices thought that if the child objected following admission, some sort of formal review process should be available.

One of the major thrusts of the district court opinion was that the state should provide appropriate outpatient services for youth who no longer required inpatient hospitalization. The Supreme Court ducked that issue completely, opining that since the admission procedures were constitutional, it did not need to address the question of discharge. The Court stated: "For a child without natural parents, we must acknowledge the risk of being 'lost in the shuffle,'" (Ref. 14, p. 619) but remanded the issue to the district court. For the Supreme Court, the issue in the case was about how children got into the hospital; for the plaintiffs, the case was about how children got out.

Where Are They Now?

As noted earlier, Joey Lister committed suicide while living with his father. J. R. was never publicly identified and has been lost to follow-up. The federal Legal Services Corporation, so important in funding attorneys to represent poor plaintiffs in civil litigation such as Parham, suffered severe cutbacks in the Reagan administration. After some growth through the 1990s, the Republican Congress attacked it for promoting welfare, and it was largely dismantled. Although the Georgia Legal Services Program continues, the young lawyers involved in the Parham case have moved on. David Goren, the guardian *ad litem* for the children, practices as an immigration attorney in Maryland,[4] and John Cromartie, Jr., who argued the case for the children before the Supreme Court, left the law and became a Methodist minister.[12]

Impact on Practice

Today, when the average length of stay in most acute child inpatient units is around seven days, and many states have cut all of their state hospital beds for children in order to save money, the concern that children will stay too long in inpatient units is seldom heard. The cost of inpatient hospitalization has changed the calculus of maintaining children (and adults, for that matter) in the hospital. Outpatient services have not sprung up to fill the gap; there is still a great shortage of such services for children, and a major shortage of child psychiatrists, especially in rural areas. Although inpatient units continue to wrestle with the problem of how to place difficult-to-place youth, long stays are rare.

In many ways, the *Olmstead* case (also from Georgia, see Chapter 6) is a more recent adult version of *Parham*, in which the question was the extent to which the state must provide outpatient services to adults, justified not on constitutional grounds, but on an interpretation of the Americans with Disabilities Act. The issue of the provision of outpatient services for discharged inpatients remains a live one. Again in Georgia, the state signed an agreement with the federal government in 2010, following an investigation of its inpatient facilities, that required it to improve its outpatient services for discharged inpatients. The need to provide services in the least restrictive environment continues to come into conflict with states' arguments that they do not have the funds to pay for such services.

In *Parham*, the Supreme Court held for the status quo – that parents decide for their children, subject only to a doctor's agreement that the treatment is indicated. That practice continues to be the general rule. Prior to *Parham*, some states passed laws allowing adolescents to file a protest to hospitalization, triggering a judicial review of the admission. Even in states that allow such a challenge, actual hearings are uncommon. In part this reflects that with short lengths of stay, many children are discharged before the court gets around to actually conducting the hearing, and in part it reflects that oppositional adolescents, angry at being admitted and eager to sign the protest form when it is offered, often withdraw their objection prior to the hearing, not infrequently leaving their court-appointed attorney wondering what all the fuss was about. Some states allow "mature minors" to consent to treatment on their own, and others allow adolescents to consent to specific treatments, such as outpatient psychotherapy. As a practical matter, since the parents usually get the bill for these services, they tend to have much to say about whether the treatment will continue.

Research done in the 1980s and early 1990s tended to show that adolescents 14 years of age and older make about the same types of medical decisions as adults, results that have been used to bolster legal arguments that pregnant adolescents are able to make decisions about abortion without parental consent. The Supreme Court has consistently held that "mature" pregnant girls have the right to consent to abortion, and for immature girls, there needs to be a judicial bypass mechanism in which a judge can decide whether abortion is in the girl's best interests without her having to notify her parents or obtain their consent. Two situations in which the parents' interests and the child's may diverge are consent for medical research and when the child is a donor for transplantation. For federally funded research that is not likely to benefit the minor subject, children do have a right to refuse,[15] and when a child is to be a donor in a situation where there is risk to him or her, such as when donating a kidney to a sibling, the American Medical Association has taken the position that ethically such decisions require judicial review.[16]

With the decrease in inpatient treatment of children, some of the *Parham* concerns have moved to the outpatient arena, particularly concerns about the care that the state provides to those in state custody. One current example is the concern being raised about overmedication of children in foster care. The typical pattern has been that the caseworker, who may not know the behavior of the child well, still consents to psychotropic medication. The rates of medicating this population are high, with studies suggesting that over a quarter of children in foster care are receiving psychotropic medications, and, compared to children not in foster care, are receiving some psychotropic medication at three times the rate,[17] and for antipsychotic medications, at over seven times the rate.[18] In response to these high rates, professional associations have developed guidelines for medicating youth in foster care,[19] states have begun to develop programs to review such treatment, and some states allow adolescents in state custody to refuse medication. The question of who decides what for a child continues to be debated.

NOTE

The author would like to thank David Goren and John L. Cromartie, Jr., for their willingness and help in discussing their roles and the history of the case.

REFERENCES

1. Scott J: Affidavit, in *Parham v. J.L. and J.R.* Docket No 75–1690 evidence *compendium*. Washington, D.C., Supreme Court of the United States, 1978, pp. 59–61
2. Exhibit 9-A-2: District Court Revised Statement of Facts, p. 66, in Parham v. J. L. and J.R. Docket No 75–1690 evidence compendium. Washington, D.C., Supreme Court of the United States, 1978, pp. 62–6
3. Georgia Legal Services: *Annual Report*. Atlanta, Author, 1972
4. Goren D: Personal communication, Mar. 8, 2011
5. *In re Gault*, 387 U.S. 1 (1967)
6. *Tinker v. Des Moines Independent Community School District*, 393 U.S. 503 (1969)
7. *Planned Parenthood of Central Missouri v. Danforth*, 428 U.S. 52 (1976)
8. *Carey v. Population Serv. Intl.*, 431 U.S. 678 (1977)
9. Complaint: p. 9, in Parham v. J. L. and J. R. Docket No 75–1690 evidence compendium. Washington, D.C., Supreme Court of the United States, 1978, pp. 1–9
10. *J.L. and J.R. et al. v. Parham et al.*, 412 F. Supp. 112 (Mid Dist. Ga.) (1976)

11. You can hear the oral argument at the Oyez Project website: U.S. Supreme Court: Parham v. J.R. – Oral Argument. Available at: www.oyez.org/cases/1970–1979/1977/1977_75_1690/argument Accessed Apr. 22, 2017

12. Cromartie JL Jr: Personal communication, Nov. 10, 2010

13. Brief of American Psychiatric Association, American Society for Adolescent Psychiatry, American Academy of Child Psychiatry, and American Association of Psychiatric Services for Children, as Amici Curiae, Parham v. J. L. and J. R., U.S. Sup. Ct. No. 75–1690 (1977)

14. *Parham v. J.R.*, 442 U.S. 584 (1979)

15. Protection of Human Subjects – Additional Protections for Children, in 45 Code of Federal Regulations [CFR], Subtitle A, Part 46, Subpart D, 10-1-99 Edition

16. American Medical Association: Code of Medical Ethics: *Current Opinions with Annotations. The Use of Minors as Organ and Tissue Donors.* Chicago, IL: American Medical Association, 1997

17. Zito JM, Safer DJ, Sai D, et al.: Psychotropic medication patterns among youth in foster care. *Pediatrics.* 121: e157–63, 2008

18. Simpson S, Domon S, Miller LH, et al.: Antipsychotic medication prescription trends in foster care children enrolled in Arkansas Medicaid following implementation of prior authorization policies. *J Am Acad Child Adolesc Psychiatry.* 55: S201-2, 2016

19. American Academy of Child & Adolescent Psychiatry: Recommendations about the use of psychotropic medications for children and adolescents involved in child-serving systems. Available at: www.aacap.org/App_Themes/AACAP/docs/clinical_practice_center/systems_of_care/AACAP_Psychotropic_Medication_Recommendations_2015_FINAL.pdf Accessed Apr. 22, 2017

5   The Right to Refuse Treatment

Rogers v. Commissioner of Department of Mental Health (1983)

Alec Buchanan

What should a doctor do when a patient refuses medication? What mechanisms are available for overriding such a refusal? Who decides whether a refusal will be overridden and, if it will be, which medication will be given?

In April 1975 Ruby Rogers, a patient of Boston State Hospital, and six other patients sued their doctors in federal court. Rogers was represented by Richard Cole, an attorney with the publicly funded Greater Boston Legal Services. Rogers and Cole were challenging the hospital's practice of secluding and medicating patients against their will without a court order. Rogers' suit alleged that the hospital's practices violated not only her constitutional rights, but also state law and accepted medical standards. The case had a high profile at the time it was argued. Many staff at the hospital held faculty appointments at Tufts and at Boston University.

The case highlighted the differences between psychiatric and other patients. By 1975 it was already clear that medical and surgical hospital patients across the country had the right to refuse prescribed treatment.[1] For psychiatric patients, the situation differed from state to state. In Massachusetts, a patient could either be "voluntary" or be committed to the hospital. Voluntary patients signed a document at the time they were admitted saying that they were willing to accept treatment. When a patient declined to sign, the hospital had a choice to make. It could allow the patient to remain in the community or make the person an "involuntary" patient. The decision was made by hospital staff based on the patient's condition and on what alternatives were available to admission. Involuntary patients were treated against their wishes, including with medication, if staff felt this was clinically what was required.

Treating the same patient for heart disease without the patient's consent would have been more complicated. The difference between psychiatry and the rest of medicine with respect to a patient's right to choose whether or not to accept treatment had its origins in earlier lay and professional beliefs concerning the nature of mental illness. By 1975 it was accepted that mental illness did not affect all aspects of a person's functioning in the same way or to the same degree.

People whose perceptions were distorted to the extent that they suffered from hallucinations were nevertheless permitted, and in some circumstances expected, to manage their money, for instance.

By contrast, 19th-century conceptions of mental illness often treated sufferers as "uniformly incompetent."[2] People admitted to a mental hospital lost the right to manage their own affairs, to vote, and to dispose of property.[3] For many the loss of the right to refuse treatment had been but one aspect of a more general loss of autonomy. By the late 20th century these perceptions had changed. The movie *One Flew Over the Cuckoo's Nest* was released in the same year Rogers filed suit. It won five Academy Awards and portrayed the removal of autonomy from and compulsory treatment of people detained in a psychiatric hospital as inhumane and, at times, cruel.

This is not to say that in 1975 everyone thought that the changes wrought by Rogers' case were desirable. The Boston press described the case of a man with mental illness who had assaulted his father and a policeman, and suggested that he had committed the assault after refusing medication and that his refusal was related to his being emboldened by coverage of the Rogers case.[4] But the lasting impact of Rogers' suit is less controversial. Admission, even involuntary admission, to a psychiatric hospital is less likely to entail a general loss of legal rights or responsibilities. Until a court determines otherwise, a psychiatric patient now has the right to refuse treatment.

Legal Course

Federal District Court

Ruby Rogers moved to Boston after attending high school in rural West Virginia. Her sister was later to say that she had left to better herself.[5] Rogers had worked as a nurse's aide and had six children before developing psychiatric symptoms and being admitted to the hospital. The trial, in front of the judge who had authored the agreement to improve conditions in a state-run school for the intellectually disabled in Belchertown, Massachusetts, two years earlier, lasted for 74 days. The hospital's seclusion and medication practices were found to accord with acceptable medical standards and the patients were denied damages.[6]

Judge Tauro found against the hospital, however, on most of the larger questions that Rogers and Cole had raised. Psychiatric patients who had not been adjudicated and found incompetent had a constitutional right to refuse treatment in non-emergency situations. This right derived from their First Amendment right to freedom of speech, which included the freedom to generate thoughts and ideas free from the effects of medication. The only exceptions were emergencies, defined by the judge as "circumstances in which a failure [to medicate forcibly] would bring about a substantial likelihood of physical harm to the patient or others."[7]

Michael Gill, the senior psychiatrist on the unit where several of the patients were housed, saw the case as extremely damaging.[8] The unit had been designed to run as a therapeutic community with an emphasis on open communication and trust. William Kantar, a psychiatrist on a different unit in the hospital, described the sense of betrayal felt by staff when they were sued by people they were seeking to help. Michael Gill reported a doubling of the number of hours that patients spent in seclusion following the suit.[9] Richard Cole has subsequently written that the patients' decision to act when they did was in part driven by the effects of a statewide strike by mental health workers and the consequences of hospital funding cuts.[10]

Nearly 40 years later, during the preparation of this chapter, it was clear that these disagreements persisted. The medical staff from Boston State Hospital to whom I spoke pointed to the value of the therapeutic community. Richard Cole asked what kind of therapeutic community forcibly medicated patients and kept them in seclusion rooms for extended periods. The medical staff pointed to the impact on the treatment milieu of some of their colleagues giving evidence against the hospital. Cole pointed to the openness of the legal and investigative process that led to the suit being brought.

Beyond the walls of Boston State Hospital, some psychiatrists welcomed the outcome of the Rogers case.[11] Others were appalled. The president of the American Psychiatric Association at the time referred to Judge Tauro's as an "impossible, ill-considered judicial decision."[12] Anger among medical staff stemmed both from the judge's language, which had included a reference to the "mind control" exerted by medication,[13] and a fear that treatment refusal would now become widespread. People who refused treatment would deteriorate and, in one psychiatrist's words, "rot with their rights on."[14]

The case was appealed, first to the federal Court of Appeals for the First Circuit[15] and then to the U.S. Supreme Court. The latter chose not to become involved, noting that patients in Massachusetts might already have more rights than the U.S. Constitution guaranteed.[16] The case was resolved after the federal Court of Appeals asked nine questions of the Supreme Judicial Court of Massachusetts.

The Questions Asked of the Supreme Judicial Court

Questions 1 to 3 concerned whether, under Massachusetts law, involuntary commitment meant that someone was automatically incompetent to make treatment decisions. The Supreme Judicial Court held that it did not. As the federal courts had decided, committed psychiatric patients were presumed competent to make treatment decisions until a probate court determined that they were not.[17]

This was not the outcome that the American Psychiatric Association had hoped for. Citing the earlier U.S. Supreme Court case *Youngberg v. Romeo*[18] to the effect that federal courts should allow hospital professionals to decide whether and when a patient could be restrained, the APA had argued in its legal brief:

Whether the patient was competent and/or whether he consented to the treatment was not deemed [in *Romeo*] to be an element of the constitutional test. Rather, the use of restraints, even as a form of compulsory treatment, was to be measured against professional standards. The same constitutional analysis should govern the use of involuntary medication.[19]

The Supreme Judicial Court rejected this view.

Questions 4 and 5 concerned what should happen if medication was required and the person was not competent to consent. The court held that in these circumstances the probate court should make an initial treatment decision and, using a "substituted judgment model," approve a treatment plan. Financial resources should be made available to enable the parties to argue their case in court, for the appointment of a guardian *ad litem*, and to allow the retention of expert witnesses. After making his or her initial decision and approving a treatment plan, the judge was to delegate the day-to-day monitoring to the guardian *ad litem*.

The substituted judgment model required the court to consider five factors before approving a treatment plan. These were the patient's expressed wishes, his or her religious convictions, the impact of the decision on the family, the probability of adverse effects from the treatment, and the prognosis with and without treatment. The same five factors had been proposed in *Roe*, an earlier Massachusetts case, and in a brief submitted by the American Orthopsychiatric Association.[20] The probate court order would provide for periodic reviews. It would be for the guardian to seek modification of the order if this was necessary before the next review.[21]

Questions 6 to 9 concerned exceptions. The Supreme Judicial Court permitted treatment over objection if the patient posed an "imminent threat of harm to himself or others."[22] In the absence of such a threat, a hospital could override a patient's refusal only where failure to treat would cause an "immediate, substantial and irreversible deterioration of a serious mental illness."[23] In all other circumstances where it wished to treat without consent, a hospital would have to apply to the probate court in the usual way.

Related Cases

Two years after Ruby Rogers brought her case in Massachusetts, John Rennie, then a 38-year-old patient at Ancora State Hospital in New Jersey, sued in federal court to prevent the hospital from treating him against his will with medication. The court's finding in *Rogers* had taken four years to appear, and the two judgments were handed down within six weeks of each other.

In New Jersey, Federal District Judge Brotman had initially responded to Rennie's request for an injunction by ordering that his dose of anti-psychotic medication be lowered to one that his psychiatrists regarded as insufficient to improve his condition. The judge had then held 14 days of hearings between January and April of 1978. After issuing an initial ruling and expanding Rennie's case into a class action involving involuntarily committed patients in all five of New Jersey's state-run mental hospitals, Brotman then held a further 17 days of hearings.

In the meantime, in March 1978 the New Jersey Division of Mental Health had developed new procedures covering compulsory treatment. *Administrative Bulletin 78-3* initiated a system whereby a refusing patient's case had to be reviewed by a hospital's medical director, who would be authorized to obtain the opinion of an independent doctor. The final judgment in Rennie's case was to include an assessment of these procedures.

Brotman found that Rennie had a right to refuse treatment, but that this right was not "absolute." Consideration was also to be given to the rights of other patients not to be assaulted by an untreated patient. The concept of the "least restrictive alternative" was used to determine whether the patient's refusal should be accepted. The examples given by the court contain considerable detail. It is clear, for instance, that Brotman regarded lithium as less restrictive than antipsychotic medication. *Administrative Bulletin 78-3*, he held, did not provide sufficient safeguards for patients.

Most New Jersey supporters of a right to refuse treatment cited the First Amendment in the same way that the *Rogers* court did in Massachusetts, inferring from the right to freedom of speech a right to compose that speech using unmedicated thoughts.[24] Others cited the Eighth Amendment, claiming that compulsory treatment was cruel or unusual punishment. Brotman's analysis took a third approach, grounding the right to refuse in a constitutional right to privacy.[25] Although not evident in the holding of the Supreme Judicial Court, this "privacy" justification for a right to refuse had appeared in *Rogers* also, both in the legal team's initial presentation[26] and in one of the *amicus curiae* briefs that were lodged on appeal.[27]

After appeals to the U.S. Court of Appeals for the Third Circuit[28] and to the U.S. Supreme Court, Rennie's case had been remanded back to the Federal District Court. The U.S. Supreme Court had held that the least restrictive alternative was not a concept that could be applied to treatment refusal. "Accepted professional judgment," the standard that the Supreme Court had described in *Youngberg v. Romeo*[29] and that the American Psychiatric Association had argued unsuccessfully should be applied in *Rogers*, was an acceptable alternative. Both the Court of Appeals for the Third Circuit and the U.S. Supreme Court had held that *Administrative Bulletin 78-3* provided sufficient safeguards.[30] The Federal District Court then ordered all parties to abide by the *Bulletin*.

The *Rennie* decisions thus left the decision-making process in the hands of medical professionals to a much greater extent than did the judgment in *Rogers*. In Brotman's later words, the courts were to allow, "medical judgments to be made by medical people."[31] By concentrating on the patient's stated refusal and using this as the starting point of any review it also placed less emphasis on the concept of competency. All patients not yet found incompetent by a court were covered by *Administrative Bulletin 78-3*; some would be able to make decisions in many areas of their lives, while others would not. Patients found competent to refuse under *Rogers* might still receive compulsory treatment under the law of New Jersey.

Where Are They Now?

Ruby Rogers died in January 2009 in a nursing home in Turner Falls, Massachusetts. The Ruby Rogers Center in Somerville, Massachusetts, was founded in 1985 by Dr. Dan Fisher and others to provide support, advocacy, and assistance to people with mental health problems. Judge Tauro continued to serve on the federal bench in Massachusetts, where he later held unconstitutional that part of the federal Defense of Marriage Act that defined marriage as "a legal union exclusively between one man and one woman."[32] Cole became assistant attorney general and civil rights division chief in the Massachusetts Attorney General's office. Gill and Kantar are psychiatrists in Massachusetts.

Impact on Practice

The Law and Patient Rights

Rogers and related litigation represented a break with legal tradition, and particularly with appellate court tradition. Until the 1970s, the courts had been reluctant to interfere in the running of mental hospitals in the

United States.[33] As a result, the assumption that patients could be com-pelled to accept whatever treatment those hospitals deemed appropriate had remained legally unchallenged.[34]

This judicial reluctance to become more involved does not seem to have stemmed from any general satisfaction with the status quo. Alan Stone, one of the psychiatrists who had criticized Judge Tauro's original decision, was to note in 1984 that "Once a litigating attorney succeeds in getting a judge to visit a public mental institution, there is a very good chance that the judge will conclude that something has to be done."[35] Instead, the courts may have been reluctant to intervene because they feared that once they became involved it would be difficult to know where to stop. In *Rogers*, for instance, the Court of Appeals for the First Circuit had found itself seeking to establish exactly when a patient who refused medication should be discharged.[36]

As the other chapters in this book demonstrate, *Rogers* and *Rennie* were two of a number of legal changes affecting American psychiatry during the 1960s and 1970s. The criteria for civil commitment came to place less emphasis on care and treatment and more emphasis on the manage-ment of dangerousness.[37] Commitment based on dangerousness permits hospitalization without treatment. The series of "right to treatment" cases that followed can be seen as an effort to encourage consideration of clinical needs once those needs had been deemed less relevant to the process of civil commitment.[38]

The Right to Refuse Treatment in Other States

Judge Tauro's approach in *Rogers* was followed in other states. In the late 1980s the California courts held that, absent an emergency, a refusal of medication could not be overridden unless the incompetence of the patient to make treatment decisions had been established judicially.[39] Oklahoma, New York, Colorado, and Wisconsin all modified their laws similarly. Because of the power it grants to a patient's expressed choices, this approach is sometimes referred to as "rights driven."

In following the "rights driven" approach of *Rogers*, however, not all states adopted the "substituted judgment" standard whereby the incom-petent patient was to receive the treatment that a court decided he or she would have wanted. Some states followed a "best interests" approach, whereby the decision-maker was required to weigh the risks and benefits of treatment, as well as the alternatives to it, from an "objective" stand-point.[40] *Rogers* notwithstanding, the "best interests" standard is now the one most frequently used.[41]

A second approach to treatment refusal, sometimes described as "treatment driven," has followed the principles laid down in *Rennie*. While the first choice of the American Psychiatric Association in *Rogers* had been preservation of the status quo, a treatment-driven approach had been the association's preferred alternative. Following this approach, treatment refusal is addressed by an administrative review or panel convened by the hospital.[42] The court in *Rennie* required that this panel include an independent psychiatric consultant or the medical director of the facility in which the patient was to be treated. Other courts have mandated that the review be undertaken by the state's Department of Mental Health.[43]

A third approach follows the logic of one Wisconsin court that, "Nonconsensual treatment is what involuntary commitment is all about."[44] This approach incorporates incompetence to make treatment decisions into civil commitment criteria.[45] Under this scheme, any detained patient has by definition been found by a court to lack competence to refuse treatment. This formula was adopted in the 1970s by Utah.[46] An attempt to implement the proposal in Florida was struck down on the grounds that commitment courts did not have the authority to make competency decisions.[47] Outside the United States practices vary. Utah's solution most closely resembles practice in other Western countries.[48]

Clinical and Legal Responses

The *Rogers* decision in Massachusetts was followed by discussion of the implications of the decision for other states. Richard Cole pointed to the benefits of people being allowed to make their own choices, even if those choices seemed unreasonable. He noted the "privacy of mental acts" and argued that this privacy had an intrinsic value that was now protected.[49] He also pointed to practical benefits and questioned the utility of forced treatment. He noted the severity of side effects and argued that patients were better able to weigh the importance of these side effects than were doctors acting on their behalf.

What happened in Massachusetts? Following the court decision significant numbers of patients were reported to be refusing treatment,[50] and increased rates of post-refusal patient violence were also described.[51] Many patients who initially refused medication subsequently changed their minds, however. And in instances where physicians recommended treatment, the courts usually seem to have agreed.[52] Even at the time, a lack of data interfered with attempts to assess the impact of the case.[53] Nearly 40 years later, the merits of the different empirical claims are even more difficult to assess.

To some extent, however, the relative merits of the competing claims have been rendered less important by changes to the way in which mental health care is delivered in the United States. The majority of patients who would once have lived in institutions now live in community settings. In many cases this has removed, for all practical purposes, the possibility of treatment without consent. Increasing but patchy use of outpatient commitment and "leverage" notwithstanding, giving medication to a symptomatic but ambivalent patient has become one of persuasion and negotiation. Admission to one of a severely reduced number of inpatient beds is usually an option only in extreme circumstances. The inpatient units described in *Rogers*, where lengths of stay were measured in months or years, are difficult for present-day clinicians, patients, and relatives to imagine.

Patients are still admitted to hospitals, however, and rules and procedures are still required to establish what will happen when a patient refuses treatment either there or in the community. Psychiatrists need to know how those rules and procedures apply in the state in which they practice. That the law should make explicit provision for something as serious as treating someone without the person's consent now seems uncontroversial. It was not uncontroversial when Rogers brought her case.

Whether this provision should be built into commitment legislation or achieved by a hospital making a separate application to a probate court is less clear. One factor impeding inclusion of decisional competence into commitment criteria seems to be a continuing desire on the part of legislators to permit the detention of mentally disordered people who are dangerous whether or not they have the capacity to make a proper choice about the treatment they will receive.[54] The most controversial example is that of sex-offender commitment.

The unwillingness of the U.S. Supreme Court to pronounce on how treatment refusal should be addressed suggests that future legal developments will take place at the state level. One conclusion has been that this will favor the "rights-based" approach of the Rogers court over the "treatment-based" approach seen in *Rennie*.[55] It is also possible, however, that changes in the way psychiatric care is delivered, combined with the increasing use of coercion in community settings, will give rise to a new generation of mental health legislation that employs both approaches.

NOTE

The author thanks Richard Cole, Michael Gill, and William Kantar. The opinions expressed are his own.

REFERENCES

1. *Schloendorff v. Society of New York Hospital*, 105 N.E. 92 (1914)
2. Appelbaum P. *Almost a Revolution*. New York: Oxford University Press, 1994, p. 118
3. Brakel S, Rock R. *The Mentally Disabled and the Law* (2nd ed.). Chicago: American Bar Foundation, 1971
4. Refusal to take drug leads to a tragedy. *Boston Herald*, Nov. 17, 1979, p. A4
5. Obituary. Ruby Rogers, 71; helped win key rights for mentally ill. *Boston Globe*, Feb. 20, 2009, p. B11
6. *Rogers v. Okin*, 478 F. Supp. 1342, 1380–1389 (1979)
7. *Rogers v. Okin*, 478 F. Supp. 1342, 1371 (1979)
8. Gill M. Side effects of a right to refuse treatment lawsuit: the Boston State Hospital experience. In A Doudera, J Swazey (Eds.), *Refusing Treatment in Mental Health Institutions: Values in Conflict* (pp. 81–82). Ann Arbor, MI: AUPHA Press, 1982
9. Gill M. Side effects of a right to refuse treatment lawsuit: the Boston State Hospital experience. In A Doudera, J Swazey (Eds.), *Refusing Treatment in Mental Health Institutions: Values in Conflict* (pp. 83–87). Ann Arbor, MI: AUPHA Press, 1982
10. Cole R. Patients rights vs. doctors' rights: which should take precedence? In A Doudera, J Swazey (Eds.), *Refusing Treatment in Mental Health Institutions: Values in Conflict* (pp. 56–73). Ann Arbor, MI: AUPHA Press, 1982
11. Hallek S. Legal and ethical aspects of behavior control. *Am J Psychiatry*. 131: 381–5, 1974
12. Schaeffer P. Court rules that mental patients have right to refuse treatment. *Clinical Psychiatry News*, January 1980
13. *Rogers v. Okin*, 478 F. Supp. 1342 (1979), p. 1367
14. Gutheil T. In search of true freedom: drug refusal, involuntary medication, and "rotting with your rights on." *Am J Psychiatry*. 137: 327–8, 1980
15. *Rogers v. Okin*, 634 F.2d 650 (1980)
16. *Mills v. Rogers*, 457 U.S. 29 (1982)
17. *Rogers v. Commissioner of Department of Mental Health*, 390 Mass 489 (1983), p. 491
18. *Youngberg v. Romeo*, 102 Sup. Ct. 2452 (1981)
19. *Rogers v. Mills*. Amicus Curiae Brief of the American Psychiatric Association to the Massachusetts Supreme Judicial Court, SJC-2995 (1982), p. 7
20. Guardianship of Roe, 383 Mass. 415 (1981)
21. *Rogers v. Commissioner of Department of Mental Health*, 390 Mass 489 (1983), p. 507
22. *Rogers v. Commissioner of Department of Mental Health*, 390 Mass 489 (1983), p. 510
23. *Rogers v. Commissioner of Department of Mental Health*, 390 Mass 489 (1983), p. 511
24. Winnick B. *The Right to Refuse Mental Health Treatment*. Washington D.C.: American Psychological Association, 1997
25. *Rennie v. Klein*, 462 F. Supp. 1131 (1978), pp. 1144–45
26. See *Rogers v. Okin*, 478 F. Supp. 1342, p. 1389

27. *Rogers v. Mills*. Amicus Curiae Brief of the Mental Health Legal Advisors Committee to the Massachusetts Supreme Judicial Court, SJC-2995 (1982), p. 4

28. *Rennie v. Klein*, 476 F. Supp. 1294 (1979)

29. *Youngberg v. Romeo*, 457 U.S. 307 (1982), p. 323

30. *Rennie v. Klein*, 720 F.2d 266 (1983)

31. Brotman S. Behind the bench in Rennie v. Klein. In A Doudera, J Swazey (Eds.), *Refusing Treatment in Mental Health Institutions: Values in Conflict* (pp. 31–41). Ann Arbor, MI: AUPHA Press, 1982

32. *Gill et al. v. Office of Personnel Management*, 682 F.3d 1 (1st Cir. 2012)

33. Appelbaum P. *Almost a Revolution*. New York: Oxford University Press, 1994

34. Wettstein R. The right to refuse psychiatric treatment. *Psychiatr Clinic North Am.* 22: 173–82, 1999

35. Stone A. *Law, Psychiatry and Morality*. Washington D.C.: American Psychiatric Association, 1984, p. 128

36. *Rogers v. Okin*, 634 F.2d 661 (1980)

37. Appelbaum P. *Almost a Revolution*. New York: Oxford University Press, 1994, pp. 17–70

38. Geller J. The right to treatment. In R Rosner (Ed.), *Principles and Practice of Forensic Psychiatry* (2nd ed.) (pp. 121–28). London: Arnold, 2003

39. *Riese v. St. Mary's Hospital and Medical Center*, 243 Cal. Rptr. 241 (1987)

40. *Rivers v. Katz*, 67 N.Y.2d 485 (1986)

41. Wettstein R. The right to refuse psychiatric treatment. *Psychiatric Clinic North Am* 22: 173–82, 1999

42. *Project Release v. Prevost*, 551 F. Supp. 1298 (1982)

43. *Project Release v. Prevost*, 551 F. Supp. 1298 (1982) at 1309.

44. *Stensvad v. Reivitz*, 601 F. Supp. 128 at 131

45. Stromberg C, Stone A. Statute. A model state law on civil commitment of the mentally ill. *Harvard Journal on Legislation* 20, 275–396 (1983)

46. *Colyar v. Third Judicial District Court*, 469 F. Supp. 424 (1979)

47. *Bentley v. State ex rel. Rogers*, 398 So.2d 992 (1981)

48. Gray J, O'Reilly R. Supreme Court of Canada's "Beautiful mind" case. *International Journal of Law and Psychiatry* 32, 315–322, 2009

49. Cole R. Patients rights vs. doctors' rights: which should take precedence? In A Doudera, J Swazey (Eds.), *Refusing Treatment in Mental Health Institutions – Values in Conflict* (pp. 56–73). Ann Arbor, MI: AUPHA Press, 1982, p. 70

50. Binder R, McNeil D. Involuntary patients' right to refuse medication: impact of the Riese decision on a California inpatient unit. *Bulletin of the American Academy of Psychiatry and the Law* 19: 351–358, 1991

51. Levin S, Brekke J, Thomas P. A controlled comparison of involuntarily hospitalized medication refusers and acceptors. *Bulletin of the American Academy of Psychiatry and the Law* 19:161–171, 1991

52. Hoge S, Appelbaum P, Lawlor T et al. A prospective, multi-center study of patients' refusal of antipsychotic medication. *Archives of General Psychiatry* 47: 949–956, 1990

53. Roth L, Appelbaum P. What we do and do not know about treatment refusals in mental institutions. In A Doudera, J Swazey (Eds.), *Refusing Treatment*

in Mental Health Institutions – Values in Conflict (pp. 179–196). Ann Arbor, MI: AUPHA Press, 1982

54. Buchanan A. The treatment of mentally disordered offenders under capacity-based mental health legislation. *Journal of Mental Health Law* 20: 40–46, 2010

55. Appelbaum P. *Almost a Revolution*. New York: Oxford University Press, 1994, p. 132

6   The Least Restrictive Alternative
Olmstead v. L. C. (1999)

Megan Testa

Why do individuals with mental illness live in our communities, rather than in state institutions?

When making treatment plans for their patients, mental health professionals often discuss the concept of the "least restrictive alternative." This principle holds that individuals with mental ailments deserve to live their lives in settings with minimal restrictions on their freedom. When mental health professionals make efforts to provide their patients with the treatments and services they require to live in the community, they do so in accordance with legal concepts.

Judge David Bazelon first advanced the idea of the *least restrictive alternative* in 1965 in his decision in the federal case *Lake v. Cameron.*[1] That decision created a right to treatment in the least restrictive setting. His purpose in creating this right, initially, was to protect people from being civilly committed on unjust terms during a time when society in the United States was taking a critical look at the institutionalization of individuals with mental illness.[2] Although the case itself only had a formal legal effect in the District of Columbia, Judge Bazelon's decision influenced clinical and legal thinking related to suitable alternatives to institutionalization for the care of people with mental disorders.

Today, psychiatrists understand the concept of the least restrictive alternative as meaning much more than providing people with protection from undue confinement in locked institutions. They interpret it to confer numerous rights to patients, including a right to community integration, which is defined as "the opportunity for people with mental illnesses to live in the community and be valued for their uniqueness and abilities like everyone else."[3]

This chapter focuses on the landmark Supreme Court case *Olmstead v. L. C.*,[4] which changed the practice of psychiatry by making consideration of the least restrictive alternative an essential element of psychiatric decision-making.

The People Before the Case

Lois Curtis was born in the late 1970s in the American South. Her mother realized early on that she was not like other children. Curtis, who had an intellectual disability, had difficulties at home and at school. She engaged in disruptive behavior at school, which interfered with her ability to succeed both academically and socially. When not in school, Curtis would leave her mother's home and wander in unsafe areas of her neighborhood. Her mother called authorities frequently, out of fear for her daughter's safety. Police responding to her mother's calls took Curtis to Atlanta Regional Hospital on many occasions, and beginning at age 11 she could frequently be found on the hospital's Child and Adolescent Psychiatric Unit.[5] Doctors diagnosed Curtis with schizophrenia. The medications that she took to treat her mental illness sedated her. A nurse who worked with her in the hospital described Curtis as having been "lackluster and isolated ... unkempt and uncared for ... sullen and depressed," and also stated, "She was withdrawn into herself and rarely smiled."[5]

Curtis grew into adulthood within the walls of a locked psychiatric ward. She spent most of her young adult years living a routine and restricted existence. "She sat around and didn't do much of anything productive ... mostly she sat around and smoked to kill time," said the Atlanta Legal Aid attorney, Sue Jamieson, who would later join Curtis in her fight to be released from the institution.

Curtis was joined in her case with another patient plaintiff, Elaine Wilson. Wilson was born in Georgia in 1951. When she was a baby, Wilson contracted a severe febrile illness that left her with physical, mental, and developmental disabilities. During her childhood she displayed severe behavioral problems. She was not able to succeed in public or private schooling. Her mother enrolled her in an out-of-town school that specialized in the education of children with disabilities, with the hope that Wilson would do well in this environment. However, Wilson continued to have problems. School authorities sent Wilson back to her mother when she was 15 years old. Wilson's mother was unable to take care of her when she returned home, and, "with a broken heart" she took Wilson to a state psychiatric facility.[6] Doctors diagnosed Wilson with mental retardation and a personality disorder.[7] Wilson was kept in psychiatric institutions for the remainder of her adolescence and much of her adult life. She spent only short interludes of time outside of hospitals, and during these times she was homeless.[6] As was the case with Curtis, Wilson's existence was restricted. She described it as living life "in a little box" with "no way out."[6]

What Led to the Case

It was not unusual in the United States in the 20th century for people who suffered from mental illness to live their entire lives in psychiatric institutions. The first insane asylums in the United States appeared during the first quarter of the 19th century, and by the time Curtis and Wilson were born asylums were erected all across the country. These institutions housed a population of nearly 560,000 individuals with mental illnesses.[8] In his writing for the *Houston Law Review*, Perlin[2] opined that the history of psychiatric institutions was one of institutional segregation. He wrote, "The mode of commitment of the insane was so easy and free from formality that a few words hastily scribbled upon a chance scrap of paper were sufficient to place a supposed insane person in the hospital and deprive him of personal liberty." Committing individuals was easy. A large number of people with mental illnesses were thus dependents of the state during the 1800s and early 1900s.

In 1950 scientists created a new medication, chlorpromazine, and serendipitously discovered that it was very effective in the treatment of psychosis.[8] After chlorpromazine was developed, people with severe mental illnesses such as schizophrenia could reduce their disabling symptoms by taking a medication. Doctors watched institutionalized patients achieve a degree of symptom resolution previously thought to be impossible, and many psychiatric inpatients were able to be released from hospitals.

As the deinstitutionalization movement accelerated, fueled in part by the civil rights movement,[8] the general public adopted the outlook that recovery from mental illness would be better achieved in the community because the well-being of individuals would increase if they lived outside of locked hospital wards.[3] In 1963 President John F. Kennedy signed the Community Mental Health Centers Act, a national bill to create centers that could administer treatment to individuals with mental illness within the communities where they would live.[8] Psychiatric institutions continued to exist; however, they ceased to be the mainstay of treatment for individuals with mental illnesses. The patient census among the state psychiatric hospitals began a precipitous decline.[8] As per diem costs of inpatient stays grew, state governments found a significant financial incentive in reducing the number of inpatient beds, but the savings from deinstitutionalization were not reinvested in outpatient community services.

Lake v. Cameron (1966)

In the early 1900s individuals with mental illness could be easily committed, but by the end of the 20th century, putting a person into a psychiatric hospital against his or her will was not an easy task. *Lake v. Cameron* likely played a role in this trend because it narrowed the states' ability to place individuals under involuntary commitment in institutions.

Catherine Lake was a woman in late middle age who doctors in 1962 described as suffering from "senility," a chronic brain syndrome that she developed from cerebral atherosclerosis. Senility rendered Lake subject to periods of disorientation and confusion, and she was prone to aimlessly walk the streets of Washington, D.C., at night. On one such night in September 1962 city police picked Lake up while she was wandering the streets, confused and exposed to the elements. They took her to the District of Columbia General Hospital. Physicians at D.C. General Hospital evaluated Lake and determined that the 60-year-old woman was unable to care for herself. They admitted her to the hospital.

Lake wanted to be sent home from the hospital but was not successful in negotiating with her physicians to achieve a hospital discharge. Her physicians believed that she posed a danger to herself. They insisted that she stay in the hospital and recommended that she be sent to St. Elizabeth's Hospital for psychiatric observation. In response, Lake filed a legal petition, a writ of habeas corpus, demanding her discharge. She was subsequently transferred to St. Elizabeth's and faced civil commitment proceedings. Psychiatrists evaluated her and asserted that, although she did not pose a purposeful threat of dangerousness to herself or others, due to her senility, Lake would be unable to survive outside an institutional setting because she would not be able to care for herself. The court dismissed her habeas corpus petition.

Lake then appealed the denial of her release. She argued, through her appeal, that she did not need the level of care provided at St. Elizabeth's. She demonstrated to the court that she had arranged to have the support of her husband and sister, both of whom came forward and expressed their intentions to help care for her if she were discharged. Her psychiatrists testified that although Lake did not need the level of care provided at St. Elizabeth's, she would need more assistance and supervision than could be provided by her family in the community. They told the court that Lake could do quite well in a nursing home type of setting. After hearing the evidence, the court denied Lake's appeal and advised her to ask for discharge again only after she could demonstrate that she had found an adequate alternative to living at St. Elizabeth's, such as a nursing home or other step-down facility.[1]

Lake then appealed her case to a higher court. The appeals court examined the facts of Lake's case and recognized that Lake was being provided treatment in a setting that was very restrictive of her liberties. The court noted that the district court had advised Lake that she could reapply for release if she could demonstrate that an alternative less-restrictive facility existed that could provide her with the care and supervision that she needed. The appeals court decided that it was the responsibility of the mental health system to place individuals in settings that provided them with the most appropriate level of care and that were not unduly restrictive of their liberties. The court remanded the case back to the district court with instructions that a more appropriate treatment facility be found for Lake. The idea that patients with mental illness have the right to treatment in the setting that is the least restrictive alternative was born.[1]

The Americans with Disabilities Act

In 1990, Congress passed the Americans with Disabilities Act (ADA) with the aim of protecting individuals with disabilities from discrimination. The ADA defined disability to be an "impairment that substantially limits one or more of the major life activities of (an) individual."[7] The definition was inclusive of mental disorders, as these impairments were likely to lead to discrimination. During discussion of the ADA among members of Congress, one representative said, "Historically, society has tended to isolate and segregate individuals with disabilities ... this continue(s) to be a serious and pervasive social problem ... in such critical areas as ... institutionalization."[7]

The ADA included many regulations. The regulation of greatest interest in this discussion of the least restrictive alternative is included in Title II, which mandates that individuals with disabilities be provided the same opportunities to benefit from governmental "programs, services, and activities" as individuals without disabilities.[3] Furthermore, Title II includes a regulation called the "integration regulation," which requires public entities to provide their services in the most integrated settings appropriate to the needs of the individuals served.[9] Congress decided that states would be exempt from following the integration regulation if doing so would "fundamentally alter the nature of the service, program, or activity."[7]

A congressional committee called the ADA a "clear and comprehensive national mandate to end discrimination against individuals with disabilities," and some compared the ADA to the Civil Rights Acts of the 1960s.[7] Importantly, the ADA was enforceable, because if a state acted in a way that violated it, such action was seen as violating the Constitution's equal protection clause. Passage of the ADA gave courts the ability to intervene on behalf of individuals and require "reasonable modifications" to programs offered by a state if the programs were not administered in accordance with the principles set forth by the ADA.[10]

Legal Course

It is in the context of this background that we return to the story of Curtis and Wilson. Both women were living at Georgia Regional Hospital in the 1990s. Curtis lived on a psychiatric unit where she had been admitted voluntarily for symptoms of schizophrenia. Wilson also lived on a psychiatric unit, having signed herself in to the hospital for treatment of a personality disorder.

When Curtis decided that she wanted to leave the hospital, her psychiatrist assessed her and determined that she had made sufficient progress with regard to her mental illness that she could be discharged. Similarly, when Wilson reached the point that she desired to leave the hospital, her doctor thought that the symptoms of her personality disorder had improved to a point that discharge from the hospital was warranted. At that time, the Medicaid program in Georgia paid for the provision of community-based services. Although the government had approved several thousand living spaces to be community placements for people being discharged from institutions, Georgia's Medicaid program only funded about a third of the spots. Because there were not enough community placements for everyone who needed one, the hospital had nowhere to move Curtis and Wilson. The women were thus placed on wait lists for community-based services, and their discharges were put on hold.[10]

Years passed by while Curtis and Wilson remained institutionalized at Georgia Regional Hospital, waiting to be discharged. Eventually, Curtis called an Atlanta Legal Aid office and told the attorneys that she had been held in the hospital for years, against her will, simply waiting for a community placement. The attorneys believed that her civil rights were being violated and filed a lawsuit against the commissioner of Georgia's Department of Human Resources, Tommy Olmstead. The suit alleged that Mr. Olmstead violated the ADA by failing to provide Curtis with integrated, community-based mental health services.[11] Wilson later joined in the suit.

The Legal Question

The legal question that the attorneys for Curtis and Wilson raised seemed straightforward. Would the court consider the state's failure to discharge them to the community for integrated care a violation of their civil rights under the ADA?

The Case

The U.S. District Court for northern Georgia heard the case brought by Curtis and Wilson, who, to protect their confidentiality as patients, became known as L. C. and E. W. Represented by Atlanta Legal Aid, L. C. and E. W. argued that prolonged hospitalization violated their rights under the ADA. The state made several opposing arguments. First, it argued that the discharges of L. C. and E. W. were denied because of funding inadequacies, not because of discrimination based upon disability. Second, it argued that requiring the state to discharge patients despite a lack of available funding for community care would violate the "fundamental alteration" clause included in the ADA. The district court ruled that the failure of the state of Georgia to place L. C. and E. W. in community-based care did indeed violate the ADA.[4]

Appeals

The state of Georgia filed an appeal, and the case went to the U.S. Court of Appeals for the Eleventh Circuit. The appeals court affirmed the district court's decision.[12] However, it also requested that the U.S. Supreme Court hear the case to decide the issue of whether community care was indeed so expensive that if it were provided to all individuals like L. C. and E. W. it would fundamentally alter the state's ability to provide care to its citizens with mental disabilities. The U.S. Supreme Court granted *certiorari*, meaning it agreed to hear the case.

Olmsted v. L. C. reached the Supreme Court in 1999. The justices faced the task of determining how the ADA applied to protection of persons with mental disorders. The main question was whether the state of Georgia was violating voluntary patients' rights when it did not make community care available when patients had recovered to the extent that they, and their doctors, believed they no longer needed to live in institutions. Additionally, if the Supreme Court decided affirmatively on that question, the Court then needed to determine what the difference between a reasonable modification and a fundamental alteration was in practice.[10]

Five justices agreed that failing to move Curtis and Wilson to community placements did amount to discrimination based on mental illness and was a violation of the ADA. Three justices dissented, arguing that Curtis and Wilson did not have a case for discrimination. As they read the ADA, they understood that it simply did not address the issue of whether mental health dollars should be spent on outpatient or inpatient care. The ninth justice, Anthony Kennedy, did not think the plaintiffs had brought a genuine case of discrimination. He pointed out that the plaintiffs did not identify any class of similarly situated individuals, such as individuals with physical illness, who were given preferential treatment – in this case, integrated community treatment – instead of institutional-based care. Nevertheless, he became part of the 6–3 majority in favor of the plaintiff's claim requiring treatment outside of institutions for individuals for whom this would be clinically appropriate. The case was sent back to the lower court.

Justice Ruth Bader Ginsburg wrote the majority opinion, which held that the ADA required community placement of individuals who did not oppose such placement if professionals of the state determined that it was appropriate and that such placement could reasonably be accommodated when consideration of available mental health resources and mental health needs of state residents was made. She stated that failure to find community placement for individuals such as Curtis and Wilson amounted to discrimination on the basis of disability. She advanced several points to support the majority's conclusion. She wrote that "institutionalization severely diminishes the everyday life activities of individuals," causing them to be less able to interact with others and less able to contribute to the community through work. She further noted that "unnecessary institutionalization perpetuates unwarranted assumptions that the persons so isolated are incapable of participating in community life, which results in stigmatization, one of the most serious consequences of discriminatory action." A final point Ginsberg made was that individuals with physical illnesses are not required to give up community life to get treatment, so requiring individuals with mental illnesses to do so in order to receive care is discriminatory.

Justice Clarence Thomas wrote the minority opinion, arguing that Curtis and Wilson were not discriminated against because no group without disability existed to which they could be compared. He said that community placement "simply is not available to those without disabilities. Continued institutional treatment ... establishes no more than the fact that (states) have limited resources."

Only five justices who agreed Georgia had violated the ADA addressed the second question posed: the request for clarification regarding the "fundamental alteration" clause in the ADA. Justice Ginsberg, writing for the majority, stated that the fundamental alteration clause of the ADA did not make Georgia exempt from providing community services to Curtis and Wilson. Any state claiming a fundamental alteration exemption would have to show that providing immediate placement of the women, even if possible, would not be equitable, given the particulars of the mental health system in that state.

The majority opinion was careful to clarify that the *Olmstead* decision was not intended to mandate closing of all state-run mental institutions. It made the point that institutions had a place in the treatment of individuals with mental illnesses. It warned that *Olmstead* should not be used as an excuse for sending patients to inappropriate settings, such as homeless shelters, in lieu of taking care of them: "[For some psychiatric patients] no placement outside the institution may ever be appropriate." For most, the opinion stated, however, this is not the case, and continued institutionalization creates the notion that they are "unworthy or incapable" of participating in community.

Justice Anthony Kennedy wrote a concurring opinion to highlight his concerns about the potential ramifications of the decision. In his opinion, he stated that "the depopulation of state mental hospitals has had its dark side ... if the principle of liability announced by the Court is not applied with caution and circumspection, States may be pressured into attempting compliance on the cheap, placing marginal patients into integrated settings devoid of the services and attention necessary for their condition."

Where Are They Now?

By the time the case reached the Supreme Court, both Wilson and Curtis had been discharged from Georgia Regional Hospital and were living in the community.[2] They were both present at the Supreme Court when the case was heard.[13]

On the day the Supreme Court announced the decision, Wilson, who was then in a group home, said she was pleased to be able to eat M&M's whenever she wanted, instead of being told what to eat and when to eat it, as she was in the hospital. Living in a community group home, she made her own decisions about how to spend her days, with the assistance of the Circle of Support, an organization that helped people with developmental disabilities live in integrated community settings. She learned to do her own grocery shopping. Her quality of life improved greatly. Three years before dying of complications from a fall, she moved into her own place.[14]

Curtis also made a life for herself in the community after leaving Georgia's state hospital. She lived in an unlocked home where she could complete the tasks necessary for daily life with the assistance of a "microboard" of individuals committed to supporting her life in the community. She spent much of her time creating and selling artwork, mainly paintings. She became an activist and traveled the United States as a motivational speaker. In 2007 she was awarded the Harriet Tubman Act of Courage. In 2011 she met President Barack Obama, and shared with him not only her story, but one of her paintings, "Girl in the Orange Dress."[6]

Impact on Practice

Some have called the *Olmstead* decision the "first coherent answer to the question of the right of institutionalized persons with mental disabilities to community services under the ADA."[2] Not only did the Supreme Court decide that institutionalization of people with mental disorders without sound clinical grounds constituted a violation of the ADA, but it also held that it was not enough for states to provide services for individuals with mental disorders or intellectual disabilities only in institutional settings, particularly when these persons could be equally served or better served in the community. *Olmstead* mandated that services for people with disabilities must be provided in integrated settings, and this ensured that those living with mental illnesses would have the opportunity to live their lives in community with others, rather than endure segregated living in institutions.

Olmstead changed the way mental health providers made decisions in the care of hospitalized patients. During the 1970s and 1980s, psychiatrists routinely considered the least restrictive alternative doctrine when making clinical decisions regarding involuntary commitment. However, they did not typically make consideration of the least restrictive alternative a part of decision-making when working with institutionalized patients. After *Olmstead*, it became the norm for mental health providers to think of all patients as having a right to community integration.[3] The focus of clinical decision-making shifted. This was especially true for patients in long-term care institutions, where the focus shifted to how to provide psychiatric care in the community and how to put in place the social services necessary to support such care.[9] In addition, clinicians made more efforts to identify resources that might best accommodate individuals deemed "discharge-ready" who were awaiting community placement. Finding community placements became one of the most significant early goals set during psychiatric hospitalization.

Olmstead also affected the practice of psychiatry at the systems level. The decision required states to administer disability services "with an even hand." In practice, this meant that if a state fully funded institutional care, but had only minimal availability of poor-quality community care, it would be in violation of the ADA.[15] Health policy experts started looking at existing mental health systems to determine whether they were providing services to individuals in a manner that would comply with the ADA. In order to prove compliance, states had to show that they provided a "range of facilities" for the treatment of individuals with disabilities. If a state could not prove compliance with the ADA, and policymakers determined that modifying the system to make integrated services available indeed would alter fundamentally that state's existing mental health system, the state would have the burden of proving that point.[10]

The Supreme Court's *Olmstead* decision did not set compliance deadlines. Although the decision made it illegal for states to fail to offer integrated mental health services, the states did not have any real legal charge to improve their community services.[10] In February 2001, President George W. Bush announced the "New Freedom Initiative," the purpose of which was to encourage states to implement compliance with *Olmstead*, and to do so with urgency. Four months later, President Bush signed an executive order regarding integrating individuals with disabilities into communities across the United States, Executive Order 13217—Community-Based Alternatives for Individuals with Disabilities. This gave federal agencies such as the Office for Civil Rights power to implement *Olmstead*, by giving them an order to enforce.[9]

Following President Bush's executive order, the National Conference of State Legislatures (NCSL) tracked states' efforts to develop and implement initiatives that would bring them into compliance with the mandates put forth in the decision. The NCSL found that by the year 2003, 48 out of 50 states had created task forces or work groups dedicated to planning *Olmstead* initiatives, and 21 of those states had issued plans or reports regarding how they would improve their community mental health services.[11]

Implementation was slow, however, because funding difficulties presented roadblocks for many states in developing integrated community services. The money that came into states for treatment of individuals who were institutionalized went directly to institutions; it did not go towards the care of particular patients. Therefore, the money used to care for an individual who was in a psychiatric hospital could not be used to care for him or her in the community. In many states, individuals continued to live in institutions far longer than they needed to because community placements simply were not available, despite the *Olmstead* mandate. Federal civil rights agencies and disability advocates filed lawsuits in many states to push them towards implementation.[16]

President Obama highlighted the importance of states working to implement *Olmstead* when he called for 2009–2010 to be a "Year of Community Living" for individuals with disabilities. The Obama administration committed to increased litigation against states for failing to implement systems that could provide integrated care for individuals with mental illnesses in communities. The governmental departments involved in housing and health provided $40 million worth of housing vouchers to provide individuals with the means to afford community living as an alternative to continued institutionalization, and created initiatives for federal money to follow individuals from institutions into communities, further removing barriers to implementation of the Supreme Court's *Olmstead* decision.[13]

REFERENCES

1. *Lake v. Cameron*, 364 F.2d 657 (D.C. Cir. 1966)
2. Perlin M. The promises of paradise: Will Olmstead v. L. C. resuscitate the constitutional least restrictive alternative principle in mental disability law? *Houston Law Rev.* 37: 999–1028, 2000
3. Salzer M, Kaplan K, Atay J. State psychiatric hospital census after the 1999 Olmstead decision: Evidence of decelerating deinstitutionalization. *Psychiatric Serv.* 57(10): 1501–5, 2006
4. *Olmstead v. L. C.*, 527 U.S. 581 (1999)
5. Nelson RR. Unlocked: The Lois Curtis story. *Dixie's Land*, Nov. 27, 2010. Available at: http://assignmentatlanta.wordpress.com/2010/11/27/unlocked-the-lois-curtis-story/Accessed Apr. 23, 2017
6. Henry D. Elaine Wilson, beat disability, discrimination. *Atlanta Journal-Constitution*, 2004. Available at: www.legacy.com/obituaries/atlanta/obituary.aspx?pid=2907375 Accessed Apr. 23, 2017
7. Herbert P, Young K. The Americans with Disabilities Act and deinstitutionalization of the chronically mentally ill. *J Am Acad Psychiatry Law.* 27(4): 603–13, 1999
8. Testa M, West SG. Civil commitment in the United States. *Psychiatry (Edgemont).* 7(10): 30–40, 2010
9. Jackson SR, Hafner G, O'Brien D et al. Approaches to implementing the Olmstead ADA Ruling. *J Law Medicine Ethics.* 31(s4): 47–8, 2003.
10. Teitelbaum J, Burke T, Rosenbaum S. Olmstead v. L. C. and the Americans with Disabilities Act: Implications for public health policy and practice. *Public Health Rep.* 119(3): 371–4, 2004
11. Priaulx E. Integrating the disabled into the community in the wake of Olmstead. *Caring.* 22(9): 6010, 2003
12. *L. C. v. Olmstead*, 138 F.3d 893 (11th Cir., 1998)
13. Office of the Press Secretary. On anniversary of Olmstead, Obama administration recommits to assist Americans with disabilities. Washington DC: The White House, 1999. Available at: www.whitehouse.gov/the-press-office/2011/06/22/anniversary-olmstead-obama-administration-recommits-assist-americans-dis Accessed Apr. 23, 2017
14. Reynolds D. Elaine Wilson dies: Her Supreme Court case is landmark. *Ragged Edge Magazine*, 2004. Available at: www.raggededgemagazine.com/drn/12_04.html#803 Accessed Apr. 23, 2017

15. Under court order. Washington, DC: Bazelon Center for Mental Health Law, 1999. Downloaded from: www.bazelon.org/News-Publications/Publications/List/1/CategoryID/11/Level/a/ProductID/14.aspx?SortField=ProductNumber,ProductNumber Accessed Apr. 23, 2017
16. Bazelon Center for Mental Health Law. Still waiting … the unfulfilled promise of Olmstead. Washington, DC: Bazelon Center for Mental Health Law, 2009. Available at: www.bazelon.org/wp-content/uploads/2017/01/Still-Waiting…The-Unfulfilled-Promise-of-Olmstead.pdf Accessed Dec. 31, 2017

7   Informed Consent
Canterbury v. Spence (1972)

Debra A. Pinals

When we go to a physician today, we expect our doctors to disclose infor-mation in order to assist us in making decisions regarding our medical care. This expectation, however, is relatively new in the world of doctor–patient relationships. How did the thinking evolve regarding disclosure of information about medical treatments and procedures? Have there always been standards related to the need for such disclosure?

In the 1950s the United States had come to a quiet, settled place. With Eisenhower as President and World War II well in the past, it was a time of hope and promise. Yet, in 1958, the ground began to shift as the Vietnam War was emerging on the horizon, and the United States was teetering on decades of social reform. It was during that year that Elvis Presley signed up for the military, the National Aeronautics and Space Administration was formed, Elizabeth Taylor was heading into another marriage, and the Lego Company patented Lego bricks. It was a time of growth and a time of loss, with World War II fresh in the minds of many. During this time Jerry W. Canterbury, at the age of 19, left his widowed mother in Cyclone, West Virginia, to work as a clerk-typist for the FBI in Washington, D.C.,[1,2] setting the stage for what the court would refer to as a "depressing tale" of a youth beset with back pain who underwent a surgical procedure without being told of the potential risk of paralysis that could ensue.

Canterbury's time in Washington, D.C., was complicated by devel-oping medical issues. In August of 1958 he had notable weight loss and low energy and went to a physician for consultation. He was hospitalized and diagnosed, after a through medical work-up, with neurosis. He was prescribed vitamins and liver extract injections. Several months later, in December 1958, Canterbury developed sharp pains between his scap-ulas and across his neck. The pains came and went and were modified based on position. After seeing another physician who provided no relief from his symptoms, it was recommended that he consult with a neuro-surgeon, William T. Spence.

It was no surprise that Spence's name came up as someone who could help Canterbury. A prominent neurosurgeon in the Washington, D.C., area, Spence was viewed as "innovative and courageous" throughout his professional life.[3] After serving in the military during World War II, he developed and held a patent for an acrylic cranioplasty and in 1951 performed the first successful carotid endarterectomy for artherosclerotic plaques.

Despite the hope this consultation may have engendered in Canterbury, Spence's neurological examination and X-rays (which were basically negative) seemed to provide no leads as to the cause of the former's pain. A myelogram, then a relatively new procedure, which involved injecting dye into the spinal column and then x-raying the image, was ordered. In Canterbury's case this test showed a defect at the fourth thoracic vertebra that may have been related to a ruptured disc. Spence recommended a procedure called a laminectomy, which involved surgery of the spine to correct the problem of the suspected ruptured disc.

At the time, anyone under age 21 was unable to consent to surgery, and thus Canterbury asked Spence to speak with his mother about the procedure. When they spoke, Spence explained that her son had a possible ruptured disc and that he needed an operation. She asked if the operation was serious, to which he responded "not more than any other operation" (Ref. 2, p. 777). He further told her that he was aware of her financial limitations and that her presence in Washington at the time of surgery would not be necessary. Records included contradictory evidence as to whether she, as the legally authorized representative of Canterbury, explicitly expressed consent to the operation. There were no further conversations between Canterbury and Spence prior to the operation, which was scheduled and postponed for a few days while an abdominal infection was resolving.

On February 11, 1959, the day of Canterbury's surgery, Mrs. Canterbury, who had little means for travel, was able to make the journey and arrived in Washington. She came to the hospital after the operation had concluded, and signed consent forms for the procedure after her arrival. The operation had revealed several abnormalities, including a nonpulsating spinal cord, local swelling, an accumulation of swollen veins, and an absence of fat in the particularly problematic area surrounding the spine in the thoracic vertebrae region. Spence attempted to relieve pressure in this area during the laminectomy procedure by widening the outer wall of the spinal cord.

The subsequent course of Canterbury's hospitalization was complicated. The first day after surgery he was doing well and seemed to be experiencing a normal recovery. According to Murphy, whose work summarizes the facts behind the Canterbury's clinical backdrop and legal case,[1] 3½ hours after surgery he was able to move all his limbs; the next day he was turning himself from side to side, had been out of bed, and went to the bathroom where he voided without difficulty. Later in the evening, he needed to be catheterized because of trouble going to the bathroom and also had an elevated temperature, but he was still moving all his limbs and was feeling "comfortable." In the early morning hours of February 12, he fell facedown out of bed while attempting to urinate without an attendant present. He rose to his knees and with the assistance of nursing staff was able to go back into bed. Of note, the medical record was unclear as to how the physician's orders had changed from requiring Canterbury to remain in bed while voiding to orders that allowed him to be alone without hospital staff nearby and out of bed while urinating.[1] Canterbury himself later indicated that a nurse had given him a portable urinal to use, but he was left unattended and there was no side rail to prevent the fall.

Hours after his fall, Canterbury complained he was having trouble breathing, and by the evening he was unable to move his legs. Upon notification that his patient was experiencing near total paralysis from the waist down, Spence returned urgently to the hospital on February 12. Mrs. Canterbury signed another consent form for a new surgery and Canterbury was operated on again for a second time, during which the wound and the passageway were opened further to allow the spinal cord sufficient space.

According to case records, Canterbury again showed improvement but it was incomplete. Still unable to urinate properly, he was referred to and was cared for by a urologist. By April, he had a procedure involving removal of bladder stones, and in May he was discharged from the hospital. In August he was readmitted to the hospital for additional urological problems. Canterbury's functioning over the years required oversight by several specialists, and his paralysis stabilized to become partial in the lower extremities with ongoing urinary incontinence.

Later in 1959, Spence recommended that Canterbury be transferred to the FBI offices in warmer climates where he could swim and exercise more readily, and in the fall that same year, Canterbury transferred to the Miami FBI office. During the first year after the operation, there were notably friendly correspondences between Spence, Canterbury, and Canterbury's mother. He worked in offices in Miami, Los Angeles, and Houston, and resigned his duties finally in 1962. He worked at several jobs after that, but he had difficulty finding steady employment due to his need to remain seated and near a bathroom. On March 7, 1963, Canterbury filed suit in the District Court against the Washington Center

Hospital and Spence, seeking damages for extensive pain and suffering, medical expenses, and lost earnings for the amount of $250,000.[1] Among the complaints alleged, Canterbury argued that Spence had been negligent in the performance of the surgery and in failing to inform him of the risk involved. Canterbury also filed suit against the hospital for negligent postoperative care, especially related to leaving him unattended and unprotected from the fall.

Legal Course

The litigation between Canterbury and the defendants (Spence and Washington Center Hospital) took years to take shape as the litigant and defendants were preparing for trial. The defendants to the matter argued that the statute of limitations for the complaint had been exceeded when examined in the context of an argument of battery. Further, they contended that the claim should not go forward due to a lack of certainty as to the true cause of Canterbury's paralysis.

At the initial hearings, Spence described Canterbury's disabilities as resulting from his preoperative condition and possible trauma, although the full nature of the condition was unclear. Spence also noted that even without trauma, paralysis could occur in approximately 1% of cases involving a laminectomy. He referenced this risk as a "very slight possibility" (Ref. 2, p. 778). Spence also remarked that communicating such a risk to a patient would not be good medical practice because patients might feel deterred from getting surgery, and because it might instill negative psychological reactions that could further the risk the success of the operation. Over the course of the ensuing trials and appeals, it was never entirely clear what caused Canterbury's injury, though advances in arteriography helped defense experts to ultimately express more consistent opinions that vascular blockage at the site and things related to collateral circulation were at issue.[1]

In 1968, at the time of the trial, Canterbury appeared to require crutches to walk and still suffered from urinary incontinence and bowel paralysis (Ref. 2, p. 778). The trial court judge granted motions for directed verdicts that had issued from both defendants, citing that Canterbury had failed to produce medical evidence that supported negligence by Spence in diagnosing him or in performing the laminectomy, and that there was no proof that the treatment itself was responsible for the subsequent disabilities. Further, although there was evidence that showed negligent postoperative care, the lack of evidence directly linking that negligent care to the cause of Canterbury's problems did not support allowing the case to go forward to the jury.

On appeal the directed verdict decision of the trial court judge was reversed, citing the testimony of Canterbury and his mother that demonstrated sufficient question as to whether there had been a violation of the physician's duty to disclose the risk of paralysis from the laminectomy, as well as testimony related to the performance of the laminectomy itself and the care rendered surrounding the fall. The heart of the matter, therefore, was the nature of the disclosure that would have been necessary to ensure that a decision to have the surgery was properly informed. Taken together, the United States Court of Appeals for the District of Columbia Circuit Court found that there was sufficient evidence produced by Canterbury and his mother that should have entitled him the opportunity for a full trial on his claims. This meant that the court was not going to make a quick decision just based on facts presented to date, and instead a trial was needed to allow the judge to hear both sides of the issue of proper informed consent procedures.

Background on the Legal Case Analysis

The decision of the U.S. Court of Appeals in this case has become one of the most commonly cited cases on the issues related to informed consent. To understand its ruling, it is necessary to journey back to the model of the doctor–patient relationship and the underpinnings of disclosure of information prior to medical interventions.

In the earliest times of recorded medical practice under Hippocrates, the idea of providing informed consent did not exist as currently known. Encompassing sharp demarcations in roles, Hippocrates viewed the physician as powerful healer, while the patient was viewed as a passive recipient of care from the trusted and protective physician. Hippocrates[4] himself admonished disciples to uphold the importance of protecting a patient even from information:

Do everything in a calm and orderly manner, concealing most things from the patient while treating him. Give what encouragement is required cheerfully and calmly, diverting his attention from his own circumstances; on one occasion rebuke him harshly and strictly, on another console him with solicitude and attention, revealing nothing of his future or present condition.

In this admonishment, a physician is regarded almost as parent to a child and as one who would know what is best for the patient. Over the course of medical advances and many centuries of discourse, the notion of consent has evolved, and this evolution has progressed at an accelerated pace, especially in the 20th and 21st centuries. Consent to medical research evolved through a path of regulation and legislation, including national and international oversight in large part after the atrocities of Nazi experimentation on human subjects in the absence of consent.[5]

Consent related to medical treatment has taken a different course, primarily through the lens of numerous examples of individual legal claims against physicians as well as through evolving standards related to medical ethics, informed by growing expectations of self-determination. Notably, the development of these principles and practices has taken different paths for medical patients and for patients in institutions for mental disorders.[6] For persons in the confines of mental institutions, it had long been thought that a patient had no right to refuse treatment, regardless of a treatment's intrusive nature. (For further discussion of the right to refuse treatment among psychiatric patients, see Chapter 5.) For medical patients for whom treatment involved invasive procedures, early American case law dating back to the 18th century reveals a requirement to at least attempt to obtain some form of consent from the patient. In the 1767 case of *Slater v. Baker and Stapleton,*[7] a physician was held liable for re-breaking a patient's leg in order to reset a fracture in the absence of expressed consent of the patient. In that case, some form of expressed consent of a patient seemed to carry the day, especially for treatments involving medical procedures with a more invasive quality.

The doctrine of informed consent evolved further as legal decision-makers attached significance to taking action on a patient – even well-meaning action – without proper permission. There was a growing acceptance in the early 20th century that a physician who committed some act upon a patient, regardless of motive or intent, could be construed as having committed battery in the absence of the patient's consent. In an oft-cited 1914 case in which a hospital was sued after a physician removed a tumor from a patient without proper consent, Justice Benjamin Cardozo opined that "Every human being of adult years and sound mind has a right to determine what shall be done with his own body; and a surgeon who performs an operation without his patient's consent commits an assault for which he is liable in damages."[8] In that case, the tenet that a physician could be found guilty of "battery" for touching a patient without specific consent was upheld, along with the idea that people have a right to make personal decisions about their healthcare.

Fast forward after years of case law related to consent when other, perhaps more nuanced issues started to come to light. For example, the decision in *Salgo v. Leland Stanford Jr. University Board of Trustees* (1957), decided just a year prior to Canterbury's surgery, emphasized the importance of disclosure of information to a patient.[9] In that case the court ruled that information provided to a patient should include a discussion of risks and alternatives of treatment. The *Salgo* court left it to the discretion of the physician to determine how much detail needed be given to patients.

Several years later, in *Natanson v. Kline* (1960), a physician was treating a patient for breast cancer.[10] When she underwent radiation treatment, she did not realize that it could result in serious burns and deep wounds to her chest. After her injury, she sued her physician for a failure to provide a fully informed consent. In a courtroom closed to spectators, she bared her chest, showing only a skin flap covering what remained of her deteriorated rib structure and weak skin.[11] The judge had to give the jury instructions on how to decide the case by setting a standard regarding how much information a physician needed to disclose to a patient. According to one author who summarized the case,[11] the court was placed in an awkward position, given the facts of a clearly injured patient and a doctor who had revealed no information as to the risks inherent in radiation treatment. In determining the standard for disclosure, there were two options: siding with the patient to determine what information was needed, or siding with the physician to determine the right information-disclosure balance. To side with the patient would mean eschewing years of relying upon a physician's professional judgment to decide what information about treatment risks needed to be shared with the patient. To side with the physician, the court would minimize the importance of an individual patient's ability to determine for herself whether to have a procedure if told the risks. The case was decided in 1960, at the cusp of the civil rights movement, yet the Kansas Supreme Court ultimately gave deference to the medical professional. Judge Alfred G. Schroeder articulated carefully, "The duty of the physician to disclose, however, is limited to those disclosures that a reasonable medical practitioner would make under the same or similar circumstances. How the physician may best discharge his obligation to the patient in this difficult situation involves primarily a question of medical judgment" (Ref. 10, p. 409).

This is where case law stood until Jerry Canterbury encountered his physical problems and sought relief by appealing the original dismissal of the directed verdicts, which were in favor of the defendant Spence and the Washington Hospital. The case was argued on December 18, 1969, before three well-known jurists of their time.

The Judges

Judge Skelly Wright was a remarkable man who spent almost 40 years as a federal judge. His decisions helped propel civil rights and liberties forward into the 21st century.[12] He moved from New Orleans after presiding over numerous desegregation cases and encountering tremendous vitriolic passion from those supporting segregation.[13] When appointed to the District of Columbia Circuit Court by President John F. Kennedy, he may not have realized he would be in the throes of significant cases litigating informed consent practices. Perhaps his earlier case, the *Application of the President and Directors of Georgetown College* (1964), in which he made an emergency decision to allow the transfusion of a Jehovah's Witness patient,[14] provided him the opportunity for reflection related to the multitude of issues encompassed in patient self-determination and set the stage for his views in the *Canterbury* case. Regardless, his role in the case likely was critical in shaping the position of the other judges in this case.

Judge Harold Leventhal was well recognized for his abilities to decipher complex matters of administrative law.[15] Having worked on the Hoover Commission Task Force on Independent Regulatory Agencies, he was notable for considering aspects of fairness, and was considered a friend of Supreme Court Chief Justice Warren Burger.

And finally, last but certainly not least, among the three jurists reviewing the *Canterbury* appeal was Judge Spottswood W. Robinson III, the primary author of the opinion. Judge Robinson had been considered a "pioneering civil rights lawyer" earlier in his career,[16] when he argued the case of *Davis v. County School Board of Prince Edward County* (1952),[17] which became consolidated with several other cases before the U.S. Supreme Court as *Brown v. Board of Education* (1954).[18] In 1961, President Kennedy named him to the U.S. Commission on Civil Rights, and he was appointed to the U.S. District Court for the District of Columbia three years later. Then, in 1966, President Lyndon B. Johnson appointed him to serve on the U.S. Court of Appeals for the D.C. Circuit, where he became the first African American jurist to serve there.

Thus, with three strong jurists, whose backgrounds included an emphasis on equality, fairness, and individual rights, *Canterbury* was perhaps poised to shape a new direction furthering the importance of self-determination for patients in the informed consent process with their physicians.

The Decision

The appellate court decided the *Canterbury* case on May 19, 1972. The judges noted that suits claiming a failure to adequately disclose risks of procedures were not new over the last half-century and, in fact, had multiplied significantly in the ten years prior to the appellate case.

To begin with, the appellate court cited the important nature of the *Schloendorff* decision in elucidating that a patient provides true consent when able to evaluate "knowledgeably the options available and the risks attendant upon each" (Ref. 2, p. 780). The court further emphasized that the duty to disclose the needed information depends primarily upon the physician. Thus, informed consent entails both adequate disclosure and consent by the patient, but each aspect relates intrinsically to and relies upon the other. A physician can only have met his burden to disclose after making a reasonable effort to convey sufficient information to the patient. In reviewing prior "duty-to-disclose" cases, the court cited the duty of physicians to do more than merely diagnose and treat, but also to communicate specific information, such as notifying the patient as to the nature of his or her condition, the limitations of treatment, the alternatives to treatment, and any risks of treatment. Thus informed, the patient would then be best situated to make a personal choice regarding whether to agree to any recommended procedures. Self-determination of the patient would thereby be paramount with regard to the patient's ultimate decisions.

In contemplating the sufficiency and nature of the disclosure by Spence, the appellate court considered prior cases that emphasized the duty to disclose as one based on the "custom of physicians practicing in the community" (Ref. 2, p. 783). However, the appellate court was unwilling to adopt this as the standard, since it would be at odds with the patient's right to make personal medical decisions. The judges noted that "both the patient's right to know and the physician's correlative obligation to tell him are diluted to the extent that its [the patient's prerogative to decide] compass is dictated by the medical profession" (Ref. 2, p. 786). They therefore turn the emphasis toward the patient, stating, "the patient's right of self-decision shapes the boundaries of the duty to reveal ..." (Ref. 2, p. 786).

The court expounded that a patient's intelligent decision could only be made when the patient was given sufficient information upon which to base a choice. Thus, the court ruled that the "scope of the physician's communications to the patient, then, must be measured by the patient's need, and that need is the information material to the decision. Thus the test for determining whether a particular peril must be divulged is its materiality to the patient's decision: all risks potentially affecting the decision must be unmasked" (Ref. 2, pp. 786–787). Recognizing the concern that a physician might not know specifically every nuance of information that would be considered important by an individual patient, the court rejected a subjective (i.e., specific to that individual in that circumstance) standard of disclosure and instead emphasized that the standard must be objective (i.e., general to what other reasonable persons who were similarly situated might feel, choose, or believe). The court decision reflected that the risk is material when a "reasonable person, in what the physician knows or should know to be the patient's position" (Ref. 2, p. 787), would consider it significant for the purposes of rendering a decision whether to accept or reject a proposed treatment. Areas for disclosure considered significant might include the risks of treatment, alternatives to the treatment, factors that might contribute to the dangerousness of a procedure, and information related to even a low-probability risk of serious bodily injury or death. The court cautioned that "there is no bright line separating the significant from the insignificant; the answer in any case must abide by a rule of reason" (Ref. 2, p. 788). Information commonly known, such as the risk of infection from procedures, or information already known to the patient, or immaterial to the patient's decision, might fall outside the scope of the disclosure.

Citing two common exceptions, the court noted that there are cases in which disclosure could be withheld. For example, in the emergency situation in which a person is unconscious or unable to consent, a disclosure may be abandoned so that treatment can begin. Further the court noted there may be situations in which the physician might assert privilege (i.e., the so-called "therapeutic privilege") in not revealing information to a patient if the information itself might be inherently damaging or foreclose the ability of the patient to make a rational decision. Even in these situations, however, a physician would probably be seeking the consent of a relative.

In considering the disclosure element, the *Canterbury* court noted that in a legal claim of negligence related to this issue, it must be clear that there is a relationship between the failure to disclose the appropriate information and the damage to the patient. Such a causal nexus can only exist when the disclosure of the risks would have led to a decision to reject the treatment. The court recognized that it might be easy for a patient, soured against the doctor after a bad outcome from a medical procedure, to stride into court and state that if she had only known about a particular risk, she would never have undertaken the procedure, and thereby establish causation. Here again, the court admonished that the finder of fact should rely upon an objective standard related to the causality issue in thinking about what a "prudent person in the patient's position would have decided if suitably informed of all perils bearing significance" (Ref. 2, p. 791). Thus, although the patient's testimony would be relevant, the jury, as legal fact finders, would and should additionally rely upon other evidence if available to determine the reasonableness of the disclosure and the linkage between the purported lack of disclosure to the subsequent bad outcome. Also, as in other tort claims, the burden would necessarily fall to the side of the case that acted as moving party (such as the plaintiff in a malpractice claim) to prove a cause of action, unless the physician is asserting a therapeutic privilege, in which case it would be the physician that would need to prove that the disclosure was reasonably withheld.

Following the logic related to the disclosure further, because the disclosure element primarily would rest with the patient to prove that a reasonable person would have made an alternative choice if given proper information, the question as to who would be best able to testify on this was also addressed by the court. In the *Canterbury* case, the court reasoned that expert testimony should be limited to describing the risks of the treatments and the risks of no treatment, as well as whether the procedure actually led to the injury.

As to the question of statutory limitations of Canterbury's claim, once it established that he was entitled to file claim beyond the age of 21 (which was considered the age of majority), the court relied upon a distinction as to whether the case involved a battery claim or a claim of negligence. This distinction was in part the fulcrum upon which the *Natanson* court had been balanced.[19] In *Canterbury* as well, the court identified factors beyond unauthorized surgery that established this as a negligence case, allowing for a longer, three-year time frame to file suit. Had they found the suit to constitute a battery claim, the statute of limitations from the age of majority would have only been a year, and Canterbury's claim, which he filed almost two years after turning 21, might not have been heard. Taken together, the trial court's decision for directed verdicts for defendants was reversed and remanded for a new trial.

The New Trial

W. J. Murphy (1975–1976) outlines the aftermath of the case involving Canterbury and Spence as follows.[1] After the appellate case reversed the decision of the trial court, the litigation continued. A petition for the case to be heard by the U.S. Supreme Court was filed but denied. The case was tried from April to May 1973 and resulted in a jury verdict for both defendants.[1] The defense asserted successfully that Spence's disclosure had been reasonable. Testifying experts agreed that there was a proper disclosure, although one expert who testified for the plaintiff argued that risk of paralysis should have been specifically disclosed. All the neurosurgeons who testified agreed that the laminectomy was indicated. In fact, Spence's efforts at disclosure were noted to be the greatest compared to the disclosures other physicians had provided Canterbury at the time. Other data used in the defense were that there had been a cordial relationship between Canterbury and Spence during the year subsequent to the surgery. Moreover, another laminectomy, performed about two years after the first trial, was utilized as demonstrable proof against Canterbury's contention that he would not have had the operation had the risks been sufficiently known to him at the time. Subsequently, the verdicts for the defense were again appealed, but in a memorandum opinion filed January 28, 1975, the U.S. Court of Appeals affirmed the verdict in favor of the defendants.[1] Shortly thereafter, on March 6, 1975, 12 years after the litigation began and almost 16 years after the initial surgery, a final petition for a judicial hearing was denied.[1]

Where Are They Now?

Canterbury v. Spence continues to be one of the most oft-cited cases on the issue of informed consent since the decision was rendered. Earl H. Davis, counsel for Canterbury, became a mentor for promising attorneys in Washington, D.C., and an award was created in his honor by one of his mentees.[20] Spence passed away in 1992, having been recognized for his contributions to the field of neurosurgery throughout his career.[3] Jerry Watson Canterbury continued working for law enforcement and died March 15, 2017.[21]

Impact on Practice

In many ways the decision by the appellate court may have been viewed by physicians as one involving radical judicial activism, leaving physicians with concerns that deference to medical judgment would fall to the wayside. It is hard to ignore the weight of the judges and their histories. However, an alternative view is that these judges, who together had this case land on their docket list among many other cases, reviewed the factual merits and the evolving views of self-determination, and fairly rendered a decision weighing the evolution in thinking related to a matter this complex. Although it may never fully be known how or why the case was decided as it was, the case was ultimately remanded for new trials. Each time, the juries at the trial court level ruled for the defendants, further supporting in some ways that the fate of this appellate case and its subsequent impact on informed consent disclosures likely resulted in large part from the leanings and influence of the judges who rendered the opinion.

Physicians' own attitudes about what information to disclose to patients has markedly shifted over the ensuing years, and one study demonstrated that between 1961 and 1976, over 90% of physicians shifted from believing that they should not tell their patients about their cancer diagnoses to preferring to disclose this information.[22] This reported shift took place during the years that the *Canterbury* case unfolded. The reasons for this are likely multifactorial, and although the *Canterbury* case may have hinged upon the particular judges who rendered its decision, they may well have been influenced by the principles of autonomy and civil rights that commanded the day. Further, the case decision inspired continuing discussion of informed consent and disclosure standards.

Under tort law, a person who owes a duty to another, such as a physician to a patient, who breaches that duty and causes damages may be held liable for such action. Failure to provide adequate informed consent continues to provide a steady flow of litigation. Subsequent case law included the standard that a reasonably prudent individual would also need to be educated with regard to information provided about the risks related to the refusal of a recommended treatment or procedure.[23] The voluntariness of the consent is also a relevant factor in the overarching informed consent framework, especially pertaining to informed consent with institutionalized or incarcerated individuals.[24] In addition to voluntariness and disclosure, the competence of the individual to provide an adequately informed consent, as opposed to just providing assent to a procedure, has become the well-established third prong of the informed consent process.[5,25]

Providing informed consent to a patient is now accepted as an ethical duty of the physician,[26] and all states but one have law that requires it. (Georgia only requires informed consent for a limited set of procedures.[27]) The question of whether informed consent was actually provided most typically arises when a patient suffers an adverse outcome and sues on the grounds that he or she was inadequately informed. State laws vary as to the standard to be used for assessing just what information the physician must share. *Canterbury* utilized a "reasonable person" or materiality of the information standard, which looks to what a reasonable patient would want to know. About half the states utilize this standard.[28] Some have argued that this approach creates the potential for hindsight bias (i.e., bias that exists because one is already aware of the outcome of a decision) in suggesting that one could second-guess what information might have been material to a reasonable person faced with a complex decision.[29]

The alternative standard, utilized by the other states, is known as the "professional standard," generally defined as what a reasonable physician in the same or similar circumstances would have disclosed. This standard avoids the problem of determining whether the patient really would have declined the procedure had he or she been informed of the particular adverse outcome the patient subsequently suffered. Although the *Canterbury* court explicitly rejected this approach because at the time physicians were not held to providing all the elements of what we now think of as informed consent, states that currently utilize a professional standard typically have laws or court holdings that specify the elements of informed consent[28] and leave it to expert testimony to inform the jury of just what that means in the particular fact situation that is before the court. Thus, similar arguments to those heard in *Canterbury* continue to be litigated to this day.

REFERENCES

1. Murphy WJ: Canterbury v. Spence – the case and a few comments. *Forum* 11(3): 716–26, 1976
2. *Canterbury v. Spence*, 464 F.2d 772 (D.C. Cir. 1972)
3. Laws E: William T. Spence (1908–1992)[obituary]. *Neurosurgery* 30:971, 1992
4. Hippocrates: *Hippocratic Corpus* [Excerpts]. Translated by J. Longrigg. *Academic Medicine*: 88(1): 80, 2013. Translated by Michael North. History of Medicine Division, National Library of Medicine, National Institutes of Health. Available at: https://journals.lww.com/academicmedicine/Fulltext/2013/01000/Hippocratic_Corpus___Excerpts_.25.aspx Accessed January 23, 2018
5. Pinals DA, Appelbaum PS: The history and current status of competence and informed consent in psychiatric research. *Isr J Psychiatry Relat Sci* 37:82–94, 2000
6. Appelbaum PS: *Almost a Revolution: Mental Health Law and the Limits of Change.* Oxford: Oxford University Press, 1994
7. *Slater v. Baker and Stapleton,* 95 Eng. Rep. 860 (K.B. 1767)
8. *Schloendorff v. Society of New York Hospital,* 211 N.Y. 125, 105 N.E. 92 (1914)
9. *Salgo v. Leland Stanford Jr. University Board of Trustees,* 317 P.2d 170 (Cal. 1957)
10. *Natanson v. Kline,* 186 Kan. 393, 1960
11. Leopold E: Irma Natanson and the legal landmark Natanson v. Kline. *Breast Cancer Action Newsletter* #83C, Fall 2004.
12. Brennan WJ: Tribute to the Honorable J. Skelly Wright. *The Yale Law Journal* 98: 207–209, 1988
13. Schwartz GT: J. Skelly Wright. *Encyclopedia of the American Constitution,* The Gale Group, 2000 (Entry written 1992). Available at www.encyclopedia.com/politics/encyclopedias-almanacs-transcripts-and-maps/wright-j-skelly-1911-1988 Accessed 1/24/18
14. *Application of the President and Directors of Georgetown College, Inc., A Body Corporate* 331 F.2d 1000 (D.C. Cir. 1964)
15. Burger WE: Harold Leventhal (1915–1979). *Columbia Law Rev.* 80: 879–81, 1980

16. Boyer EJ: Obituaries: Spottswood W. Robinson; Lawyer challenged segregation. *Los Angeles Times*, Oct. 14, 1998

17. *Davis v. County School Board of Prince Edward County*, 103 F. Supp. 337, 1952

18. *Brown v. Board of Education of Topeka*, 347 U.S. 483 (1954)

19. Beauchamp T, Faden RR: History of informed consent, meaning and elements of informed consent, paternalism. In S. Post (Ed.), *Encyclopedia of Bioethics* (3rd ed.). New York: Macmillan Reference, 2004.

20. Devorah C: D.C.'s Malpractice magi. *The Common Denominator*, March 21, 2005. Available at www.thecommondenominator.com/032105_carrie.html Accessed Apr. 25, 2017

21. The Register-Herald.com: Jerry Watson Canterbury, Mar 12, 1939–Mar 15, 2017. Available at http://obituaries.register-herald.com/stories/obituaries/jerry-canterbury-1939-2017-895204172/bc54ccb218554208 b926c05f1383 Accessed May 1, 2017

22. Laine C, Davidoff F: Patient-centered medicine: A professional evolution. *JAMA*. 275: 152–3, 1996

23. *Truman v. Thomas* (165 Cal. Rptr. 308) 1980

24. *Kaimowitz v. Michigan DMH* (1973), 42 U.S.L.W. 2063 Civil No. 73-1934-AW, 1973

25. Appelbaum PS, Gutheil TG: *Clinical Handbook of Psychiatry and the Law* (4th ed.). Philadelphia, PA: Lippincott Williams & Wilkins, 2007.

26. American Medical Association, Council on Ethical and Judicial Affairs. 2.1.1 Informed consent. In *Code of Medical Ethics of the American Medical Association*. Chicago, IL: American Medical Association, 2017. Available at www.ama-assn.org/delivering-care/informed-consent Accessed Feb. 4, 2018.

27. *Blotner v. Doreika*, 678 S.E. 2d 80 (2009)

28. For a list of state statutes and holdings as of 2000, see the Appendix in *Ketchup v. Howard*, 543 S.E.2d 371 (2000) at 381. The actual holding in *Ketchup* was later reversed (see reference 25)

29. Hutchinson D: Comment: Marsingill v. O'Malley: The duty to disclose becomes the duty to divine. *Alaska Law Rev.* 25: 241–61, 2008

8 The Right to Die and End-of-Life Decision-Making

Cruzan v. Director, Missouri Department of Health (1990)

Richard Martinez

Do incompetent persons in a persistent vegetative state maintain rights to control medical treatment decisions? Does the state have a legitimate interest in protecting incompetent persons? Do families of incompetent persons have protected rights to decide on behalf of their loved ones? Why do we have advance directives and what do psychiatrists need to know about the law and end-of-life care?

General psychiatrists and other mental healthcare professionals are familiar with informed consent and informed refusal of treatments, but not all mental health professionals, including general psychiatrists, are well informed about the unique and complex medical–legal dynamics that shape the dying process in the United States. While a small percentage of psychiatrists work in the area of end-of-life care, those with expertise in hospital-based medical and surgical consultation and those who work on palliative care teams, as well as general psychiatrists, can benefit by understanding the implications of the U.S. Supreme Court's 1990 *Cruzan* decision. In hospital-based practices, psychiatrists are considered medical experts in determination of competency to make medical decisions, and therefore often are involved in assessments of patients refusing treatments. They are often asked to participate in family meetings regarding such decisions, which may involve conflict and disagreement. On rare occasions, psychiatrists may also be asked to consult in complex cases where questions of suicidal intent must be evaluated before decisions to withdraw life-sustaining technologies can be concluded. Lastly, general psychiatrists, especially those who work with the elderly in nursing homes and hospices, should be familiar with the law pertaining to end-of-life care.

On January 11, 1983, 25-year-old Nancy Cruzan crashed her 1962 two-toned Rambler on a narrow two-lane blacktop road south of Carthage, Missouri. She was heading home after a night out with friends. Nancy lived with her husband, Paul Davis, in a small two-bedroom home on what locals called Krummel Nursery Road, a twisting rural roadway with few streetlights. Around 12:30 a.m., a neighbor, Dale Lappin, who lived about a mile from Nancy and Paul, heard a loud noise and rushed to the front of his home. He and his stepfather were the first to arrive at the Rambler, which was sitting upside down about 35 yards off the road. They pounded on the car window, but no one responded. Dale ran up to a nearby house to see if someone had left the car. No answer. On his return, he almost stumbled over a young woman lying facedown and motionless, her face bruised and bleeding, and her clothes torn. Shortly thereafter, two highway patrolmen arrived, one of whom checked the woman's pulse. He rolled her body over and could detect neither pulse nor breathing. He concluded she was dead. Several minutes later, an ambulance and fire truck arrived. They worked frantically to restore the woman's heartbeat. At 3 a.m., Nancy's father and mother, Joe and Joyce Cruzan, received a call from their older daughter, Chris, who had been called by Nancy's husband. They all rushed to Freeman Hospital in Joplin, where Nancy was being taken after an initial stop at a small hospital in Carthage. When his daughter was wheeled through the emergency door on a gurney, Joe Cruzan did not recognize her. Joyce later said that she recognized the socks that she had recently given all of her daughters for Christmas.[1]

This begins the tragic story that led to the U.S. Supreme Court decision in *Cruzan vs. Director, Missouri Department of Health*, 497 U.S. 261 (1990), a case in which the justices of the Court weighed in on the national "right to die" debate, addressing withdrawal of nutrition and hydration in incompetent persons in a persistent vegetative state.[2] Although the New Jersey Supreme Court had opined on constitutional questions in granting Karen Quinlan's father guardianship to remove her ventilator 14 years earlier,[3] a case that will be discussed later in this chapter, the journey of the Cruzan family and their attorney, William Colby, stands as the first involvement of the U.S. Supreme Court in the national controversy. In *Cruzan*, the Court addressed the moral and legal complexities of end-of-life care. The tension among the rights of the incompetent person in a persistent vegetative state, the appropriate involvement of substitute decision-makers, and the state's interests in the protection of vulnerable individuals involved a seven-year process that culminated in the landmark decision in 1990.

In the aftermath of this decision, the concepts of proxy decision-making, durable power of attorney in medical decision-making, and living wills – all forms of advance directives – became more important considerations for individuals and families facing serious illness across the United States. Numerous state legislative bodies and the federal government enacted laws that transformed the conversation among healthcare professionals and patients and their families on the subject of end-of-life care, and furthered the evolving practice of shared decision-making between healthcare providers and patients for all healthcare decisions. Fourteen years after the *Quinlan* decision, the *Cruzan* case further established the involvement of both hospital ethics committees and psychiatrists with expertise in hospital-based competency consultation in hospital settings, where the withdrawal of life-sustaining technologies are often decided.

Legal Course

The Supreme Court released the *Cruzan* decision on June 25, 1990, affirming in a 5–4 decision the Missouri Supreme Court's requirement that a clear and convincing evidence standard reflecting Nancy's wishes for the removal of her feeding tube was necessary before it could be removed by her family. Chief Justice William Rehnquist wrote the majority opinion, with Justices Antonin Scalia and Sandra Day O'Connor offering concurring opinions, and Justices Anthony Kennedy and Byron White joining the majority position. Justices William Brennan, Thurgood Marshall, Harry Blackmun, and John Paul Stevens dissented.

To understand the Supreme Court decision in *Cruzan*, some background on the case is necessary. In March 1988, William Colby represented the Cruzans before Judge Charles E. Teel, Jr., in the Jasper County Probate Courthouse in Carthage, Missouri. His strategy was to convince the judge that Nancy was in a persistent vegetative state, that she would not want the medical treatment that she was receiving, and that it was legally and ethically appropriate to withdraw her feeding tube at the request of her parents. Colby argued that a number of legal considerations supported the Cruzans' request. Since constitutional privacy rights and common-law developments in self-determination had been successful in other end-of-life cases, Colby utilized several legal justifications to argue the case.

The lengthy trial reached national prominence, including an appearance on *Nightline*. Following the trial, Joe, Joyce, and Chris (Nancy's father, mother, and sister), and her two nieces, Angie and Miranda, sat in their living room in Carterville, Missouri, in July 1988 when the courier from the courthouse delivered Judge Teel's decision. Betsy Arledge and members of her film crew from PBS's *Frontline* were present as well. Betsy had been documenting the Cruzan story for some time and would follow the case through the 1990 Supreme Court decision and Nancy's subsequent death. Reading through Judge Teel's decision, Joe Cruzan struggled to find the bottom line. Did Judge Teel grant their request to have Nancy's feeding tube removed or not? After several minutes, he read: "There is a fundamental right expressed in our Constitution as the right to liberty which permits an individual to refuse or direct the withholding or withdrawal of artificial death-prolonging procedures when a person has no more cognitive brain function than our Ward.... The Respondents, employees of the state of Missouri, are directed to cause the request of the Co-guardians to withdraw nutrition or hydration to be carried out" (Ref. 1, p. 232). Initially, Joe and his family were confused. He read the order again, and according to William Colby's reconstruction of the event, stated: "So, if that's winning, we won" (Ref. 1, p. 233).

There was no joy in the room as Joe walked away from the table. Judge Teel had ruled in favor of Nancy and her family and had directed state employees at the Missouri Rehabilitation Center in Mt. Vernon, Missouri, to remove the feeding tube.

The relief and sorrow they felt were short-lived. Thad McCanse, who had been appointed by Judge Teel as the guardian *ad litem* for Nancy and who believed the Cruzan family was acting in her best interests, filed an appeal. Colby writes that he later learned that Judge Teel, recognizing the importance of the Cruzan case, had asked McCanse to appeal to the Missouri Supreme Court immediately after he released his decision.

According to Colby, the behind-the-scenes decisions leading to the appeal were complicated. Apparently, the chief justice of the Missouri Supreme Court, William H. Billings, was familiar with the Cruzan case and its importance and had asked Teel to arrange for an immediate appeal. The State of Missouri had passed a new definition of death in 1982, and while not directly related to the Cruzan case, Chief Justice William H. Billings was aware of the case. Billings, who had been Teel's law school classmate, had already been scheduled to hear another case (Philip Radar) with different circumstances than Nancy Cruzan's, but that clearly shared the complicated legal and moral problems of end-of-life and withdrawal of medical treatments. Once the appeal was submitted by McCanse, the two cases were scheduled to be reviewed by the Missouri Supreme Court, bypassing the appellate court. Missouri Attorney General William Webster, with the support of then governor John Ashcroft, joined the appeal as well.

In September 1988, the Cruzans drove up to Jefferson City, Missouri, for the hearing before the Missouri Supreme Court. In brief, the court formed its opinion based on a Missouri State Living Will statute that was passed after Nancy's accident, but before the hearing in Teel's court. While recognizing the common-law doctrine of informed consent and right to refusal of treatment, the Missouri Supreme Court opined that the right was not unrestricted and that a right to privacy in refusing medical treatment was not in the U.S. Constitution. In a split decision, the majority justices argued that the State Living Will statute strongly favored the preservation of life, and that the evidence of Nancy's wishes presented to the probate court did not meet the "clear and convincing evidence" standard. Thus, the state had an interest in continuing to feed Nancy through her gastrostomy feeding device. The Cruzan family, after some reflection and frustration, decided to appeal the Missouri Supreme Court decision to the U.S. Supreme Court.

The Cruzan Arguments to the U.S. Supreme Court

William Colby, the attorney who had represented the Cruzan family since 1987, did not sleep well on the night of December 5, 1989, the night before he would argue on behalf of the Cruzan family in front of the U.S. Supreme Court. Colby had first met Joe Cruzan, Nancy's father and guardian, in May 1987 when he was 31 years old. A graduate of the University of Kansas Law School, he had worked in Washington, D.C., for several years before moving back to the Midwest and joining the firm of Shook, Hardy, and Bacon in Kansas City. In order to gain experience in trial litigation, he volunteered for *pro bono* work on behalf of the firm. In the spring of 1987, a colleague approached him with the Cruzan case. Initially, he believed that this "probate case" would be "an opportunity," since he was looking for experience. It did not occur to him that two and a half years later he would be arguing his first case in front of the justices of the U.S. Supreme Court. As he acknowledged in a talk at the Midwest Bioethics Center in Kansas City on the 20th anniversary of the Cruzan decision in November 2010, he had no idea that his relationship with Nancy and her family would transform his life.[4]

After representation through the initial probate decision and subsequent appeals by the State of Missouri, Mr. Colby found himself opposite the U.S. Solicitor General Kenneth Starr on a cold December morning in 1989. Earlier in the fall, the American Medical Association had submitted one of 21 additional *amicus* briefs in support of the Cruzan family position. In October 1989, the solicitor general decided to enter the case on the side of Missouri. In addition, more than 19 *amicus* briefs, including a brief from the U.S. Catholic Conference, were submitted in opposition to the Cruzan family's position.

Colby struggled with what strategy would stand the best chance of success, given the makeup of the Supreme Court. While a privacy argument was considered, it was clear to him and others that recent Court decisions had barely upheld the arguments presented in *Roe v. Wade*.

Colby correctly understood that the Court had no interest in expanding any constitutional claim for a right to privacy in other areas. Therefore, he approached the Court with the argument that "all persons have a fundamental liberty interest to stop unwarranted bodily intrusions by the state" (Ref. 1, p. 288). Colby developed a three-step approach that he would present to the Court. First, incapacitated individuals do not lose fundamental constitutional rights. Since competent persons clearly had a right to refuse medical interventions, Colby argued that this right also extended to incompetent persons. Second, legal precedent recognized that families were the rightful persons to speak on behalf of those who could no longer speak for themselves. Third, a general claim by the state to protect life is inadequate to override a family decision. The state must articulate a specific interest for such an override. Thus, Colby avoided the privacy argument in favor of Nancy's liberty interest.

The U.S. solicitor general's approach troubled Colby as he entered the Court. Starr had not argued against Nancy's liberty interest, but instead had emphasized that the state had "a profound interest in preserving human life" (Ref. 1, p. 293). Since Nancy had lost the ability to speak on her own behalf, the state had an obligation to require that a third party was making a decision that she would have wanted. This switched the burden from the state having to prove a specific interest in overriding a family's decision to the family proving that their decision was reflective of the wishes of the incapacitated family member. Starr argued that since a state had an interest in protecting vulnerable individuals, Missouri was correct in requiring the Cruzan family to demonstrate by a clear and convincing standard of evidence that they were reflecting Nancy's wishes if she could have spoken for herself. Given the Court's reluctance to expand privacy rights and its history of showing respect for states developing their own approaches to this question, Colby and his colleagues believed this might be a persuasive argument.

Colby's concerns about the Court's respect for states' rights were warranted. As the arguments proceeded, Justice Scalia peppered him with questions revealing his skepticism of the Cruzan position. He challenged Colby to consider other cases where the state could override family decisions, asking him if the parents were Christian Scientists or for other reasons refused a relatively ordinary surgical procedure "would the state have to accept that determination, or would the state not be able to appoint a guardian and the guardian make it?" (Ref. 1, p. 303). As an example, Colby acknowledged that some Jehovah's Witness cases were examples where the state could take steps to override parental decisions, but those cases were situations where the medical profession was attempting to save a life, far different than Nancy's persistent vegetative state. Colby argued that in the Cruzan case, the medical profession was not offering Nancy or her family any possibility of recovery, but only continuing nutrition and hydration for purposes of continuing her life in a state that was irreversible and unacceptable to Nancy as well as her parents.

After 30 minutes that included questions from Justices O'Connor, Scalia, White, and Blackmun (the author of *Roe v. Wade*), Colby sat down. Robert Presson of the Missouri attorney general's office was up next. He allotted 10 of his 30 minutes to Solicitor General Starr, then spent most of his remaining 20 minutes struggling with Justices Stevens and Blackmun. Justice Blackmun asked the final question before Mr. Presson's time was exhausted: Had Presson ever seen a person in a persistent vegetative state? Presson replied that he had seen Nancy Cruzan.

In his ten minutes, Kenneth Starr provided the Court with a way out of the difficult situation. His argument was simple. He conceded that Nancy had a liberty interest and that the family had a legitimate role in deciding on her behalf. However, he argued that the state should not be placed in an inflexible position, but must be allowed a reasonableness standard in exercising its interest in protecting vulnerable individuals. Starr argued that the clear and convincing evidence standard required of surrogate decision-makers acting on what Nancy would have wished was the proper balance, allowing states to exercise their interest. He conceded that where there is clear evidence of an incapacitated person's wishes, a liberty interest to be free of unwanted intrusions under the Constitution "is implicated."

Colby had one minute to respond. He was concerned about the persuasiveness of Starr's argument and even more worried about the burden it placed on individuals in a persistent vegetative state as well as on their families. He tried to remind the Court that if the solicitor general's position would stand for "the proposition that this state hospital cannot be forced to remove a tube that they didn't insert," there would be a terrible practical result (Ref. 1, p. 311). It would leave Nancy, her family and future individuals and their families with the choice of not inserting a tube in the early stages of such a catastrophic injury for fear that once the tube had been inserted, there would be no way to remove it. Nancy had no place else to go to remove the tube that she did not want. In essence, the argument was comparable to the arguments made in *Quinlan* and other previous cases in which the removal of a ventilator had been the issue.

Judge Rehnquist and the Majority Opinion

In the Supreme Court opinion, Justice Rehnquist reviewed the extensive history and diversity by which states have reasoned and ruled on the question of the rights of incompetent patients to refuse medical treatment. While recognizing that states have a variety of legal bases, including state constitutions, common law, and statutes not available to the question before the Court, Rehnquist wrote: "In this Court, the question is simply and starkly whether the United States Constitution prohibits Missouri from choosing the rule of decision which it did. This is the first case in which we have been squarely presented with the issue whether the United States Constitution grants what is in common parlance referred to as a 'right to die'" (Ref. 2, p. 277). He made clear that the narrow question was the one before the Court, acknowledging that while the "principle that a competent person has a constitutionally protected liberty interest in refusing unwanted medical treatment may be inferred from our prior decisions" (Ref. 2, p., 278), the incompetent patient belonged to a separate and different class of individuals requiring a different balance between their rights and the interests of the state. He then reviewed the intermediate standard of proof from previous cases, acknowledging that the standard of proof was "to instruct the fact finder concerning the degree of confidence our society thinks he should have in the correctness of factual conclusions for a particular type of adjudication" (Ref. 2, p. 282). The Court reviewed the various cases where the clear and convincing evidence had been determined as the proper balancing standard, situations that included proceedings involving deportation and denaturalization, civil commitment, and termination of parental rights.

The Supreme Court supported Missouri, Rehnquist writing that the Constitution did not forbid the state from requiring a higher standard of proof from the family in order to grant their request on behalf of Nancy. While recognizing the common-law doctrine of informed consent as well as previous arguments involving constitutional rights of privacy and state constitutions and statutes, the Court addressed the narrow question of whether Missouri's requirement was constitutional. Rehnquist and the majority reasoned that this was a reasonable standard in balancing the state's interest against Nancy's and her family's interests.

In addition to the narrow question, the Court did recognize in *dicta* a liberty interest under the due process clause in the Fourteenth Amendment in refusing unwanted medical treatment for competent patients, including the refusal of nutrition and hydration. The fact that Nancy was incompetent changed the balance between the state's interests in protecting an incompetent person and preservation of life in general, and the continuation of that right in an individual who could no longer make an informed and voluntary choice. For the Court, the Missouri procedural protections, including the requirement for a "clear and convincing evidence standard," was an acceptable way of balancing these conflicting values. Rehnquist opined that the standard effectively considered the risk of error involved in an irreversible decision. The Court expressed concern that an erroneous decision to terminate life-supporting medical treatment was irreversible, and therefore that maintaining the status quo in the absence of such evidence was consistent with the state's general duty to protect and preserve life.

In addition, the Court ruled that the Missouri Supreme Court had not erred in concluding that the evidence of Nancy's wishes failed to meet the clear and convincing standard at the original probate trial, and therefore agreed with overturning Judge Teel's decision. Lastly, while recognizing that states could defer to family members to determine the wishes of the incompetent, the due process clause did not require that states accept the "substituted judgment" of family members. In other words, there was no constitutional requirement that the state recognize the primacy of the family in situations such as Nancy's. Although states could look to family members to determine the wishes of the incompetent, since Missouri could require the clear and convincing evidence standard to determine Nancy's wishes, it could discharge its responsibility to her through proper procedures to determine what those wishes were, rather than simply accepting the family's wishes on her behalf.

Justice O'Connor wrote an important concurring opinion. She agreed with the majority in recognizing a liberty interest flowing from the idea of physical freedom and self-determination in refusal of medical treatments for competent patients, acknowledged the preservation of certain rights of refusal, including the refusal of nutrition and hydration in incompetent patients, agreed with the decision not to require that states recognize family surrogates as the final word on the intentions of the incompetent, and upheld the Missouri requirement for clear and convincing evidence to determine the incompetent person's intent. She also suggested several approaches that might decrease error and increase confidence that decisions reflected the intention of the incompetent. For example, she proposed that appointment of a proxy or healthcare agent to make decisions in the event that a competent person became incompetent, along with written advance directives and living wills, would increase confidence that those speaking on behalf of incompetents accurately reflected their wishes. She highlighted durable power of attorney statutes that included authority to make medical decisions. O'Connor thus offered future direction in the face of the absence of national consensus on "this difficult and sensitive problem" (Ref. 2, p. 292). She wrote: "Today we decide only that one State's practice does not violate the Constitution; the more challenging task of crafting appropriate procedures for safeguarding incompetents' liberty interests is entrusted to the 'laboratory' of the States" (Ref. 2, p. 292).

The Dissent

In dissent, Justices Brennan, Marshall, and Blackmun objected to the majority's decision to uphold and justify the state's interest in "protecting" Nancy Cruzan. Simply put, they argued that the Missouri procedures "impermissibly burden[ed]" Nancy since she was "entitled to choose to die with dignity" (Ref. 2, p. 302). The four justices took issue with the opinion that the "clear and convincing evidence" standard was the proper "accuracy" necessary to discharge the state's interests, arguing that placing the burden on the family rather than on the state to demonstrate that an incompetent would wish to live in a persistent vegetative state was a major flaw of reasoning and prejudice. The dissenting justices argued that few people executed living wills or other directives, and since the likelihood of a persistent vegetative state was low, few felt any urgency to create formal evidence of their wishes. The Missouri procedure was not protective of Nancy's true wishes, but assumed that the state was in a better position than her loved ones were to determine those wishes. Quoting from *In re Jobes*, "Family members are best qualified to make substituted judgments for incompetent patients not only because of their peculiar grasp of the patient's approach to life, but also because of their special bonds with him or her... It is ... they who treat the patient as a person, rather than a symbol of a cause."[5] The dissenting justices thus reasoned that the state was a "stranger" to the patient and, given political and other considerations, was not equipped to make more accurate or better decisions than the family.

Lastly, Justice Stevens offered a separate and more strident dissent, arguing that the majority decision perverted the liberty interests upon which it determined that Missouri had an interest in protecting Nancy. Most concerning to Stevens was the fact that the guardian *ad litem*, the parents and family, and an impartial trial judge had all agreed that Nancy's wishes would have been to remove the feeding tube and be allowed to die. Through the attorney general's office, the state had decided to pursue the case, thus turning Nancy's best interests into an abstract examination of her intent, limiting "an innocent person's constitutional right to be free from unwanted medical treatment" to a small class of incompetents "who had the foresight to make an unambiguous statement of their wishes while competent" (Ref. 2, p. 339). Stevens was critical of the state's actions: "There can be no doubt that her life made her dear to her family and to others. How she dies will affect how that life is remembered. The trial court's order authorizing Nancy's parents to cease their daughter's treatment would have permitted the family that cares for Nancy to bring to a close her tragedy and her death. Missouri's objection to that order subordinates Nancy's body, her family, and the lasting significance of her life to the State's own interests" (Ref. 2, p. 344).

Review of Competent and Incompetent Patient Rights to Refuse Medical Treatments

In order to fully appreciate the importance of the *Cruzan* decision, it may be helpful to review several court cases that established the competent patient's fundamental right to be free of unwanted medical treatments and devices, which then informed the cases that addressed the incompetent patient's rights. Justice Benjamin Cardozo, who heard the case *Schloendorff v. Society of New York Hospital* while on the New York Court of Appeals in 1914, authored the opinion that most consider the birth of the informed consent doctrine: "Every human being of adult years and sound mind has a right to determine what shall be done with his own body; and a surgeon who performs an operation without the patient's consent commits an assault for which he is liable in damages."[6]

With the development of technologies that allowed for extending life, the courts were confronted with situations where participants grappled with decisions that shaped the dying process. At age 21 in a vegetative state in which her life continued through mechanical ventilation and artificial nutrition and hydration, Quinlan's father petitioned the New Jersey courts to allow him to have his daughter's ventilator removed. After a lower court denied his request, the New Jersey Supreme Court agreed to allow it, opining that since a competent patient had a constitutional entitlement to reject life-sustaining medical intervention, an incompetent was also protected. The court selected a protected privacy right, citing the reasoning in *Griswold v. Connecticut* and *Roe v. Wade*.[3]

In *Quinlan*, the New Jersey court stated: "We think that the State's interest contra weakens and the individual's right to privacy grows as the degree of bodily invasion increases and the prognosis dims. Ultimately there comes a point at which the individual's rights overcome the State interest." (Ref. 3, p. 41). Justice Hughes reasoned that since Quinlan was not competent and could not speak for herself, her father could speak on her behalf. Otherwise, her constitutional interests would be unprotected. The court provided several additional opinions that would become standards of practice and understanding in the end-of-life debates. Hughes indemnified health professionals and institutions against criminal prosecution when withdrawing mechanical ventilation, arguing that "if there is no reasonable possibility of Karen's ever emerging from her present comatose condition ... the present life-support system may be withdrawn and said action shall be without any civil or criminal liability on the part of any participant" (Ref. 3, p. 54).

The 1983 President's Commission for the Study of Ethical Problems in Medicine and Biomedical and Behavioral Research provided additional support for the proposition that an unconscious patient had the same rights as a conscious patient in refusal of unwanted medical technologies.[7] While recognizing the state's interest in preserving life, upholding the integrity of the medical profession, protecting vulnerable individuals, and preventing suicide, the commission made clear that a mixture of constitutional and case law firmly established a right of refusal for the incompetent patient through identified surrogates.

In 1986, the AMA Council on Ethical and Judicial Affairs (CEJA) adopted a statement entitled "Withholding or Withdrawing Life-Prolonging Medical Treatment," concluding that:

The social commitment of the physician is to sustain life and relieve suffering. Where the performance of one duty conflicts with the other, the choice of the patient, or his family or legal representative if the patient is incompetent to act on his own behalf, should prevail.... Life-prolonging medical treatment includes medication and artificially- or technologically-supplied respiration, nutrition or hydration. In treating a terminally ill or irreversibly comatose patient, the physician should determine whether the benefits of treatment outweigh its burdens. At all times, the dignity of the patient should be maintained.[8]

In *Elizabeth Bouvia v. Superior Court of California*, the California Court of Appeals overruled a lower court that had denied the plaintiff's request to have a nasogastric tube removed.[9] Bouvia had suffered with cerebral palsy since birth and was quadriplegic and bedridden. At the time of the California appellate decision, she was 28 years old and resided in a county hospital in Los Angeles. All parties agreed that she was competent to make medical decisions and did not suffer a terminal illness. In the lower court decision, the judge ruled against her request, reasoning that the removal of the nasogastric tube involved suicidal intent. In addition, attorneys for the hospital and the state argued that she was not uncomfortable, that it was in her interests to maintain the status quo in order for other aspects of the legal proceeding to move forward, and therefore that she continued to have an acceptable legal remedy to the hospital's decision.

At the trial court hearing, the hospital argued that while recognizing a basic right to refuse medical treatment for competent patients, Bouvia's situation was different. Maintaining that the state had an interest in preserving life, preventing suicide, protecting third parties, and maintaining the ethical standards of the medical profession, the hospital noted that Bouvia was in a public facility, thereby making the state a party to her actions. She was not comatose, terminally ill, or in a persistent vegetative state. She asked for medical treatment and could not accept part of the treatment and refuse the rest. Furthermore, she was trying to commit suicide by starving herself to death, and the state could not assist in this activity. In addition, the hospital argued that Bouvia could live another 15 or 20 years with the nasogastric tube.

The appellate court disagreed with all the arguments, stating that they were insufficient to deny Bouvia her fundamental right to refuse treatment. According to the court, "The trial court mistakenly attached undue importance to the *amount of* time possibly available to petitioner, and failed to give equal weight and consideration for the *quality* of that life" (Ref. 9, p. 1142). Associate Justice Beach wrote: "Here Elizabeth Bouvia's decision to forego medical treatment or life-support through a mechanical means belongs to her. It is not a medical decision for her physicians to make. Neither is it a legal question whose soundness is to be resolved by lawyers and judges. It is not a conditional right subject to approval by ethics committees or courts of law. It is a moral and philosophical decision that, being a competent adult, is hers alone" (Ref. 9, p. 1143).

In *In re Conroy*, the same court that had decided *Quinlan* determined that a nasogastric tube could be removed from an 84-year-old patient who was suffering irreversible mental and physical problems.[10] However, the court abandoned the federal right to privacy, reasoning in favor of the common-law right to self-determination and informed consent. Reasoning that the right to self-determination in competent patients included decisions that might result in death, this right was preserved in the incompetent patient. In addition, the court argued that the right could be fulfilled through the surrogate decision-maker utilizing a substituted judgment standard. In the absence of clear evidence, a best-interest standard was acceptable. Several subsequent decisions upheld this reasoning in New Jersey and supported deference to family members.

Aftermath

Initially, Colby and the Cruzan family were disappointed, even devastated. In a careful reading of the opinion, Colby recognized a short eight-word sentence fragment that he believed might be a solution to Nancy and her family's seven-year journey. Chief Justice Rehnquist wrote:

An erroneous decision not to terminate (life support) results in a maintenance of the status quo; the possibility of subsequent developments such as advancements in medical science, *the discovery of new evidence regarding the patient's intent* [italics added], changes in the law, or simply the unexpected death of the patient despite the administration of life-sustaining treatment at least create the potential that a wrong decision will eventually be corrected or its impact mitigated. [Ref. 2, p. 283]

Colby began to organize for a new trial back in the court in the Jasper County courthouse in Carthage, with the judge who had originally sided with the Cruzan family in July 1988.

Following the U.S. Supreme Court decision, Colby waited several months before filing for a new hearing. Interestingly, the Missouri attorney general had decided to depart from the case, stating to the lower court that the state no longer had an interest in the outcome. Most important, new witnesses stepped forward who learned of Nancy's predicament because of the national attention and media coverage during the Supreme Court hearing. Debi Havner and Marianne Smith had worked with Nancy at Stapleton Elementary School in Joplin, Missouri, in 1977. The school specialized in working with children with disabilities including mental retardation, deafness, and blindness. At that time, Nancy was using her married name, so Havner and Murphy did not recognize her under the Cruzan name until they saw her photo in the news coverage at the time of the Supreme Court hearing. Both women remembered several conversations with Nancy during their time working with disabled children, in which she had made statements declaring that she would not want to remain alive if found in the predicament of some of the children for whom she was providing care. Both women would provide credible and convincing testimony in the trial to Judge Teel. On November 1, 1990, the new trial began.

Besides the testimony of the new witnesses, Thad McCanse, Nancy's guardian *ad litem*, told Colby that he had an obligation to challenge Colby and the Cruzan family. Initially, Colby was irritated with this stance, but once the trial began, it was clear that what McCanse was describing as his obligation ultimately supported Nancy and her family. He examined Dr. James Davis, the physician responsible for Nancy's care at the Missouri Rehabilitation Center. In his initial testimony in the original trial three years earlier, Dr. Davis had equivocated on his assessment of Nancy's prognosis. In the second trial, McCanse asked him whether it was in Nancy's best interests to remain in her current state. On this occasion, without any hesitation or equivocation, Dr. Davis made it clear to the court that he had come to the conclusion that it was not in her best interests. On cross-examination from Colby, Dr. Davis stated that her existence was likely "a living hell."

In December 1990, seven years after Nancy's accident, Judge Teel offered an opinion that would finally release her from the feeding tube. Colby immediately drove to the Missouri Rehabilitation Center (MRC) with the order in hand, telling Joe, Joyce, and Chris to meet him there. He entered the office of Don Lamkins, the center's director. Although Colby presented Judge Teel's decision together with an affidavit from the Department of Health Director, John Bagby, stating that the MRC and the Department of Health would carry out the order, Lamkins argued that he needed to check with authorities in Jefferson City, the state capital. Soon, Lamkins was told that the MRC must comply. Discussion began about when was the best time, who would talk with the press, and other details that had not been agreed. While Colby and Joe Cruzan were attempting to make it clear to Lamkins that they did not wish to delay and wanted the gastrostomy tube removed that day, Dr. Davis walked to Nancy's room and pulled it out. According to Colby, he then placed gauze strips over the hole, charted his action, and "with no fanfare" did what the Cruzan family had wanted for Nancy over the previous four years.

It took Nancy until the early hours of December 26, 1990, to die. In the twelve days between Dr. Davis' removal of the feeding tube and Nancy's death, Operation Rescue mobilized and camped out on the doorstep of the MRC. According to Colby, at one point in the vigil, members of the group attempted to enter the center, intending to replace the feeding tube. The local sheriff's office had been tipped off to the plan and stopped the intruders on the elevator as they attempted to go up to Nancy's room. In addition, Lamkins told Dr. Davis that Governor Ashcroft wanted the tube reinserted, even though there were no legal avenues for such an action. The attorney general's office had decided not to enter into the retrial, and did not see any justification for further involvement.

On December 28, 1990, the Cruzan family buried Nancy in the Carterville Cemetery, a short distance from their home and the site of the accident in 1983. Her grave marker had three dates:

> Born: July 20, 1957
> Departed: January 11, 1983
> At Peace: December 26, 1990

On August 17, 1996, after suffering with depression requiring a psychiatric hospitalization, medication, and electroconvulsive therapy, Joe Cruzan hanged himself in his carport after leaving a note to his wife telling her to call the police and not to come to his rescue. Joyce Cruzan was diagnosed with cancer in 1998 and died six months later at home in the arms of her daughter Chris after refusing chemotherapy. After some difficult years, Chris founded the Cruzan Foundation, an organization devoted to helping others making decisions at the end of life. She, her husband, and her children, now adults, all live in Missouri. William H. Colby, the lawyer who entered the "little *pro bono* case" in 1987, continues to practice law in Missouri, has authored two books on the subject of healthcare ethics and end-of-life decisions, works with various philanthropic and service organizations, and remains a close friend to Chris Cruzan and her family.[4]

Impact on Practice

Since the *Cruzan* decision in 1990, a national consensus has developed through case law and legislative advance-directive enactments. Although there is no absolute "right to die," there does exist a limited right that involves refusal of life-sustaining medical interventions, including nutrition and hydration, for both competent and incompetent patients.[11] *Cruzan* acknowledged clearly the "principle that a competent person has a constitutional protected liberty interest in refusing unwanted medical treatment" and also recognized that such a right extends to an incompetent patient, building on a concept first addressed in the *Quinlan* case. However, the Court recognized that the incompetent person could not truly "choose," instead retaining the right of refusal through decision-making processes that could involve an individual's surrogate, but preserving the state's interests in protecting vulnerable persons.

In the months following the *Cruzan* decision, the Society for the Right to Die distributed over a million living wills. While not directly in response to the *Cruzan* decision, Senator John Danforth, a Missouri Republican, proposed the Patient Self-Determination Act, which took effect in November 1991. Now part of standard admission practice in all American hospitals, this legislative directive requires healthcare facilities to inform patients about their rights to control medical interventions, including offering all patients the opportunity to create an advance directive. Although the U.S. Supreme Court did not address the practice of physicians involved in active assistance in dying in *Cruzan*, it made clear in its 1997 decisions in *Washington v. Glucksberg*[12] and *Vacco v. Quill*,[13] that there was no constitutional right to die and that states had the option of excluding active interventions that hasten death. At the same time, the Court supported the concept of palliative care, stating that making patients comfortable during the dying process was an acceptable practice consistent with the Court's decision in *Cruzan*, even if those interventions hastened death.

In summary, the courts, including the Supreme Court, have supported a decision-making process that occurs in the clinical setting, including the use of ethics committees to help in decision-making. The courts should be utilized when there are disputes that cannot be resolved in the clinical setting. Surrogates making decisions for incompetent patients should first use a substituted-judgment standard where the patient's own preferences guide the decision, and when this information is not available, should resort to a best-interest standard.

Advance healthcare directives have become the process by which individuals maintain control over their fate at times near death or, in some circumstances, when individuals become transiently incapacitated and cannot make decisions. Also known as living wills or personal healthcare directives, these instruments are usually a set of written instructions to healthcare providers that indicate what a person wishes in terms of life-sustaining technologies in the situation of incapacitation and serious illness. In addition, advance directives can include the appointment of a durable power of attorney or a healthcare agent designated to make decisions. Lastly, active euthanasia and assisted suicide are distinct, morally and legally, from withdrawal of life-sustaining treatments, and are prohibited except in the growing number of jurisdictions where specific laws have been established.

There are variations on these settled principles. *Cruzan* supported the view that surrogates must provide a high level of proof of an incompetent's wishes before removal of life-sustaining technologies is permissible. Some jurisdictions require separate procedures and decision-making processes for withdrawing nutrition and hydration. A variety of legal approaches shape the end-of-life discussion and the "right" to refuse treatment. Federal constitutional considerations of privacy, liberty, and religious freedom, state constitutional rights, common-law rights to be free from unwanted bodily intrusion, and various statutory and regulatory rights have emerged.

With *Cruzan*, the doctrine of informed consent and informed refusal was extended to include a mechanism for the incompetent patient in a persistent vegetative state to exercise "choice." Although some were disappointed with the Supreme Court's position in the case, it became clear that incompetent persons retain their liberty interests in refusing life-sustaining treatments through their surrogates and loved ones. The informed consent and informed refusal doctrines further evolved and were strengthened by *Cruzan* and other end-of-life legal decisions. Advance directives and conversations about values pertaining to the balance between longevity and quality of life moved to center stage, fully

illuminated in many American families either experiencing or antici-
pating the journey that is inevitable for us all.

REFERENCES

1. Colby WH: *Long Goodbye: The Deaths of Nancy Cruzan*. Carlsbad, CA, Hay House, 2002
2. *Cruzan vs. Director, Missouri Department of Health*, 497 U.S. 261 (1990)
3. *In Re Quinlan*, 355 A.2d 647, 70 N.J. 10 (1976)
4. Personal communication with Mr. Colby in November 2010
5. *In re Jobes*, 108 N.J. 394, 416, 529 A.2d 434, 445 (1987)
6. *Schloendorff v. Society of New York Hospital*, 211 N.Y. 125, 129–130, 105 N.E. 92, 93 (1914)
7. President's Commission for the Study of Ethical Problems in Medicine and Biomedical and Behavioral Research: Deciding to forego life-sustaining treatment: A report on the ethical, medical, legal issues in treatment decisions, Library of Congress, March 1983. Available at https://repository .library.georgetown.edu/bitstream/handle/10822/559344/deciding_to_ forego_tx.pdf?sequence=1&isAllowed=y Accessed Jan 30, 2018
8. AMA Council on Ethical and Judicial Affairs: Witholding or Withdrawing Life-Sustaining Treatment. Available at www.ama-assn.org/delivering-care/withholding-or-withdrawing-life-sustaining-treatment Accessed Jan 30, 2018
9. *Elizabeth Bouvia v. Superior Court of California*, 179 Cal. App. 3d 1127, 225 Cal. Rptr 297 (1986)
10. *In re Conroy*, 98 N.J. 321, 486 A.2d 1209 (1985)
11. Meisel, A, Cerminara, KL: *The Right to Die: The Law of End-of-Life Decisionmaking* (3rd ed.). Frederick, MD: Aspen Publishers, 2004
12. *Washington v. Glucksberg*, 521 U.S. 702 (1997)
13. *Vacco v. Quill*, 521 U.S. 793 (1997)

9 Prohibiting Psychiatrist–Patient Sex
Roy v. Hartogs (1976)

Jacob M. Appel

Can sexual relationships between psychiatrists and patients ever have a place in therapy or are such interactions inherently malpractice? If such relationships are prohibited, do they qualify as acts of professional negligence to be covered by malpractice insurance, or do they fall within a category of intentional transgressions that lies beyond the scope of coverage?

Background on the Case

On June 12, 1972, *New York Magazine* ran a cover story by psychiatrist Phyllis Chesler on patient–therapist sexual relationships that began with the provocative question: "Are you sure you want to sleep with your psychotherapist?"[1] In the course of interviews with eleven female patients who reported having sex with their psychiatrists, the author mustered evidence that "many therapists are lousy lovers" and that "they may not be very good doctors either."[1] Yet what remains striking about the article, "The Sensuous Psychiatrists," is that some figures within the psychiatric profession stepped forward to defend therapist–patient sex. Chesler quoted one "Greenwich Village psychologist" who argued that "doctors should sleep with patients, but "very rarely," and another New York psychiatrist who claimed, "There may be occasions where sleeping with a patient might be catastrophic. I have known it to occur where nonetheless the therapy has proceeded pretty well."[1] Chesler noted that, shortly before the publication of her article, psychoanalyst Martin Shepard (who later lost his license as a result of liaisons with patients) wrote in *The Love Treatment: Sexual Intimacy between Patients and Psychotherapists* (1972) that "sexual involvement can indeed be a useful part of the psychotherapeutic process."[1] This is not to say that the acceptance of psychiatrist–patient sex was the norm in the early 1970s, although it may have been more common in an earlier era, when pioneers like Wilhelm Reich and Sandor Rado married former patients. Rather, the practice existed under the radar, but was likely widespread.[2] Chesler cited research by renowned sexologists William Masters and Virginia Johnson that concluded: "If only 25 per cent of these specific reports are correct, there is still an overwhelming issue confronting professionals in this field."[1]

A handful of surveys conducted in the 1970s confirmed the concerns of Masters and Johnson. For example, a 1972 sampling of Los Angeles psychiatrists performed by Sheldon H. Kardener found that 10% reported sexual contact with patients.[3] In 1977, Holroyd and Brodsky surveyed psychologists and found that 5.5% of male therapists had entered sexual relationships with patients during treatment, while another 2.6% had done so within three months of terminating therapy.[3] In fact, the American Psychiatric Association did not formally proscribe psychiatrist–patient sex until 1973.[4] It was against this backdrop that in March 1971 a 32-year-old secretary named Julie Ellen Roy filed a lawsuit against prominent New York City psychiatrist Renatus "René" Hartogs that brought the issue of psychiatrist–patient liaisons out of the closet and onto America's front pages.

Hartogs was 62 years old in 1971 and cut a well-known figure in the field. A German-born Jewish refugee who had immigrated to the United States via Belgium in 1940 and later earned a medical degree at the University of Montreal, he had served for many years as chief psychiatrist at the Youth House of New York and later as medical director of the Community Guidance Service. In the former capacity, he was the therapist who evaluated a 13-year-old delinquent named Lee Harvey Oswald in 1953.[5] Hartogs testified before the Warren Commission during its investigation of the Kennedy assassination and subsequently coauthored a book with Lucy Freeman, *The Two Assassins*, which purported to expose "the hidden causes behind the crime of our generation."[6] (Hartogs' inconsistent testimony before the Warren Commission has since become a crucial piece of "evidence" mustered by those who challenge the commission's finding that Oswald acted alone.[7]) Although never a leading researcher, Hartogs carved out a niche for himself as a minor authority on the subject of profanity and, somewhat ironically, the causes of "sexual delinquency."[8,9] He was best known to the lay public as the author of a serial column, "The Analyst's Couch," in *Cosmopolitan Magazine*.[10] He had also penned a guide for female patients, *Questions Women Ask*, and (with Helen Jill Fletcher) a popular book for teens entitled *How to Grow Up Successfully*. By 1969, when Julie Roy first sought his help, he was a married father of two adult children with an office on Manhattan's Upper East Side.

Roy came to Hartogs for treatment of depression in March of 1969.[11] At age 31, she had already suffered a lifetime of setbacks: abandonment by her father at age three; a brother's suicide; and, most recently, the collapse of her three-year marriage to a Lebanese immigrant. In the words of journalist Susan Braudy, "She'd always been a depressed person" who "for years wore the same blue dress to hide her body." Roy felt as though she were "dying, dead, withered inside" and wished she could "evaporate" (Ref. 11, p. 33). Years later, she would write of believing herself to have been "a melancholy person, doomed to sadness" who "had nothing" to live for (Ref. 11, pp. 36–37). In a third-person recounting of her own predicament, she added: "[Roy] did not feel stifled, for that meant you had ideas to express that were bottled up. She felt empty, not even aware of how she would [have] like[d] her life to change" (Ref. 11, pp. 36–37).

Roy's path to Dr. Hartogs' office included "a stormy lesbian relationship" and a series of one-night stands with men she picked up at a jazz club.[12] Hartogs attributed her divorce to her supposed "homosexuality" and her "fear of men" and sought to cure her of these "lesbian" tendencies.[13] His primary mode of treatment consisted of sexual interactions during so-called "therapy" sessions that rarely lasted longer than ten minutes.[13] Although Hartogs informed Roy that she was making considerable progress in her recovery, she continued to feel depressed.[13] When she complained to Hartogs that her symptoms had not abated, he reportedly dismissed her concerns as unimportant.[13] He soon waived his $10-per-session fee and was paying her to type his correspondence. The pair met approximately twice weekly for a combination of talk therapy and sexual intercourse over a period of 14 months, both at Hartogs' office and at his apartment, until Hartogs terminated the "treatment" without warning in 1971.[14] According to Roy, after refusing to see her again, Hartogs refused to refer her to another therapist for additional care.

The consequences of the relationship proved devastating for Roy. She quit her job as a secretary in the advertising department at *Esquire* magazine and briefly contemplated traveling to the Grand Canyon and jumping over the rim. She also considered murdering Hartogs (Ref. 11, p. 128). In her third-person account of the affair, she wrote, "Dr. Hartogs had taken away what little identity [Roy] had, reducing her to a messy pulp" (Ref. 11, p. 119). Ultimately, she was twice hospitalized at Metropolitan Hospital for suicidal thoughts – once for eleven days and a second time for five weeks.[15] During her ensuing care, she encountered mental health professionals who expressed shock and indignation at Hartogs' conduct. As a result, she phoned the Legal Aid Society of New York to ascertain what rights she had vis-à-vis her former therapist (Ref. 11, p. 107). For a second opinion, she consulted Robert Stephan Cohen of Lans, Feinberg & Cohen, the 32-year-old attorney who had handled her earlier divorce action.

Cohen found his former client to be like "a lost bird with a wounded wing."[16] Once he'd been persuaded that Roy was telling him the truth regarding her liaisons with Hartogs, the self-described "insensitive New York lawyer" grew outraged by her story.[16] "What happened to her could have been called statutory rape. Even incest," he recalled. "She believed in her psychiatrist; the process of therapy was working. It was as if she were hypnotized ... When it was over, she was much worse off than before."[16] Nonetheless, Cohen recognized that any claim Roy might file against Hartogs faced steep odds; prior to that time, no patient had ever won a malpractice suit against a therapist for sexual misconduct in an American court. A year earlier, in *Zipkin v. Freeman*, a Missouri court had upheld an award for outrageous conduct that included therapist–patient sex, but the therapist's conduct also included encouraging the patient to sue her own family members and commit burglary; it is not clear whether a sexual relationship alone would have triggered an award.[17] Undeterred by the obstacles, Cohen accepted the case on a standard contingency and filed suit for $1.25 million.

Legal Course

After numerous delays engineered by Hartogs' legal team, the trial took place before Manhattan Civil Court Judge Allen Murray Myers from March 10 to March 19, 1975. Myers, a Democrat who subsequently enjoyed a distinguished career as a state appeals court judge, had a long record of social activism prior to joining the bench – including spearheading a campaign against antiquated school buildings in the 1950s – and his courtroom seemed a promising forum for Roy's claims.[18] An editorial in his local newspaper once described the judge as "a man with a conscience and the courage to match it" (Ref. 11, p. 135). In addition to Cohen, Roy's legal team included future entertainment law heavyweight Loren H. Plotkin. Hartogs retained attorneys Samuel Halpern and Jesse Cohen for his defense.

Roy's lawyers had two tasks. The first goal was to convince jurors that Hartogs had indeed seduced Roy under the guise of therapy. The second goal was to persuade the jury that this conduct deviated from the accepted standard of psychiatric care and therefore constituted malpractice. In order to accomplish this second mission, Cohen called to the stand a series of experts in medical ethics, including pioneer bioethicist and Hastings Center founder Willard Gaylin. Gaylin had never previously been willing to testify in court, but he agreed to serve as a witness for Roy's team free of charge (Ref. 11, p. 157). Psychiatrist Charles Clay Dahlberg, author of the first modern study of physician–patient sexual relationships, also testified on her behalf.[19] Both men argued that when a psychiatrist engages in sexual activity with a patient, it is a violation of ethical standards and thus inherently medical malpractice. These experts argued that the phenomenon of transference, an inherent aspect of the psychotherapeutic process in which the patient redirects her feelings about an important figure in her life (such as a parent) towards the therapist, rendered meaningful consent impossible. Roy's attorneys also cited the 1973 American Psychiatric Association guidelines as evidence.

In his defense, Hartogs did not attempt to justify his sexual relationship with Roy either as meeting the psychiatric profession's ethical standards or as serving his patient's therapeutic interests. In fact, he readily conceded that such conduct would be both unethical and malpractice. Instead, he denied the existence of any sexual relationship between them at all.[20] Hartogs "diagnosed" Roy to be an "incurable schizophrenic" who would "have delusions for the rest of her life,"[20] delusions that, coupled with personal antipathy, motivate her lawsuit, he claimed. "She hated me and she continued to hate me until the last day of treatment," he testified.[20] "She insulted me, she threw things at me and she treated me like nothing."[20] One piece of evidence he mustered to support his denials was the claim that he had been unable to have intercourse since the mid-1960s as the result of a worsening testicular hydrocele that he attributed to a kick from a guard at a concentration camp in 1940 (Ref. 11, p. 86). The other contention he advanced was that the pair could not have had relations on his analytic couch, as Roy testified, because the couch was only 29 inches wide. Hartogs even submitted a photograph of the narrow couch into evidence.[21]

The downside of Hartogs' denial of his sexual capabilities was that it permitted Roy's attorneys to introduce evidence of sexual contact between the psychiatrist and additional patients since the onset of his alleged impotence. Cohen and Plotkin found three other women who reported similar encounters. One was 50-year-old Manhattan schoolteacher Corinne Stern, who reported that she had sex regularly with Hartogs during seven years of treatment.[22] "I tried to stop," she told the court. "He kept talking me into it.... He kept saying, 'Trust me. You need this love. You've been deprived.'"[21] The second patient was celebrated actress and civil rights activist Madeleine Thornton-Sherwood, whose credits included Miss Lucy in Tennessee Williams' *Sweet Bird of Youth* and Reverend Mother Placido on the ABC sitcom *The Flying Nun*. Thornton-Sherwood testified that she had gone to Hartogs as a patient while "very disturbed" and had engaged in sex with him for several months, until he refused to see her anymore, a pattern similar to his alleged conduct with Roy.[22] A third patient, Cooper Union film student Judith Ann Cuttler, told the jury that Hartogs had fondled her breasts and propositioned her during therapy. Although Hartogs' attorneys persuaded Judge Allen to strike the Thornton-Sherwood and Cuttler testimony from the record as inflammatory, considerable damage had already been done. The jury of four women and two men returned a 5–1 verdict in Roy's favor and awarded her $250,000 in compensatory damages and an additional $100,000 in punitive damages. Judge Myers subsequently reduced the compensatory damages to $50,000, based on his observations in the courtroom regarding Roy's degree of impairment.[23]

The greatest challenge to Roy's suit occurred at the conclusion of opening statements, when Hartogs' lawyers moved for the case to be dismissed on the grounds that such litigation was prohibited by New York State's civil rights laws, specifically the legislation known as the Anti-Heart Balm Act of 1935.[24] Prior to that year, New York State allowed lawsuits for breaches of promise to marry ("seduction") or interference with another's marital relationship ("alienation of affection").[25] In response to evolving social mores, the state legislature had outlawed such actions as contrary to public policy. Another New York state court had recently rejected a similar sexual misconduct lawsuit against a gynecologist. The question Judge Myers faced was thus whether, in banning such suits, the legislature had intended to proscribe *all* seduction-based claims. He concluded that it had not. "It was never the intention of the Legislature to outlaw all actions in which sexual intercourse is an element," wrote Myers, noting that the power of transference rendered the psychiatrist–patient relationship different even from other cases of medical misconduct. "As a matter of fact, where consent could not be given or where it was coerced as in cases of statutory rape, rape or where there was a fiduciary relationship between guardian and ward, there was always an action for damages on the case…. This case involves a fiduciary relationship between psychiatrist and patient and is analogous to the guardian-ward relationship."[25] The judge added, "It is noted with regard to the defendant's claim that public policy bars this suit, that there is a public policy to protect a patient from the deliberate and malicious abuse of power and breach of trust by a psychiatrist when that patient entrusts to him her body and mind in the hope that he will use his best efforts to effect a cure."[25] That ruling sealed Hartogs' legal fate.

Hartogs appealed the verdict to New York State's Supreme Court (a first-tier appellate court), and a ruling by Justices Markowitz, Tierney, and Riccobono reduced the judgment even further.[26] The triumvirate concluded that no punitive damages were appropriate and that even $50,000 was an excessive amount for compensatory damages in light of Roy's condition, remanding the case to Judge Allen with the suggestion that total damages of "no more than $25,000" would be more appropriate.[26,27] Hartogs' insurer, Employers Mutual Liability Insurance

Company of Wisconsin, had previously committed to settling the claim for $50,000, and the firm chose not to challenge this earlier agreement.[28] However, the insurer refused to indemnify the cost of Hartogs' defense on the grounds that his conduct had been outside the scope of medical practice. Unable to afford his attorney bills and trial-associated costs, Hartogs filed for bankruptcy. He then sued the insurance company for failure to fulfill the terms of his policy.

Judge Harold Baer faced a difficult challenge in *Hartogs v. Employers Mutual Liability Insurance Company of Wisconsin*. On the one hand, he believed that what he derisively termed *"fornicatus Hartogus"* did "not constitute medical malpractice" and therefore fell beyond the scope of Dr. Hartogs' insurance.[28] On the other hand, Baer did not wish victims like Roy to go without compensation in future cases. His Solomon-style solution was to invalidate the coverage with regard to Hartogs, but not to Roy:

Defendant claims that the "treatment" which Hartogs administered did not constitute medical malpractice and was therefore not covered under the policy. Hartogs argues that the jury in the case against him has already found medical malpractice. They are both correct. A distinction should be drawn in a factual situation such as this between medical malpractice in the mind of the patient and medical malpractice in the mind of the doctor. Plainly when the patient submitted she believed that appropriate medical therapy was being administered. Only some time thereafter did she discover that she had been duped, the victim of fraud and subterfuge. On the other hand, the doctor administering the "treatment" at all times knew, and has so stated in the previous trial and on this motion, that what he was doing was in no way pursuant to the doctor–patient relationship. The obvious purpose was to permit him to accomplish his personal satisfaction.[28]

As it turned out, the ruling against Hartogs relied on narrower grounds, namely that he had failed to provide his insurer with timely notice after his transgressions. Of note, Hartogs included an affidavit with his insurance cases admitting "that he at all times knew that the therapy he was administering was a violation of professional ethics and not within acceptable medical standards."[28]

Aftermath

Hartogs hobbled away from the case with his reputation in tatters. Formal charges were brought against him at the December 1976 meeting of the New York State Board of Regents, the authority that governed medical licenses.[29] He chose not to contest the charges, saying he was unable to defend himself, and resigned his license.[29] However, this did not entirely end his career as a practicing physician. He drew legal attention again when his name arose nine years later in what Judge James K. Oakes of the United States Court of Appeals for the Second Circuit described as the "weird, if not to say bizarre" case of *Goldberg v. National Life Insurance Company of Vermont* (1985).[30] Goldberg had taken out an insurance policy in 1980 that required him "to be under the care and attendance of a licensed physician"; according to the paperwork he filed with his policy, that physician proved to be none other than Renatus Hartogs who, the defending insurers now pointed out, had not held a valid medical license at that time.[30] The degree to which Hartogs continued to practice psychiatry without a license remains unclear. He divorced during the course of his liaison with Roy, never remarried, and died in relative obscurity in New York City in 1998 at the age of 89.

Attorney Robert Cohen parlayed his courtroom victory into a career as one of the nation's most-recognized family and divorce lawyers. He headed the matrimonial department at the firm of Morrison Cohen Singer & Weinstein in New York for nearly two decades and established his own boutique, Cohen Lans LLP, in 2003. His high-profile clients have included Michael R. Bloomberg, Christie Brinkley, and Ivana Trump.[31] He also teaches divorce law at the University of Pennsylvania Law School. In 2002, the *New York Times* profiled him as "one of the most powerful matrimonial lawyers in the country."[31] During the immediate aftermath of Roy's success, however, Cohen found himself inundated with similar pleas for assistance. "I'm handling ten such cases right now," he told journalists following the trial.[16] "I get letters every day from all over the country from lawyers and women interested in filing suit." He recognized that the case was a watershed victory that would soon witness "a great surge of women in court asserting their rights not to suffer discrimination or sexual abuse of any kind."[16]

According to Cohen, Julie Roy "took the money finally awarded, moved to California, got a job and bought a harpsichord."[16] Soon thereafter, she was earning $65 a week as a clerk in a San Francisco bookstore.[15] Around this time, Roy collaborated with *New York Times* journalist Lucy Freeman on a firsthand account of her experiences, *Betrayal*, which was ultimately published in 1976. (Freeman had previously collaborated with Dr. Hartogs on *The Two Assassins*; she also wrote a best-selling account of her own experience with psychoanalysis, *Fight Against Fear* (1951), and died in 2005.[32]) The popular account was generally well received within the psychiatric community. For example, Jean Smith, reviewing the volume in the *American Journal of Psychoanalysis*, described it as "an absorbing, well-written book which leaves us with more questions than it answers."[33] The following year, *Betrayal* was adapted into a teleplay by Joanna Crawford and Jerrold Freedman and aired as an NBC movie of the week starring Rip Torn as Hartogs and Lesley Ann Warren as Roy; Paul Wendkos directed. Warren was particularly taken by the story, describing the "devastating role" as "an emotionally exhausting experience."[34] The actress told reporters, "Because of the demands of playing Julie Roy … I started to take on the same attitudes myself. I saw the show for the first time a few days ago, and I cried for an hour-and-a-half afterwards."[34] The horrific story of Julie Roy's betrayal and the secret world of therapist–patient sex had entered America's living rooms and unsettled the conscience of society.

Impact on Practice

A well-worn legal adage, first penned by Judge Robert Rolfe but popularized by Supreme Court Justice Oliver Wendell Holmes' opinion in *Northern Securities Co. v. United States*, argues that "hard cases make bad law." In other words, an extreme set of facts can often produce a binding precedent whose application is undesirable when less-extreme cases arise. *Roy v. Hartogs* offers an example of a hard case making good law. Had Dr. Hartogs admitted to his sexual conduct and defended it as lying within acceptable practice, he might have had a better chance of victory, since the law was far less settled in this area in the mid-1970s than it is today. In 1976, psychiatrist Alan Stone noted that Hartogs did not pursue two lines of argument open to him at the time: either "that the client had freely consented to an affair that had been presented to her as entirely separate from the therapeutic relationship" or that "the client had given informed consent to sex *as* therapy before transference developed."[35] As Stone observed: "Both of the defenses I enumerated, though unacceptable to the mental health profession, may still be appropriate in courts of law."[35] Malpractice law holds that when a minority viewpoint regarding appropriate care is held by a reasonable number of respected practitioners in the medical community, those following that view may be protected from claims. Paul E. Mason noted shortly after the case that Hartogs could have relied upon the writings of Martin Shepard and other defenders of therapist–patient sex to make a case that his conduct reflected a respectable minority view.[35] Jerry Edelwich and Archie Brodskyd also pointed out that Hartogs could have argued that the 1973 APA guidelines were being applied *ex post facto* to conduct that occurred several years earlier.[35] If Hartogs had attempted these tactics and won his case – not an implausible outcome in 1975 – he might well have established a troublesome precedent. Instead, his insistence on his factual innocence despite the testimony of multiple accusers assured both his own disgrace and a significant shift in both public attitudes and legal standards.

The widespread publicity surrounding *Roy v. Hartogs* and the seemingly outrageous extremes of Dr. Hartogs' behavior generated considerable professional and societal action to prevent similar conduct. Soon afterwards, for example, the Los Angeles chapter of the National Organization for Women launched a project to help victims report such cases.[36] The American Psychiatric Association took up the issue at its annual meeting in 1976 and the American Psychological Association did so at its convention in 1978. Ultimately, sixteen states have criminalized therapist–patient sex, while three now require mandatory reporting of past sexual exploitation by other therapists.[37] Moreover, the scope of prohibited conduct has increasingly expanded. In 1988, the American Psychiatric Association amended its ethical code to proscribe sex with former patients (Ref. 37, p. 609). Courts have also found malpractice for conducting affairs with patients' relatives (Ref. 37, pp. 614–617). Defending sexual relations with a patient as ethical now appears to be a losing hand in malpractice litigation.[38] Since 1976, Ralph Slovenko reported in 2009, "sexual misconduct has represented 15% of all lawsuits against psychiatrists and has accounted for one-third or more of payouts for psychiatric claims" (Ref. 37, p. 608).

The most important result of Julie Roy's lawsuit has been a significant shift in public attitudes toward sexual relations between psychiatrists and those in their care. Cohen reflected, nearly three decades after Hartogs' misconduct, that "in the wake of the Hartogs case, public attitudes and the psychiatric practice now recognize the utter inappropriateness of such conduct" (RS Cohen, personal communication, January 2013). Another consequence of *Roy v. Hartogs* and the slew of cases that followed has been considerable change in insurance coverage. As a result of numerous sexual misconduct claims, the American Psychological Association's insurer refused to renew its coverage in 1976 (Ref. 35, p. 209). The organization found a new insurer that explicitly refused to provide payment for such claims. The American Psychiatric Association followed suit in 1985. Slovenko observed that deterrence was not the primary motivation behind this change; rather, secondary insurers demanded excessive premiums unless sexual misconduct was excluded from APA policies (Ref. 37, p. 613). Although both organizations will cover some litigation costs in cases where therapists deny sexual contact, they do not make payouts to victims of sexual misconduct. Therapists who engage in such behavior are on their own. One unfortunate downside of this approach is that a victim like Roy would likely have more difficulty obtaining awarded compensation today.

Psychiatry has evolved considerably since the era when Phyllis Chesler was called a "hysterical man-hater" and accused of "making up" the phenomenon of sexual misconduct by psychiatrists (P. Chesler, personal communication, January 2012). However, Dr. Chesler is quick to note that although this behavior is "very clearly unethical, possibly criminal" and "certainly damaging to the patient," it has not entirely abated (P. Chesler, personal communication, January 2012). What has changed, as a result of Robert Cohen's perseverance and Julie Roy's courage, is the willingness of the profession to stand up against such transgressions. Their immediate victory in *Roy vs. Hartogs* may have occurred in the courtroom, but Ms. Roy's far greater long-term triumph occurred in the court of public and professional opinion.

REFERENCES

1. Chesler P: The sensuous psychiatrists. *New York Magazine,* Jun. 19, 1972
2. Riskin LL: Sexual relations between psychotherapists and their patients: Toward research or restraint. *Cal L Rev.* 67: 1000, 1979
3. Gartrell N, Herman J, Olarte S, Feldstein M, Localio R: Psychiatrist–patient sexual contact: Results of a national survey, I: Prevalence. *Am J Psychiatry.* 143: 1126–31, 1986
4. APA Ethics Committee: The principles of medical ethics with annotations especially applicable to psychiatry. *Am J Psychiatry.* 130,9: 1057–64, 1973
5. Testimony of Renatus Hartogs before the Warren Commission, Apr. 16, 1964
6. Hartogs R, Freeman L: *The Two Assassins.* New York: Thomas Y. Crowell, 1965
7. La Fontaine R, La Fontaine M: *Oswald Talked: The New Evidence in the JFK Assassination.* Gretna, LA: Pelican Publishing Company, 1996, p. 52
8. Hartogs R: *Four Letter Word Games: The Psychology of Obscenity.* New York: Delacorte Press/M. Evans, 1967
9. Hartogs, R: Discipline in the early life of sex-delinquents and sex-criminals. *Nervous Child.* 9: 167–73, 1951
10. Yoakum R: The Hartogs case. *The Telegraph* (Nashua, NH). Apr. 9, 1975, p. 4
11. Freeman L, Roy J. *Betrayal: The True Story of the First Woman to Successfully Sue Her Psychiatrist for Using Sex in the Guise of Therapy.* New York: Stein and Day, 1976
12. Braudy S: Review of *Betrayal* by Lucy Freeman and Julie Roy. *New York Times.* Aug. 8, 1976, p. 165
13. Morin LA: Civil remedies for therapist-patient sexual exploitation. *Golden Gate Univ Law Rev.* 19, 3:410–11, 2010
14. Patient awarded $350,000: doctor found guilty in 'sex therapy'. *Los Angeles Times,* Mar. 20, 1975, p. 4
15. Love thy analyst. *Time magazine.* Mar. 24, 1975, p. 76
16. Kleiman C: Sex therapy is off the couch, into court. *Chicago Tribune,* Aug. 11, 1976, p. B2
17. *Zipkin v. Freeman,* 436 S.W.2d 753 (Missouri 1968)

18. Pace E: Allen Murray Myers, 85, justice who protested outdated school. *New York Times*, Apr. 13, 1998

19. Dahlberg CC: Sexual contact between patient and therapist. *Contemporary Psychoanalysis* 6: 107–24, 1970

20. But the couch is only 29 inches wide. *Evening Independent* (Massillon, Ohio), Mar. 19, 1975

21. Psychiatrist's therapy: Patient treated with sex, jury says. *Los Angeles Times*, Mar. 19, 1975, p. 2

22. Sex therapy suit: Doctor ruled guilty. *The Modesto Bee*. Mar. 19, 1975

23. Morin LA: Civil remedies for therapist-patient sexual exploitation. *Golden Gate Univ Law Rev.* 19, 3: 410–1, 2010

24. N. Y. Laws 1935, c. 263, N. Y. Civ. PstAc. Acr (1935) §§ 61a-61i.

25. *Roy v. Hartogs*, 366 N.Y.S.2d 297 (1975)

26. *Roy v. Hartogs*, 381 N.Y.S.2d 587 (1976)

27. Metropolitan briefs: award against doctor cut to $25,000. *New York Times*. Feb. 4, 1976, p. 32

28. *Renatus Hartogs v. Employers Mutual Liability Insurance Company of Wisconsin*, 391 N.Y.S.2d 962 (1977)

29. Johnson L: Hearings are begun in psychiatrist case. *New York Times*. Dec. 23, 1976, p. 19

30. *Stephen M. Goldberg v. National Life Insurance Company of Vermont*, 774 F.2d 559 (1985)

31. Witchel A: Counterintelligence; the patch-up, from the master of the split-up. *New York Times*, Mar. 17, 2002 Available at: www.nytimes.com/2002/03/17/style/counterintelligence-the-patch-up-from-the-master-of-the-split-up.html

32. Cave D: Lucy Freeman, Times reporter and prolific author, dies at 88. *New York Times*, Jan. 3, 2005

33. Smith J: Review of *Betrayal* by Lucy Freeman and Julie Roy. *Am J Psychoanalysis*. 37: 89–92, 1977

34. Betrayal drama airs. *Herald-Journal* (Spartanburg, SC). Nov. 11, 1978, p. 13

35. Edelwich J, Brodskyd A: *Sexual Dilemmas for the Helping Professional*. East Sussex, UK: Psychology Press, 1991, pp. 205–206

36. Mall J: About women: therapist–patient sex and the courts. *Los Angeles Times*, Aug. 27, 1978, p. J8

37. Slovenko, R: *Psychiatry in Law/Law in Psychiatry*. New York: Taylor & Francis, 2009, p. 604

38. Lang DM: Sexual malpractice and professional liability: some things they don't teach in medical school – a critical examination of the formative case law. *Conn Ins L J.* 6: 151, 1999/2000

10   Psychotherapist–Patient Privilege

Jaffee v. Redmond (1996)

Jacob M. Appel

Can the confidential communications between a patient and a psychother-apist be used against that patient in court? Do protections against such forced disclosure apply to all licensed therapists, or only to psychologists and psychiatrists?

Hoffman Estates, Illinois, had a reputation as an idyllic, all-American community. When Sears, Roebuck & Company relocated its headquarters to the village from downtown Chicago in 1991, the corporation found a middle-class hamlet of "leafy subdivisions" that resembled one of the "neatly clipped suburbs in a Sears advertisement."[1] That year, a police force of 85 officers, including 8 women, served the municipality's 46,000 residents.[2] Violent crime remained relatively rare: The town experienced no homicides and only 10 robberies in 1990.[3] However, this placid exterior masked significant social tensions. Gang activity was starting to spill over from Chicago's inner suburbs, ensnaring children as young as 13; illicit drug use increasingly infected the local schools.[4] In 1989, simmering racial antagonisms between the town's white majority and its approximately 1,300 African American residents (2.8% of the population) had boiled into a bitter two-year legal battle after the town fired its only African American police officer for a minor uniform violation. So on June 27, 1991, the shooting of a black suspect, Ricky Allen, by a white patrol officer, Mary Lu Redmond, occurred against a background of ongoing racial hostility and mutual mistrust.

The 29-year-old Redmond, a five-year veteran of the Hoffman Estates force, was regarded as a first-rate cop: "very level-headed" and "very competent."[5] On the night of the shooting, she was the first officer to respond to a report of two men fighting at the Canyon Estates apartment complex on the Grand Canyon Parkway. Redmond testified that when she pulled into the complex's parking lot, she encountered two African American women who ran toward her car and told her that a stabbing had occurred inside the development. At this point, Redmond called her dispatcher for backup and an ambulance. The officer then approached the building as five African American men charged out the doors; one of

114

them carried a pipe above his head, and when he refused her commands to drop the weapon, Officer Redmond drew her 9-mm semiautomatic. Seconds later, according to Redmond, a white man (later identified as 37-year-old Thomas Jamell) fled the building, pursued by an African American (31-year-old Ricky Allen) wielding a kitchen knife. As revealed in subsequent testimony, the two men were involved in an altercation over musical instruments that Jamell accused Allen of removing from his van. Redmond described what transpired next to the trial court:

I ordered the black male subject with the knife to drop the knife several times. I told him to drop the knife and get on the ground ... I was yelling at him to drop the knife and get on the ground ... [H]e did not drop the knife and he did not get on the ground ... [I yelled] at least three times. I just kept yelling the minute I saw him. As [Allen] was gaining speed on the first subject until they were directly – he was directly in front of him, like the first subject's back, and then the second subject, as he was gaining on him the second subject, the male black subject with the knife took the knife back, raised it above his head and I waited, and as he started to come down with the knife and made the downward motion, I fired one shot at him.[6]

A crowd soon gathered around the shooting victim, including four of Allen's siblings, and witnesses claimed that Officer Redmond held the bystanders at bay with her weapon. Allen's siblings insisted that they had not seen their brother raise a knife, although a carving knife was later found by the authorities alongside his body. The second officer on the scene, Joe Graham, reported that he heard people in the crowd threatening that "they were going to sue the white bitch for shooting Mr. Allen."[6] Ten days later, Allen's mother, Carrie Jaffee, did file a federal wrongful death lawsuit under the Civil Rights Act of 1871 (42 U.S.C. §1983) for more than a million dollars on behalf of her son's estate and her grandsons against both Mary Lu Redmond and the Village of Hoffman Estates.

To the victim's family and much of the local African American population, Ricky Allen's death was caused by an unnecessary overreaction steeped in racism. Reverend Jimmie Daniels, president of the local chapter of the civil rights organization Operation PUSH, explained to the press that "the only thing Ricky's mother can see is a white officer shot her son because of another white man."[7] In contrast, the Cook County state's attorney determined that Redmond's conduct was "justifiable" and that she had "acted properly," and the Village's Use of Force Review Board concluded that Redmond had "used deadly force only after all reasonable alternatives had been exhausted."[8] The following spring, Redmond was awarded the Hoffman Estates Police Department's medal of valor for her role in the fatal incident. Deputy Chief Clint Herdegen credited her with "an overall outstanding job of handing [the] entire situation," including "preserving the crime scene" and possibly saving Jamell's life.[9]

Redmond herself remained "extremely traumatized" by the shooting[10] and sought counseling several days after the tragedy. She contacted the town's employee-assistance program and entered treatment with its director, licensed social worker Karen Beyer. Beyer was a highly experienced psychotherapist. She had assumed management of the Hoffman Estates Department of Health and Human Services in 1983 after more than a decade leading a well-regarded local nonprofit organization, the Family Services Agency of Greater Elgin. Redmond and Beyer met for two or three 90-minute sessions per week during the first six months after the shooting, terminating only after Beyer received a subpoena from Jaffee's attorneys demanding her counseling records for her sessions with Redmond and seeking her testimony regarding the content of those sessions.[10] Needless to say, Redmond's lawyer, Gregory Rogus, objected to such a hand-over. Although Illinois state law granted psychotherapy patients the right to withhold such information, no such privilege then existed in federal courts. However, against the recommendation of her lawyers, Karen Beyer refused to provide the subpoenaed documents, citing her professional and ethical duty of confidentiality to her client. Beyer's defiance of United States District Judge Milton I. Shadur, a 68-year-old Carter appointee with a reputation for both liberalism and intransigence, generated a four-year-long legal battle over the nature and scope of patient–psychotherapist privilege that would ultimately be decided by the U.S. Supreme Court.

Legal Course

Legal Background

No privilege between physicians and patients had existed in common law, and it was not until 1828 that New York became the first state to adopt such a privilege by statute.[11] Missouri followed in 1835.[12] By the early 1960s, thirty states offered at least a limited privilege under physician–patient privilege rules to psychiatrists engaging in psychotherapy.[13] However, these laws did not protect nonphysician therapists, such as psychologists and social workers, and often did not apply in criminal matters. Moreover, it was not always clear that the treatment of "mental and emotional disorders" constituted "the practice of medicine" under many of these statutes.[13] During the 1950s, six states (Arkansas, Georgia, Kentucky, New York, Tennessee, and Washington) adopted specific statutes creating a psychologist–patient privilege, modeled directly on the common law attorney–client privilege.[14] In addition, in the seminal case of *Binder v. Ruvell* (1952), Circuit Court Judge Harry M. Fisher upheld psychotherapist–patient privilege for the first time in Cook County, Illinois,[15] the location of the Allen shooting. However, prior to the 1960s, most jurisdictions offered few if any guarantees of confidentiality to therapists.[16]

Two events in the early 1960s spurred the expansion of legal protections at the state level for communications between patients and therapists.[13] The first was the defection of a pair of National Security Administration cryptologists, William Hamilton Martin and Bernon F. Mitchell, to the Soviet Union in 1960. The House Un-American Activities Committee subpoenaed Mitchell's private psychiatrist, who testified in a closed hearing to the contents of his sessions with Mitchell, including "embarrassing personal information" such as Mitchell's homosexuality and atheism.[16] A professional outcry ensued.[17] The Council of Washington Psychiatrists issued a formal protest and the Medical and Chirurgical Faculty of the State of Maryland circulated a petition asking the state medical society to investigate the breach of confidentiality.[17] Although largely forgotten today, the Mitchell incident – the culmination of FBI Director J. Edgar Hoover's decade-long campaign to get physicians to report suspicions of "espionage, sabotage and subversive activities"[18] – played an instrumental role in prompting mental health professionals to lobby for a legal right to confidentiality. Among the most important of these efforts was the draft of a model privilege statute by the Group for the Advancement of Psychiatry (GAP) for potential adoption by the states (Ref. 13, p. 736). Shortly afterwards, at the behest of state senator and mental health advocate Florence D. Finney, Connecticut became the first state to adopt a specific psychiatrist–patient privilege in response to the GAP proposal (Ref. 13, p. 737). By 1991, every state had adopted such a testimonial privilege, and the vast majority extended that privilege beyond psychiatrists and psychologists to all licensed counselors.

In contrast to the states' courts, the federal courts had proven reluctant to extend a testimonial privilege to the confidences of psychotherapy patients. However, the federal courts, to a much greater degree than most states, have clear guidelines for the circumstances under which new privileges may be created.[19] The Advisory Committee for the Federal Rules of Evidence, established by Chief Justice Earl Warren in 1965, had proposed nine "specific nonconstitutional privileges," including psychotherapist–patient privilege.[20] However, in adopting the Federal Rules of Evidence (FRE) in 1975, Congress overtly rejected such enumerated privileges in favor of a general framework that shifted the burden of adopting specific privileges to the judiciary.[21] Rule 501 of the FRE, which governs privileges, established only that the "privilege of a witness ... shall be governed by the principles of the common law as they may be interpreted by the courts of the United States in the light of reason and experience."[22] In other words, judges were charged with using "reason and experience" to determine whether, and to what degree, the confidences of psychotherapy patients ought to be shielded from subpoena.

In the two decades between the adoption of the Federal Rules of Evidence and the Supreme Court's ruling in *Jaffee v. Redmond*, the lower federal courts failed to reach any consensus on the validity or scope of psychotherapist–patient privilege.[23] Several courts embraced a limited privilege. For example, in *Doe v. Diamond* (1992), the Second Circuit Court of Appeals upheld the privilege, but one "that [was] highly qualified and require[d] a case-by-case assessment of whether the evidentiary need for the psychiatric history of a witness outweigh[ed] the privacy interests of that witness."[24] Similarly, in *In re Zuniga* (1983), the United States Court of Appeals Sixth Circuit adopted a form of the privilege that required "balancing the interests protected by shielding the evidence sought with those advanced by disclosure," but one that, on the whole, appeared to favor protecting confidentiality.[25] At the opposite end of the spectrum, the United States Courts of Appeals for the Fifth, Ninth, Tenth, and Eleventh Circuits all categorically rejected such a federal privilege.[26-29] At the time Karen Beyer appeared in Judge Shadur's courtroom, neither the District Court for Northern Illinois nor the Court of Appeals for the Seventh Circuit had ever ruled on the merits of federal psychotherapist–patient privilege. As a result, both Shadur and the Court of Appeals possessed considerable latitude regarding the handling of Beyer's claims.

In the Lower Courts

The decisive legal wrangling in the case of *Jaffee v. Redmond* occurred long before the actual opening of the trial on December 13, 1993. Judge Shadur repeatedly ruled in pretrial hearings that no privilege protected Redmond's confidential communications to her therapist. Yet during three consecutive depositions, Karen Beyer testified that she could not remember the content of her sessions with Redmond; she also continued to refuse to hand over her confidential therapy notes. Officer Redmond similarly expressed a lack of memory regarding the conversations. Judge Shadur eventually became frustrated with the defiant silence of both the therapist and the defendant.[10] He threatened to prohibit Redmond from testifying at trial on her own behalf, arguing that the officer's silence combined with Beyer's failure to disclose her notes made effective cross-examination of her impossible. Eventually, the judge partially relented, permitting Redmond to testify, but issuing the following highly unfavorable jury instruction:

You have heard evidence in this case that Karen Beyer, while an employee of the Village of Hoffman Estates, had numerous conversations with Mary Lu Redmond and made notes of those conversations ... During the course of this lawsuit the Court ordered the Village of Hoffman Estates to turn over all of Ms. Beyer's notes to plaintiff's attorneys. The Village was provided with numerous opportunities to obey the Court's order and refused to do so. During the course of this lawsuit Mary Lu Redmond also testified that she would not authorize or direct Ms. Beyer to turn over those notes to plaintiff's attorneys. During Ms. Beyer's testimony she referred to herself as a "therapist," although she is not a psychiatrist or psychologist – she is a social worker. This Court has ruled that there is no legal justification in this lawsuit, based as it is on a federal constitutional claim, to refuse to produce Ms. Beyer's notes of her conversations with Mary Lu Redmond, and that such refusal was unjustified. Under these circumstances, you are entitled to presume that the contents of the notes would be unfavorable to Mary Lu Redmond and the Village of Hoffman Estates.[30]

The implications of this instruction were even more detrimental to the defense case than they may appear on the surface, since the plaintiffs had sought to establish that Redmond had revealed to Beyer either a prior interaction with the victim or had confessed during therapy to using excessive force. Presumably, Judge Shadur's directive allowed the jury to infer that both of these speculative claims might be true. In addition, Shadur referred Beyer's case to the United States Attorney's office for potential criminal prosecution. Although federal prosecutors ultimately decided against filing charges, Beyer was not informed of this decision for some time, leading her to fear that she "might go to jail."[10]

    The week-long trial itself focused largely on the question of whether or not Ricky Allen had been about to stab Thomas Jamell at the moment of the shooting. Officer Redmond testified that no one had moved the knife found near Allen's corpse until the investigating officers arrived. However, Allen's sisters insisted that he was not carrying a knife when Redmond fired at him. A paramedic who attended to Allen on the scene also testified that he had seen no knife. The plaintiffs contended that, after the shooting, "a Hoffman Estates police officer picked up that knife by the blade, walked over to where Ricky Allen's body lay, and threw it down on the ground."[31] Forensic testing of the knife discovered beside Allen's body did not reveal any recoverable fingerprints.[32] Judge Shadur also inserted himself directly into the trial on the subject of the knife, questioning the credibility of Redmond's account.[31] Likely influenced by Judge Shadur's commentary and his sweeping instructions, the eight-member jury found that Redmond had "used unnecessary deadly force" and had "acted with the deliberate intent to harm Allen."[31] In compensation, they awarded Ricky Allen's sons $545,000.

Redmond and the Village of Hoffman Estates appealed the verdict to the Seventh Circuit Court of Appeals in Chicago on the grounds that Judge Shadur's jury instructions had been in error and that he was mistaken in failing to recognize a federal psychotherapist–client privilege. The case was argued on September 14, 1994 before a three-judge panel consisting of Reagan appointee John Louis Coffey, Ford appointee Harlingon Wood, Jr., and Johnson appointee John Cooper Goldbold, a senior judge from the Eleventh Circuit who heard the case by designation. All three judges had sterling reputations for moderation and fairness. Judge Coffey's opinion, in which his colleagues concurred, rejected Judge Shadur's approach wholesale.

The appeals court adopted a broad psychotherapist–patient privilege for the jurisdiction largely along the lines advocated by the defense. Judge Coffey, consistent with other federal court rulings, embraced a balancing test for the application of the privilege, and stated: "The privilege we recognize in a case of this nature requires an assessment of whether, in the interests of justice, the evidentiary need for the disclosure of the contents of a patient's counseling sessions outweighs that patient's privacy interests."[30] At the same time, Coffey's analysis strongly suggested that in cases like Redmond's, the officer's counseling fell well within the scope of privilege. He wrote:

We decline to speculate as to what situations would call for the abrogation of this privilege. Instead, we confine our analysis to a factual situation of this nature, where the balance of the competing interests tips sharply in favor of the privilege if we hope to encourage law enforcement officers who are frequently forced to experience traumatic events by the very nature of their work to seek qualified professional help.[30]

Coffey might have stopped here and merely overturned the lower court's verdict. Instead, he concluded with following the observation:

Officer Redmond, and all those placed in her most unfortunate circumstances, are entitled to be protected in their desire to seek counseling after mortally wounding another human being in the line of duty. An individual who is troubled as the result of her participation in a violent and tragic event, such as this, displays a most commendable respect for human life and is a person well-suited 'to protect and to serve.'[30]

The judgment for the Allen family was set aside, delivering Judge Shadur a stinging rebuke.

The Supreme Court Decision

The Allen family appealed Judge Coffey's ruling to the Supreme Court and the high court granted *certiorari* on October 16, 1995.[33] The case instantly became a matter of significant concern for both mental health providers and legal authorities. All of the major professional associations in mental health, including the American Psychoanalytic Association, the American Psychiatric Association, the American Psychological Association, the American Counseling Association, the American Academy of Psychiatry and the Law, and the National Association of Social Workers, filed *amicus* briefs in support of a psychotherapist–patient privilege. Of note, the American Psychiatric Association, which has historically sought to protect its members' prerogatives against encroachment by psychologists and social workers, advocated strongly for a broad privilege that included all licensed therapists.[34] Surprisingly, Solicitor General Drew S. Days III, representing the Clinton Administration, also filed a brief favoring such a privilege, although one that only extended to social workers within jurisdictions where the state already conferred the privilege broadly.[35] Although the Justice Department has generally opposed the creation of additional privileges, fearing the exclusion of valuable evidence from the courtroom, in this case Days argued that the significant benefits of keeping confidential counseling available to law enforcement officers outweighed any potential harm done by the loss of testimony.[35] Not one *amicus* brief was filed on behalf of the Allen family.

Oral arguments in the case took place on February 26, 1996, with Kenneth Flaxman representing the Allen family and Gregory Rogus representing Officer Redmond and the Village of Hoffman Estates. From the outset of the hearing, the Supreme Court appeared disposed to carve out some form of psychotherapist–patient privilege, but the question remained whether that privilege would be limited or absolute and to whom it would apply. Justices Anthony Kennedy and David Souter grilled Flaxman regarding this latter question, relying heavily on the American Psychiatric Association's *amicus* brief that favored inclusion of social workers.[36] In a fast-paced exchange, Souter forced Flaxman to concede that "psychiatric social workers do all sorts of things," and that the challenges of drawing a meaningful line between the work of psychiatrists and that of other licensed mental health workers were considerable.[36] In the other significant exchange of the morning, Chief Justice William Rehnquist elicited from Rogus an admission that Redmond and Beyer sought only a limited privilege subject to a presumption of confidentiality and a balancing test between the societal benefits of protecting confidentiality and of providing evidence. Justice Scalia then intervened and used his interrogation of Rogus to explain why he believed such a balancing test to be unworkable. Ironically, the Court later embraced Scalia's reasoning, but not his conclusions, opting for an absolute privilege over the mere presumption of confidentiality advocated by Rogus.

The Supreme Court's majority opinion, authored by Justice John Paul Stevens and handed down on June 13, 1996, proved a decisive victory for advocates of the psychotherapist–patient privilege. Stevens first noted the considerable public interest served by "facilitating the provision of appropriate treatment for individuals suffering the effects of a mental or emotional problem."[37] In the opinion's most memorable lines, Stevens wrote: "The mental health of our citizenry, no less than its physical health, is a public good of transcendent importance."[37] He then pointed out that the evidence lost by the creation of the privilege would be "modest":

> If the privilege were rejected, confidential conversations between psychotherapists and their patients would surely be chilled, particularly when it is obvious that the circumstances that give rise to the need for treatment will probably result in litigation. Without a privilege, much of the desirable evidence to which litigants such as petitioner seek access – for example, admissions against interest by a party – is unlikely to come into being. This unspoken "evidence" will therefore serve no greater truth-seeking function than if it had been spoken and privileged.[37]

Stevens relied in part upon the brief from the National Association of Social Workers in observing that the clients of psychiatric social workers "often include the poor and those of modest means who could not afford the assistance of a psychiatrist or psychologist."[37] Therefore, if the privilege was to serve its intended purposes, it had to be extended to *all* licensed psychotherapists. Even the presumption of confidentiality, subject to balancing, was too narrow for Justice Stevens, since it opened the privilege up to uncertainty that might lead to mistrust or lack of confidence on the part of psychotherapy patients. According to Stevens:

> Making the promise of confidentiality contingent upon a trial judge's later evaluation of the relative importance of the patient's interest in privacy and the evidentiary need for disclosure would eviscerate the effectiveness of the privilege ... [I]f the purpose of the privilege is to be served, the participants in the confidential conversation 'must be able to predict with some degree of certainty whether particular discussions will be protected. An uncertain privilege, or one which purports to be certain but results in widely varying applications by the courts, is little better than no privilege at all.[37]

Stevens's opinion offered a sweeping rejection of the Allen family's arguments and represented an extraordinarily broad endorsement of psychotherapist–patient privilege, one that went beyond even the briefs offered on behalf of Redmond and Beyer. Justices O'Connor, Kennedy, Souter, Thomas, Ginsburg, and Breyer all joined Stevens' opinion.

In dissent, Justice Antonin Scalia, writing for himself and Chief Justice Rehnquist, challenged Stevens' contention that patients would withhold information from psychotherapists in the absence of a federal privilege. To support this claim, Scalia pointed out that "psychotherapy got to be a thriving practice before the psychotherapist privilege" came into existence.[37] Even in the absence of a federal psychotherapist–patient privilege, according to Scalia, patients had continued to seek therapy. Scalia also appeared to doubt the *unique* values of psychotherapy. He acknowledged, "Effective psychotherapy undoubtedly is beneficial to individuals with mental problems, and surely serves some larger social interest in maintaining a mentally stable society," but he did not believe these benefits are "of such importance ... to justify making our federal courts occasional instruments of injustice."[37] In fact, Scalia saw nothing about the psychotherapist–patient relationship that rendered it different from numerous other social interactions not protected by rules of privilege:

When is it, one must wonder, that *the psychotherapist* came to play such an indispensable role in the maintenance of the citizenry's mental health? For most of history, men and women have worked out their difficulties by talking to, *inter alios*, parents, siblings, best friends and bartenders none of whom was awarded a privilege against testifying in court. Ask the average citizen: Would your mental health be more significantly impaired by preventing you from seeing a psychotherapist, or by preventing you from getting advice from your mom? I have little doubt what the answer would be. Yet there is no mother-child privilege.[37]

Scalia emphasized that the victim of this exclusionary rule was likely to be the person "who is prevented from proving a valid claim or (worse still) prevented from establishing a valid defense"[37] as an inevitable result of lost probative evidence.

The opinions in *Jaffee v. Redmond* defied the Court's usual ideological divides. Justice Scalia, whose judicial philosophy often favored the positions of law enforcement, found himself on the side of a working-class African American plaintiff. Justice Stevens, usually a champion of racial minorities and the poor, aligned himself with the interests of a white police officer accused of violating an African American man's civil rights.

Aftermath

After the Supreme Court's decision, the Allen's suit returned to District Court in Chicago for retrial. Without the benefit of Judge Shadur's jury instructions, and without testimony revealing the content of Officer Redmond's counseling sessions, the jury of six white men and one African American woman found that Redmond had acted "unreasonably but not maliciously" in shooting Allen.[38] The split verdict rejected the Allen family's wrongful death claim, including its foundation in racism, but agreed that Redmond had exercised poor judgment and had violated the victim's rights to due process. Both sides tried to spin the final $100,000 judgment to their advantage. Outside the courthouse, Allen's mother told the press: "I go through life with what's on my heart and in my gut. Based on that, I continue to believe in my son. I didn't lose this. So I guess what I'm doing is all right ... Is it enough? No, it's not enough. You can't put a price on somebody's life."[38] Speaking on behalf of Officer Redmond, her attorney, Gregory Rogus, argued that the jurors must have believed his client. "If they had believed she shot an unarmed man," he said, "then they would have found her guilty of wrongful death."[38]

The clear-cut winners in the case were the Allen family's attorneys. Since the jury found in favor of Allen's estate on one count, they were eligible for compensation by the Village of Hoffman Estates for their legal fees. Judge Shadur estimated the reimbursement for the initial trial alone as in excess of $300,000.[39] Allen's teenage sons, Brandon and Ricky Jr., divided the $100,000 jury award. The boys returned to New Orleans, with their mother, Lechia Allen, who subsequently was honored as a local hero for her service as a 911 operator during the aftermath of Hurricane Katrina, and whose profile in the *Times-Picayune* was the subject of a 2006 Pulitzer Prize.[40] Karen Beyer continued her work in nonprofit mental health. She is presently executive director of the Eckert Center for Mental Health in Elgin, Illinois, and a leading advocate for the rights of both psychotherapists and their patients. Her pioneering client, Mary Lu Redmond, left the Hoffman Estates Police Force on disability shortly after the shooting and, at the time of the Supreme Court ruling five years later, she had not returned to law enforcement.[41] Except for her court testimony, she has never spoken publicly about the incident. Her former boss, Hoffman Estates Police Chief Donald Cundiff, believes that it was the civil trial, not the shooting, that led his star officer to leave law enforcement. "It was her own doing. She couldn't participate in police work feeling that way," he told the media. "It was the process, not the shooting."[41]

Impact on Practice

The Supreme Court's decision in *Jaffee v. Redmond* marked the first time since the adoption of the Rules of Federal Procedure that the high court had embraced a privilege protecting an entire profession. Psychotherapists joined attorneys and spouses among the select few parties guaranteed such confidentiality. In contrast, physicians, journalists, and clergy remain without such broad protections at the national level. Yet the impact of *Jaffee* may extend well beyond the federal courts. Noted forensic psychiatrist Paul Appelbaum has observed that "most litigation, ... whether civil or criminal, occurs in state courts, and state rules are likely to be influenced by the Supreme Court's broad decision." Appelbaum sees this as the hidden importance of the ruling:

Privilege statutes are always under assault in the courts, because they undercut a fundamental tenet that every person's testimony is owed to the court. State privilege laws tend to be riddled with exceptions, and courts create new ones regularly. *Jaffee's* ... most significant impact may be to underscore the importance of confidentiality in therapy, thereby dissuading courts and legislatures from degrading protections further.[42]

Another way of looking at the impact of *Jaffee* would be to note that, had the ruling gone against a federal privilege, both prosecutors and litigants seeking to admit such evidence would have exerted efforts to have their cases heard, whenever possible, in federal courts. Inevitably, this forum-shopping would have led to a watering down of protections in state courts, as it would have made little sense to protect such confidentiality in state courts if it were not also protected at the federal level, since the whole purpose of the privilege is to ensure confidence in the confidentiality of psychotherapy, which a federal court exception would have undermined.

In contrast to other court rulings related to mental healthcare, the *Jaffee v. Redmond* decision did not have a large-scale impact on practice, principally because patients and therapists *already* acted as though their confidential exchanges were protected. However, if the Court had struck down the privilege, then the consequences for psychotherapy would likely have been drastic and devastating. "A contrary ruling would have driven people away from obtaining the therapy they often need and would not have produced evidence in most cases that is helpful to trial," argued Steven Shapiro, the American Civil Liberties Union's national legal director. "In the end, we would've sacrificed privacy with little to show on the other side of the equation."[43] Karen Beyer probably summed up the impact of the case best with the observation that "licensed therapists who had been following the case" greeted the ruling with relief.[10]

Jaffee has not entirely resolved questions regarding the scope of psychotherapist–patient privilege. Whether or not the privilege applies in situations of "dangerous patients," for example, is a controversial question on which federal courts remain divided. How to distinguish psychotherapy from non-psychotherapeutic counseling is another issue that stands unresolved.[44] A third unsettled question, and the one most likely to impact clinical practice, is how a therapist should proceed if a court rejects a claim to psychotherapist privilege under Jaffee. Melanie Stone presents the therapist's dilemma as follows:

One option is to proceed as respondents did in *Jaffee*: refuse to comply with court-ordered disclosure, receive an unfavorable jury instruction placing the presumption against the party claiming the privilege, and then appeal the instruction. The other alternative is to comply with the court order by revealing patient confidences, and then appeal the compelled disclosure. This second alternative undermines the purpose of the privilege and nullifies any protection that otherwise would be afforded.[45]

Neither of these options is without considerable drawbacks. However, it is likely only a matter of time before the courts resolve these outstanding concerns.

Few can doubt the importance of *Jaffee v. Redmond* in upholding the very foundations of the mental health professions. In fact, it is difficult to imagine psychotherapy continuing as we know it without such protections. Yet Appelbaum points out the "serendipity" of the facts that led to such a sweeping ruling:

As the first case on psychotherapist–patient privilege to reach the Supreme Court, it offered the most sympathetic facts imaginable for advocates of a privilege. The patient was a police officer, traumatized in the line of duty, and exposed to civil suit by plaintiffs whose testimony the courts appeared to view as of questionable veracity. A ruling for privilege in this case was a ruling to protect the guardians of law and order and to deny a monetary reward to the family of a probable malfeaser. Would the outcome have been different if the patient had been an accused rapist, seeking to prevent the admission at trial of a confession made to his therapist? We shall never know. Proponents of a privilege, however, clearly had the odds on their side this time.[42]

Of course, students of the Supreme Court recognize that justices choose their cases wisely. It is unlikely a coincidence that, of the many lower-court cases raising questions of psychotherapist privilege, the Supreme Court chose *Jaffee* as the vehicle for addressing this controversial issue. Most likely, the justices saw the great damage that would have been done by a continued failure of trial judges to recognize a psychotherapist–patient privilege, and when they saw an opportunity to act, they stepped into the void.

NOTE

* The precise duration of the counseling remains unclear, as the timeline of "nearly two years" provided by Ms. Beyer significantly exceeds the time between the shooting and the subpoena.

REFERENCES

1. Wilkerson I: New home in suburb seems tailored to Sears. *New York Times*, Jul. 19, 1989, A10
2. Myers L, McMahon C: Women cops: from novelty to the norm. *Chicago Tribune*, Jul. 5, 1991, p. 124
3. U.S. Department of Justice, Federal Bureau of Investigation: Uniform Crime Report Statistics 1990. Available at www.ucrdatatool.gov/Search/Crime/Local/RunCrimeJurisbyJuris.cfm
4. Fountain JW: Teens and trouble. Teenagers in the northwest suburbs are facing growing pressures to join gangs. *Chicago Tribune*, Feb. 13, 1991
5. Fountain J, Christian SE. Fight ends with officer killing man. *Chicago Tribune*, Jun. 28, 1991, p. 1
6. *Jaffee v. Redmond*, 51 F.3d 1346 (7th Cir. 1995); the minor edits are Justice Coffey's, not my own. Case text available at: http://jaffee-redmond.org/cases/appellate.htm
7. McMahon C, Ibata D: A case of heroism or racism? *Chicago Tribune*, Jun. 30, 1991, p. 1
8. Fountain JW, Christian SE: Hoffman Estates cop exonerated in fatal shooting. *Chicago Tribune*, Jul. 17, 1991, p. 5
9. Fountain JW, Kirby J: Medal for cop adds fuel to fire in fatal shooting. *Chicago Tribune*, May 28, 1992
10. Beyer K: First person: Jaffee v. Redmond therapist speaks. *Am Psychoanalyst* 34: 3, 2000
11. *NY Rev. Stat. 1829 11*, 406 Part 3, title 3.
12. Missouri Laws, 1835. P. 623, section 17.
13. Goldstein AS, Katz J: Psychiatrist–patient privilege: the GAP proposal and the Connecticut statute. *Am J Psychiatry* 118: 735, 1962
14. Louisell DW: Psychologist in today's legal world. *Minnesota Law Rev* 41: 733–5, 1956–57
15. *Binder v. Ruvell*, Circuit Court of Cook County, No. 52C2535 (1952); reprinted in the *JAMA* 150: 1241, 1952
16. Slovenko R, Usdin G: The psychiatrist and privileged communication. *Arch Gen Psychiatry* 4(5):431–4, 1961
17. Sidel VW: Confidential information and the physician. *New Engl J Med* 264: 1133–7, 1961
18. Hoover JE: Let's keep America healthy. *JAMA* 144: 1094–5, 1950
19. Appel JM: The dangers of the underprivileged ethicist. *New Mexico L Rev* 42: 1, 2012
20. House Report No. 93–650 (House Committee on the Judiciary, 1974) The nine privileges to be applied in federal courts were those that applied to relationships between lawyer and client, psychotherapist and patient, husband and wife, and penitent and clergyman, as well as those covering required reports, political vote, trade secrets, secrets of state, and the identity of an informer
21. Miller RF: Creating evidentiary privileges: An argument for the judicial approach. *Conn L Rev* 31: 772–5, 1999 (detailing the controversy surrounding the committee's proposal)

22. Federal Rules of Evidence, Rule 501 (1975)
23. See Cerveny KL, Kent MJ: Evidence law: The psychotherapist–patient privilege in federal courts. *Notre Dame L Rev* 59: 791, 1984
24. *Doe v. Diamond*, 964 F.2d 1325 (1992)
25. *In re Zuniga*, 714 F.2d 632 (1983)
26. *United States v. Burtrum*, 17 F.3d 1299 (1994)
27. *In re Grand Jury Proceedings*, 867 F.2d 562 (1989)
28. *United States v. Corona*, 849 F.2d 562 (1988)
29. *United States v. Meagher*, 531 F.2d 752 (1976)
30. *Jaffee v. Redmond*, 51 F.3d 1346 (7th Cir. 1995) The case text is available here: http://jaffee-redmond.org/cases/appellate.htm
31. Christian SE: Excessive force trial puts focus on knife. *Chicago Tribune*, Dec. 14, 1993, p. 1
32. Wiltz T: Victim was in danger, accused cop testifies. *Chicago Tribune*, Dec. 16, 1993
33. Greenhouse L: Justices to decide case on establishing therapist-client privilege. *New York Times*, Oct. 17, 1995, p. A23
34. Taranto, R: Brief of the American Psychiatric Association and the American Academy of Psychiatry and the Law as Amici Curiae in Support of the Respondents. Jaffee v. Redmond, 518 U.S. 1, No. 95–266, 1996
35. Days, DS: Brief for the United States as Amicus Curiae Supporting Respondent. Jaffee v. Redmond, 518 U.S. 1, No. 95–266, 1996
36. Oral Argument in Jaffee v. Redmond Before the United States Supreme Court, 518 U.S. 1, Feb. 26, 1996
37. *Jaffee v. Redmond*, 518 U.S. 1 (1996) Quote within Stevens quote is from *Upjohn Co. v. United States*, 449 U.S. 383, 389 (1981)
38. Tatum, C: Family awarded $100,000 in wrongful death trial. *Daily Herald (Illinois)*, Dec. 7, 1996, p. 4
39. O'Connor M, Searcey D: Victim's sons get $100,000: jury clears ex-Hoffman cop but oks damages. *Chicago Tribune*, Dec. 7, 1996
40. Thevenot B: 'Help me, please don't let me die': 911 operators confront grim task, ghastly calls. *Times-Picayune*, Sep. 19, 2005
41. Borchmann P: Ex-Hoffman Estates cop still lives with 1991 killing. *Chicago Tribune*, Mar. 27, 1996, p. 1
42. Appelbaum PS: Jaffee v. Redmond: Psychotherapist–patient privilege in the federal courts. *Psychiatric Services* 47 (1033–34) 1996
43. Greenburg, JC: High court: Counseling is confidential. *Chicago Tribune*, Jun. 14, 1996
44. Mosher, PW: Psychotherapist-patient privilege: The history and significance of the United States Supreme Court's Decision in the case of Jaffee v. Redmond. In CM Koggel, A. Furlong, C. Levin (Eds.), *Confidential Relationships: Psychoanalytic, Ethical, and Legal Context* (pp. 177 ff). Amsterdam: Brill Rodopi, 2003
45. Stone, MS: The Supreme Court adopts a federal psychotherapist–patient privilege. *Mercer Law Rev* 48: 1283, 1997

11   Protecting Others from Dangerous Patients

Tarasoff v. Regents of the University of California (1976)

Phillip J. Resnick

When a clinician learns that her patient is likely to seriously harm another person, what is she required to do? When does a clinician's legal duty to preserve confidentiality give way to her obligation to protect human life? Does a clinician's duty to third parties vary from one state to another?

In October 1968, 19-year-old Tatiana ("Tanya") Tarasoff began her freshman year at college. Although she was shy around boys, she convinced her father to let her go to Friday-night folk dance classes at the International House at University of California, Berkeley, so she could practice her foreign language skills.

Prosenjit Poddar was born in the village of Balurghat, 200 miles north of Calcutta, India. A member of the Harijan or "untouchable" caste, he was raised in a home with no electricity.[1] Meals were cooked over a fire fueled by cow dung patties. Prosenjit nonetheless managed to escape his humble origins and was accepted to the Indian Institute of Technology (IIT) in Kharagpur, the best engineering college in India, when he scored in the upper one-tenth of one percentile of applicants. He was the first "untouchable" admitted to the IIT. After studying naval architecture and graduating second in his class, he received a scholarship to attend the University of California, Berkeley, to obtain a master's degree in naval architecture. He came to Berkeley in September 1968 at the age of 23 and lived in the International House. Prosenjit had never shared a kiss, let alone a romance with a girl, and he was not at all familiar with American mores.

When Tatiana met Prosenjit at a Friday-night folk dance class in October 1968, she stepped on his foot. He was quite taken by her wide Slavic cheekbones, dark hair, and green eyes. Prosenjit's lack of confidence made Tatiana feel more self-assured.[2] She sought him out in his dorm room on several occasions.

Prosenjit took Tatiana to a movie. He viewed her as encouraging his affections because she had permitted his forearm to rest against hers. Prosenjit misread her affection for him and decided to purchase a sari to give her as a betrothal gift.

129

Tatiana later admitted to Prosenjit that she had spent the night with another man, but that he had never called her again. Prosenjit forgave her and gave her the sari, which she accepted so as to not hurt his feelings. On New Year's Eve, she kissed him. When Prosenjit proposed marriage, Tatiana said that she did not know him well enough and that she just wanted to remain friends.

Tatiana stood Prosenjit up several times. Feeling humiliated, he wanted to hurt her in return. He began to think Tatiana was laughing at him behind his back. Tatiana recognized that Prosenjit was vulnerable, but could not accept his neediness. After she rejected him, she missed his attentions and his worship of her. She called him and initiated further visits. Prosenjit believed that Tatiana had entered into a "sacred commitment" with him and then discarded him.[2] He became completely preoccupied with her, growing depressed, paranoid, and no longer attending classes. He neglected his appearance as well as his studies. He told Tatiana that he wanted to build a radio-controlled bomb and place it in her purse so he could blow her up. She did not take his initial threats seriously. Prosenjit's best friend, who was another Indian student, urged him to seek psychiatric treatment. He initially resisted seeing a psychiatrist, but on June 5, 1969, his best friend shepherded him to the Cowell Memorial Hospital at Berkeley. His friend stayed with him through his first interview with the psychiatrist, Dr. Stuart Gold.

Prosenjit's friend conveyed to Dr. Gold that Prosenjit had been dating a girl who was troubling him. When Prosenjit was seen briefly alone, he expressed concern that his best friend was trying to steal his girlfriend from him. He believed that other students at the International House were "in cahoots" against him and were laughing at him. Dr. Gold diagnosed Prosenjit with paranoid schizophrenia, prescribed the antipsychotic medications Thorazine and Compazine, and referred him to a psychologist, Dr. Larry Moore, for psychotherapy. Dr. Moore concluded that Prosenjit believed himself to be gravely injured by his "girlfriend." Feeling betrayed, he had a compulsion to get even with Tatiana.

In the summer of 1969, Tatiana accepted an invitation to spend two or three months with her aunt in São Paulo, Brazil. Prosenjit became furious that Tatiana had not written to him from Brazil after he wrote to her several times. Dr. Moore instructed Prosenjit to detach himself from Tatiana, which Prosenjit agreed would be a good plan. Dr. Moore also directed Prosenjit to stop taking the antipsychotic medication. When Prosenjit mentioned a plan to move in with Tatiana's 17-year-old brother, Alex, Dr. Moore threatened to stop seeing him if he did. Prosenjit delayed moving in with Alex, but he eventually did so without telling Dr. Moore.

At Prosenjit's sixth psychotherapy session, he told Dr. Moore he was feeling much better and that he was done with his girlfriend. Dr. Moore then received a visit from the friend who had accompanied Prosenjit on his first visit, who told him that Prosenjit had moved in with Alex Tarasoff and had muttered something about going to San Francisco to buy a gun to kill Tatiana. Dr. Moore confronted Prosenjit at their seventh session the next day. When Prosenjit would not say whether he purchased a gun, Dr. Moore said that he was going to go to the police and have him detained in a psychiatric ward. Prosenjit walked out, saying, "You are against me, too."[2]

Dr. Moore was informed by the Berkeley campus police that he needed to write a letter before they would pick up Prosenjit and take him to the hospital. He prepared the letter and personally took it to the police chief, who was preoccupied with the anti-Vietnam War riots on campus at the time. Three campus police officers went out and spoke with Prosenjit, who remained polite and assured them that he would not have anything more to do with Tatiana. Compared to the hippies protesting the Vietnam War, Prosenjit had a clean-cut appearance.[2] The police told Dr. Moore that they did not find sufficient reason to take him to the hospital.

Upon his return from a vacation, Dr. Harvey Powelson, chief of the Department of Psychiatry, asked the police to return Dr. Moore's letter and directed that all copies of the letter and Dr. Moore's clinical notes be destroyed. Dr. Paulson, who was psychoanalytically trained and placed great importance on confidentiality, ordered that no further action be taken to hospitalize Prosenjit. Dr. Paulson was specifically named in the subsequent lawsuit.

Tatiana flew back from Brazil on September 10, 1969. During the last week of her vacation she had met a man, had spent a weekend with him, and had become pregnant. Upon her return to San Francisco, she attended a housewarming party at the apartment of her brother Alex and Prosenjit. Within earshot of Prosenjit, Tatiana commented that she met a "guy" in Brazil whom she thought she was in love with.

Prosenjit told Tatiana that he wanted to talk to her to find out once and for all how she felt about him. She replied that she was not interested. He persisted in contacting her. Tatiana told him that if he continued to bother her, she planned to burn the sari that he had given her and throw the ashes in his face. Prosenjit responded by sobbing.[2] He then began to stalk her. Finding her home alone on October 27, 1969, Prosenjit insisted that she speak with him. When she refused, he forced his way into her home. Tatiana screamed. Prosenjit pulled out a pellet gun he had recently purchased and shot her repeatedly until the gun was empty. He then used the 13-inch butcher knife he brought with him "to protect himself" and stabbed her eight times. He called the police and said that he had just stabbed his girlfriend. When the police arrived, he said, "Handcuff me. I killed her."

Legal Course

Prosenjit was examined within 24 hours of the stabbing by a police department psychiatrist who agreed with the diagnosis of paranoid schizophrenia.[3] He pled not guilty by reason of insanity. At his criminal trial, Dr. Moore and others testified that he was legally insane. Dr. Moore testified regarding the details of his threats against Tatiana and his own unsuccessful attempt to secure an emergency commitment.[1]

On August 26, 1970, Prosenjit was found guilty of second-degree murder and was sentenced to five years in prison. The jury had rejected his insanity defense. After four years, his verdict was overturned by an appellate court because the jury instructions about specific intent had been incorrect. He accepted an offer by the prosecutor not to proceed with a second trial if he agreed to deportation back to India. After he returned home, his father arranged a marriage for him. Two years later he received a scholarship to resume his naval architecture studies at a prestigious institute in Hanover, Germany. Prosenjit's friend later reported that he was "leading a normal life with his wife (an attorney) and daughter."[2,4]

When Tatiana's parents learned that Prosenjit had told his treating psychologist that he was going to kill Tatiana, they brought suit against the Regents of the University of California, Dr. Moore, Dr. Paulson, and the Berkeley campus police. The trial judge dismissed the suit because he believed that Dr. Moore had no duty to a third party (Tatiana), only to his patient. A California appeals court upheld the trial court decision. However, in 1974 the Supreme Court of California held that Dr. Moore and the campus police had a legal duty to warn Tatiana of the threat to her life.[5] Because of the great consternation among mental health professionals and police officers, the California Supreme Court took the unusual step of agreeing to rehear the case in 1976. Their second ruling[6] is generally known as the case that defined mental health clinicians' duty to warn and protect third parties. After the California Supreme Court held that clinicians had a duty to protect threatened victims, the *Tarasoff* case was settled out of court for an undisclosed sum of money.

Legal Holding

In the 1976 *Tarasoff v. Regents* case (Tarasoff II), the California Supreme Court majority held that "when a therapist determines, or according to the standard of his profession should determine, that his patient presents a serious danger of violence to another, he incurs an obligation to use reasonable care to protect the intended victim from danger. It may call for him to warn the intended victim or others likely to apprise the victim of the danger, to notify the police, or to take whatever other steps are reasonable."[6]

Mental health professionals clearly have duties to their patients. For example, failure to civilly commit a dangerous patient who then harms himself may result in a malpractice case against the treatment provider. However, *Tarasoff* raises the question of whether a third-party victim can bring a malpractice case against a physician. The answer to this question is usually no, resting in the common-law principle that people do not generally have duties to "third parties" unless they have a special relationship with them. Thus, if a person is at a swimming pool and sees a stranger drowning, and a life preserver is readily available, that person generally has no legal duty to assist the drowning person. However, a few states have created a statutory duty to rescue another person.

A therapist, who clearly has a special relationship with his patient, traditionally does not have a duty towards others who might be harmed by that patient's conduct. There are, however, exceptions. Doctors have been held liable to persons infected by one of their patients for negligently failing to diagnose a contagious disease or failing to warn members of the patient's family about the risk of infection. A psychiatric hospital may be liable if the staff negligently permits the escape or premature release of a dangerous patient who kills someone, and mental health professionals have a duty to report suspected child abuse.

Legal Arguments

The defendants in the *Tarasoff* case contended that imposing a duty to exercise reasonable care to protect third persons was unworkable because therapists could not accurately predict whether a patient would become violent. This argument was supported by the *amicus curiae* briefs of the American Psychiatric Association and several other professional organizations, which quoted research showing that therapists consistently overpredict violence and were more often wrong than right.

The California Supreme Court majority responded by stating they did not require a therapist to render a perfect performance. They stated that a therapist "need only exercise that reasonable degree of skill, knowledge and care ordinarily possessed and exercised by members of his profession under similar circumstances," adding that "proof aided by hindsight" was insufficient to establish negligence. Furthermore, in this particular case, Dr. Moore had accurately predicted Prosenjit Poddar's violence.

The court went on to argue that resolving the tension between the conflicting interests of a patient and potential victim was an issue of social policy, rather than a matter of professional expertise. The justices concluded that "professional inaccuracy in predicting violence cannot negate the therapist's duty to protect the threatened victim." The majority added that the risk of unnecessary warnings was a reasonable price to pay for the lives of possible victims who might be saved.

The court majority also considered allegations by the defendants that free and open communication was essential to psychotherapy and that a therapist's duty to breach confidentiality would make patients reluctant to make full disclosures. They viewed these allegations as speculative, holding that the importance of the public interest in safety from violent assault outweighed concerns about protecting patients' privacy. Furthermore, they noted that the medical ethics of the American Psychiatric Association (APA) had stated that "a physician may not reveal a confidence unless he is required to do so by law or unless it becomes necessary in order to protect the welfare of the individual or the community." Thus, a duty to protect a threatened victim established by the courts would not require doctors to breach any medical ethics.

The dissenting judges argued that therapists would be faced with a dilemma by the majority opinion, having either to ignore the majority's duty to warn, thereby incurring potential civil liability, or to violate the California statute stating they had a duty not to disclose private information. The dissent accepted the APA's view that therapists could not accurately predict dangerousness, also expressing concern that the majority decision would cripple the effectiveness of psychiatry by deterring people from seeking psychotherapy, inhibiting psychotherapy patients from making revelations necessary to effective treatment, and forcing psychiatrists to violate their patients' trust by breaching confidentiality. They predicted that there would be a net increase in violence because many patients would no longer trust psychiatrists and would therefore not enter into psychiatric treatment.

Extensions of the Tarasoff Duty

Several state supreme courts extended the concept of the *Tarasoff* duty not just to identifiable victims, but to all persons who might be in a class who are endangered. For example, *Lipari v. Sears Roebuck*[7] extended the *Tarasoff* duty to unidentified third parties who were foreseeably endangered. The duty was even extended to property in the case of *Peck v. Counseling Service of Addison County*[8] by the Vermont Supreme Court. In *Peck*, the duty was mandated in the case of a patient's threat to burn down his father's barn. The *Tarasoff* duty was also extended to unintentional harm caused by psychiatric patients in some states. Two cases (*Petersen v. Washington*[9] and *Naidu v. Laird*[10]) ruled that psychiatrists can be liable for discharging psychiatric inpatients who are at a foreseeable risk of driving recklessly.

Two states rejected a *Tarasoff* duty. A minority of states have still taken no position on the *Tarasoff* issue. The duty of mental health professionals to protect third parties today is defined in individual states by case law (appellate court decisions) and state statutes (legislative enactments).

Impact of the *Tarasoff* Case on Practice

Paul Appelbaum has observed that "no court decision in the last generation has succeeded in so raising the anxieties of mental health professionals" as the *Tarasoff* decision.[11] Thirty years after the 1976 *Tarasoff* decision, Buckner and Firestone argued that concerns about the potential loss of confidentiality had not had the adverse impact on psychiatric practice that was predicted by the *amicus curiae* briefs and Justice Clark's strong dissent in the *Tarasoff* case.[1] *Tarasoff* did stimulate greater awareness of the violent patient's potential for violence, which encouraged closer scrutiny and better documentation of the therapist's examination of this issue.

Rosenhan (1993) found in a survey of California psychotherapists that nearly all respondents indicated that they would have warned potential victims of violence because of their ethical obligations, even if the *Tarasoff* case did not require them to do so.[12] This suggests that the case merely reinforced what therapists were already doing, based on ethical considerations, rather than creating an onerous new duty. The *Tarasoff* case has been cited throughout English-speaking countries to determine ethical codes of conduct for mental health professionals.

Binder and McNeil[13] found that psychiatry residents were interpreting California law as encouraging warnings to intended victims even when a dangerous patient was hospitalized. Their survey also found that warnings generally were appreciated by the potential victims and had little effect on the doctors' therapeutic relationship with patients. A survey of police sergeants showed that only 3% were specifically familiar with *Tarasoff* case rulings, and less than 50% indicated that they would respond to a warning by monitoring the potential victim.[14]

Soulier et al. (2010) analyzed 70 appellate *Tarasoff* cases from 1985 through 2006.[15] They determined that defendants are rarely found to be negligent on grounds of failing to warn or protect. In the early days after *Tarasoff*, courts found negligence in cases with fact patterns similar to those that are now being decided for defendants. This change is due to *Tarasoff*-limiting statutes and increased sympathy toward the clinician confronted with threats of violence. In states with *Tarasoff*-limiting statutes, courts have consistently found that there was no duty when the patient had not communicated a threat to the therapist. In states with and without *Tarasoff*-limiting statutes, courts have almost always found that defendants owed no duty to the public at large.

Tarasoff Duties Today

The variety of duty-to-warn laws across the nation is virtually unprecedented for a widespread legal doctrine.[16] In response to the *Tarasoff* decision and its broad extensions, 37 states have passed *Tarasoff*-limiting statutes[15] with the goal of reducing the potential liability of mental health professionals. These statutes fall into three primary categories:

1. *Statutes that seem to explicitly establish a duty*: These statutes contain terminology that appears to create a definite duty such as, "A mental health professional has a duty..."
2. *Statutes that prohibit liability except under specified circumstances*: These statutes are phrased in a conditional manner, such as, "There can be no cause of action and no liability ... unless ..." The majority of statutes fall within this category.
3. *Statutes that seem to be permissive*: The statutory language appears to allow disclosure, but does not require it. For example, "The psychiatrist may disclose ..."

Herbert and Young observed that if statutes and case law are combined, about half the states impose a mandatory duty to warn and another 10 jurisdictions accord psychotherapists permission to warn.[16] About 13 states have no definitive law on the issue.

1. *The duty jurisdictions*: The general formulation is that a mental health professional is obligated to notify either the potential victim or the police when a patient makes an explicit threat of serious physical harm against a readily identifiable third party, or in some states is obligated to hospitalize the patient. Other jurisdictions incorporate the therapist's judgment into the duty by using such phrases as, "The patient has the apparent intent and ability to carry out such a threat." Four states require a psychotherapist not only to warn of explicit threats by a patient but also to discern by the patient's actions or the circumstances any threat of violence and to warn of this as well.

2. *The permissive jurisdictions:* These jurisdictions leave it to the discretion of the therapist whether to warn a third party of the patient's threat of violence.

Statutes are malleable in the hands of the courts called upon to interpret them.[16] Kachigian and Felthous found in their analysis of cases after states passed *Tarasoff*-limiting statutes that in only a small number of cases did courts interpret the state statutes to circumscribe the duties owed to third parties.[17] Most left the duty-to-protect ill-defined.

Dramatic cases sometimes create bad law. In the Aurora, Colorado, *Batman* movie shooting of 2012, a psychiatrist knew of a patient's threats to kill, but the patient had expressed no specific target or plan. State legislatures are at risk of reacting hastily to a mass shooting by passing legislation that does not fairly balance patients' rights to confidentiality with the safety of the public. Less than one year after the Newtown school shooting, the New York legislature passed a law requiring therapists to notify law enforcement when they determined that a patient was a serious danger of harming himself or another person.

Conclusion

Of the 23 states with protective disclosure statutes, 18 have had cases that address potential *Tarasoff* situations.[17] Unfortunately, court approaches after statutory enactment are lacking in uniformity.[18] Although clinicians would prefer consistency and concrete rules throughout the country, they are now confronted with a patchwork of rules that vary by jurisdiction. Clinicians should determine their legal duty to protect potential victims by learning their specific legal duty in their own state. However, even in the absence of a legal duty, clinicians may have an ethical and moral duty to take reasonable steps to protect human life.

REFERENCES

1. Buckner F, Firestone M: Where the peril begins: 25 years after *Tarasoff*. *J Legal Med.* 21(2): 187–222, 2000
2. Blum D: *Bad Karma: A True Story of Obsession and Murder.* New York: Atheneum, 1986
3. *People v. Poddar*, 518 P.2d 342 (Cal. 1974)
4. Merton V: Confidentiality and the 'dangerous' patient: Implications of *Tarasoff* for psychiatrists and lawyers. *Emory L J.* 31: 263 (1982)
5. *Tarasoff v. The Regents of the University of California*, 529 P.2d 533 (Cal. 1974)
6. *Tarasoff v. The Regents of the University of California*, 17 Cal. 3d 425, 551 P.2d 334, 131 Cal. Rptr. 14 (1976)
7. *Lipari v. Sears*, 497 F. Supp. 185 (D.Neb. 1980)

8. *Peck v. Counseling Service of Addison County*, 146 Vt. 61, 499 A.2d 422 (1985)
9. *Petersen v. Washington*, 671 P.2d 230 (Wash. 1983)
10. *Naidu v. Laird*, 539 A.2d 1064 (Del. 1988)
11. Appelbaum P, Zonana H, Bonnie R, Roth L: Statutory approaches to limiting psychiatrists' liability for their patients' violent acts. *Am J Psychiatry.* 146(7): 821–8, 1989
12. Rosenhan D, Teitelbaum TW, Teitelbaum KW, et al.: Warning third parties: The ripple effects of Tarasoff. 24 *PAC L J.* 1165 (1993)
13. Binder R, McNeil D: Application of the Tarasoff ruling and its effect on the victim and the therapeutic relationship. *Psychiatr Serv.* 47(11): 1212–5 (1996)
14. Huber MG, Balon R, Labbate, LA, et al.: A survey of police officers' experience with Tarasoff warnings in two states. *Psychiatr Serv.* 51: 807–9, 2000
15. Soulier MF, Maislen A, Beck JC: Status of the psychiatric duty to protect, circa 2006. *J Am Acad Psychiatry Law.* 38: 457–73, 2010
16. Herbert PB, Young KA: Tarasoff at twenty-five. *J Am Acad Psychiatry Law.* 30: 275–81, 2002
17. Kachigian C, Felthous AR: Court responses to 'Tarasoff' statutes. *J Am Acad Psychiatry Law.* 32: 263–73, 2004
18. Felthous AR, Kachigian C: The duty to protect. In R Rosner, CL Scott (Eds.), *Principles and Practice of Forensic Psychiatry* (3rd ed.), p. 813. New York: CRC Press, 2017.

12   The Insanity Defense
United States v. Hinckley (1982)

Alan W. Newman

Under what conditions do we not punish a mentally ill person for committing a crime?

On March 30, 1982, John Hinckley shot and seriously wounded President Ronald Reagan and three others outside of the Hilton Hotel in Washington, D.C.[1] As Hinckley's act occurred before numerous witnesses and he was immediately apprehended at the scene, there was no question that he committed the act. Consequently, his trial focused exclusively on his mental state at the time of the act. His highly publicized trial ended with the unexpected verdict of "not guilty by reason of insanity," an outcome that was criticized by both the public and media, leading to an intense debate on the future of the insanity defense.[2]

Unlike most of the cases discussed in this book, *The United States v. John W. Hinckley* was a trial level case whose verdict was unaffected by the appellate process. Subsequent legislative reforms led to significant changes in laws affecting criminal responsibility in multiple states as well as in federal court. The case also led to widespread criticism of the field of psychiatry and is considered a watershed event in the development of the modern practice of forensic psychiatry, the development of improved training in forensic psychiatry, and the evolution of the ethical practices that now affect forensic practice.[3]

John W. Hinckley, Jr., was born the youngest of three children in 1955 to a successful and affluent family.[4] John's father was the founder of Vanderbilt Energy Corporation, a business ultimately run by John's older brother. Although at an early age John appeared to be outgoing, serving as class president in 7th and 9th grades and managing his school's football team in junior high, by high school he was noted to be increasingly reclusive, have few friends, and spend much of his time listening to and writing music.[5] After John graduated from high school in 1973, the Hinckley family moved from Texas to Colorado. John enrolled at Texas Tech University in Lubbock and completed his first year. After intermittent enrollment over the next year, he moved to Hollywood in April

1976, where he hoped to sell his music. After quickly depleting his funds, he requested money from his family, embellishing his letters with false stories of contacts with the recording industry as well as describing a girl-friend who in fact did not exist. It was during his time in Hollywood that became familiar with the movie *Taxi Driver*, which he saw fifteen times during its theatrical run.[6]

Hinckley's preoccupation with *Taxi Driver* would prove to be a key in understanding Hinckley's future actions. The movie had its roots in the diaries of Charles Bremer, the man who shot and paralyzed Presidential candidate George Wallace in 1972.[7] *Taxi Driver* starred actor Robert DeNiro as Travis Bickle, a Vietnam veteran coping with severe insomnia by becoming a late-night cab driver in New York City.[8] The socially inept Bickle develops a romantic interest in Daisy, a young presidential campaign staffer. He also develops a paternal interest in Iris, a 12-year-old runaway and prostitute, played by actress Jodie Foster. After being rejected by Daisy, Bickle becomes increasingly paranoid and isolated, seeing himself as a person with a mission to deal with the "scumbags" he encounters. After purchasing a cache of weapons, he goes to a pres-idential campaign rally with the apparent intent to assassinate the can-didate. Thwarted by an observant Secret Service agent, Bickle flees the scene to rescue prostitute Iris. In a violent rampage, Bickle murders Iris' pimp and others while being gravely wounded himself. In an ironic twist ending, Bickle not only survives but is regarded as a hero for his violent rampage, returning to an uncertain future driving his cab.

The character of Travis Bickle resonated very strongly with Hinckley, and Hinckley modulated many of his behaviors to mimic Bickle, including his purchase of guns, the invention of a girlfriend to manipu-late his family, and the fantasy of making a dramatic impact on society. And while Bickle's interest in the 12-year-old prostitute Iris was paternal in nature, Hinckley developed a romantic preoccupation with the now older teen actress who played her.

Hinckley became disaffected with Hollywood and returned to Colorado in late 1976, only to return briefly to California in early 1977 before returning to Texas Tech. Although he was intermittently enrolled at Texas Tech from 1973 through mid-1978, his inconsistent coursework was insufficient to obtain a degree. During that period, he was noted by his family to be nervous, and he presented to the Texas Tech clinic with a wide variety of physical complaints. During that period, he became increasingly interested in racist white supremacist ideology.

By late 1979, he had purchased his first handgun and began pub-lishing a racist newsletter, falsely claiming to be the director of an orga-nization with members living in many states. His somatic preoccupations and anxiety increased, as did his purchase of additional weapons. In May 1980, Hinckley learned from a magazine that Jodie Foster would be attending Yale University in New Haven, Connecticut. Hinckley himself had returned to Texas Tech for a summer session. During this period, Hinckley began to experience dizziness and fatigue, as well as hearing problems attributed to his time on a firing range. He was prescribed an antidepressant, and later the sedative Valium. By September, he had convinced his parents to provide him the financial means to pay for a writing course at Yale, where Jodie Foster had begun her freshman year. Hinckley moved to New Haven without enrolling in the class. His focus instead appeared to be to meet Jodie Foster. He left letters and poems in her mailbox and succeeded in having two phone conversations with her. Unsurprisingly, she was not interested and asked him not to call her. After being rebuffed by Foster, he returned to Denver, then flew to Lubbock, where he bought two .22-caliber handguns. He then flew to Washington, D.C., where he began to stalk President Jimmy Carter as he was campaigning for reelection.

Over a three-day period in early October 1980, Hinckley followed Carter from Washington, D.C., to Columbus, Ohio, and then to Dayton before flying back to New Haven to leave more notes for Foster. Next, he flew to Lincoln, Nebraska, in an unsuccessful attempt to meet the director of the American Nazi Party, and then to Nashville, Tennessee, where Carter was campaigning. Hinckley was arrested at the Nashville Airport on October 9, 1980 after he was discovered to have a handgun in his suitcase.[9] Despite his proximity to the President, Hinckley was released from custody with the primary consequences of paying a $62.50 fine and forfeiting his gun.

Following his arrest, he spent the next few weeks resuming his drifting via airline, traveling first to New Haven for two days before returning to Texas to buy two more handguns, after which he briefly returned to New Haven before briefly returning to Washington, D.C. to continue to stalk President Carter. On October 20th, he left Washington, D.C., to return to his parents' house near Denver, where he subsequently overdosed on his medications. His parents referred John to psychiatrist Dr. John Hopper, who saw John for twelve sessions between October 1980 and February 1981.[5] Dr. Hopper's impression was that John's primary problem was immaturity rather than mental illness and he recommended to John's parents that they kick him out of their house and end his financial support.

On November 4, 1980, Ronald Reagan was elected president in an overwhelming victory over Carter.[10] Hinckley returned to Washington, D.C., on November 20th. Several weeks later, on December 8th, former

Beatles singer John Lennon was shot to death outside of his New York City apartment building by Mark David Chapman.[11] A fan of the Beatles, Hinckley traveled from Washington, D.C., to New York attend a vigil for Lennon but left New York shortly thereafter for nearby New Haven to leave more poems and notes for Jodie Foster, before returning to his parents' home in Colorado for Christmas.

In early February 1981, John returned to the East Coast, where he again visited New Haven, New York City, and Washington, D.C. During these travels, he read books about assassinations and contemplated committing suicide at the spot where Lennon was murdered. He returned to Denver briefly in late February, but 11 days later returned to New York and New Haven, leaving a note to Jodie Foster saying, "Jodie, after tonight John Lennon and I will have a lot in common."[12] Not acting on the apparent suicide threat, and out of money, John begged his parents to let him return home. In his final note to Foster, he wrote, "JODIE, GOODBYE! I LOVE you SIX TRILLION TIMES. DON'T YOU MAYBE LIKE ME JUST A LITTLE BIT? (You MUST ADMIT I AM DIFFERENT) IT would make all of this worthwhile."[9]

On the advice of Dr. Hopper, John's parents allowed him to fly home back to Colorado but did not allow him to stay in the family home.[12] Instead, he spent the next few weeks isolated in motels, spending his time reading books and watching television. In late March, he flew to Hollywood to try to sell some of his songs, but left after only one day, taking a bus that arrived in Washington, D.C., on March 29.

Facts of the Case

On the morning of March 30, 1981, John Hinckley read in a local news-paper that President Reagan would be giving a speech that morning at the Washington Hilton Hotel and immediately decided to shoot Reagan.[9] Hinckley wrote a letter to Jodie Foster explaining his reasons for the assassination, stating his belief that he could be killed in the attempt and that he "would abandon this idea of getting Reagan in a second if I could only win your heart and live out the rest of my life with you." He ended the letter stating that by "sacrificing my freedom and possibly my life, I hope to change your mind about me" and that he hoped to gain her "respect and love."[13]

After arriving at the Hilton by taxi, Hinckley stood with a crowd of reporters when Reagan arrived at 1:45 p.m. Hinckley waved at the president, but did not act at that moment, nor did he try to go into the hotel where Reagan was giving a speech. After his speech, Reagan, Secret Service agents and various aides exited a side door to an awaiting limousine. Less than 30 feet away, Hinckley removed a concealed handgun and quickly fired six bullets.[9]

Four of the six bullets fired struck human targets. Press Secretary James Brady, Washington, D.C., policeman Thomas Delahanty; and Secret Service agent Timothy McCarthy were struck before the final shot struck President Reagan after ricocheting off the presidential limousine. Hinckley was immediately detained, disarmed, and arrested.

Due to rapid medical treatment, Reagan's life-threatening chest wound was successfully treated and he fully recovered. Agent McCarthy recovered from his abdominal injury. Officer Delahanty survived his disabling neck injury. Secretary Brady's brain injury proved to be permanently disabling.

Legal Course

As there were multiple eyewitnesses to the crime and Hinckley was immediately apprehended with the attempted murder weapon, it was clear that his likely defense would focus on his mental state at the time of the crime. The only logical defense available involved the insanity defense, a rarely successful legal strategy.[14] Hinckley was charged with thirteen offenses, a mixture of violations of both federal and "state" (i.e., District of Columbia) laws. Had the offense occurred in a state, rather than in the District of Columbia, the state charges would have been tried in the state court system and the federal charges in federal court. A unique quality of District of Columbia law allowed for someone with both state and federal charges to be tried simultaneously in Federal District Court.[15]

The federal standard for criminal responsibility in the District of Columbia was established in the 1972 case *United States v. Brawner*. This case replaced what had been the most lenient insanity standard in the country with a much stricter standard, typically referred to as the Model Penal Code standard. This standard, a variation of the one developed by the American Law Institute (commonly referred to in D.C. as the Brawner Rule), stated: "A person is not responsible for criminal conduct if at the time of such conduct as a result of mental disease or defect he lacks substantial capacity to appreciate the wrongfulness of his conduct or to conform his conduct to the requirements of the law."[16]

Although more restrictive than the previous standard, the Brawner Rule allowed for a consideration of both the defendant's cognitive status (i.e., "knowledge of criminality") and volitional abilities (i.e., "capacity to conform conduct to the requirements of the law"). By the time of the 1972 *Brawner* decision, the majority of states used some form of an insanity defense that allowed for both cognitive and volitional considerations; a minority of states utilized a standard that only allowed for an insanity verdict if the mental disease or defect prevented the defendant from knowing that his or her illegal act was wrong. This cognitive-only standard was also known as the "right–wrong" test and was based on rules established after the 1843 case of Daniel M'Naghten, a Scot who killed the secretary of the British Prime Minister.[17]

Under the Brawner Rule, Hinckley's defense faced two challenges: (1) they would need to prove that at the time of his actions on March 30, 1981, Hinckley experienced a psychiatric illness that would meet the threshold of a "mental disease or defect" and (2) if he had a "mental disease or defect," this condition prevented him from "appreciating the wrongfulness" of his conduct or "conforming his conduct to the requirements of the law."[16] Although the phrase "appreciating the wrongfulness" was not defined in *Brawner*, Hinckley's lawyers argued that the use of this phrase broadened the volitional arm by requiring not only "cognitive awareness" but also an "emotional understanding" of one's actions.[18]

The Hinckley family's wealth allowed John access to a well-funded defense team. His lead attorney, Vincent Fuller, was well-known for his defense of Teamster boss Jimmy Hoffa and mobster Frank Costello.[19] Fuller decided that much of the focus of the defense strategy would be on John's preoccupations with Jodie Foster, which continued well after the crime. Hinckley was not opposed to this strategy. As a condition of his cooperation, Hinckley wanted Jodie Foster to testify at his trial. It was decided that she would not have to testify in person during the trial, but she did testify on videotape before the judge, lawyers, and Hinckley himself.[4]

Hinckley's trial began approximately a year after the shooting. The case opened with the prosecution presenting the factual aspects of the case unrelated to mental state: that he had performed the shooting with premeditation.[1] After the prosecution rested their case, the defense made no attempt to contest the factual aspects of the case, but focused exclusively on Hinckley's life history and psychiatric symptoms. The defense witnesses included John's parents, who accepted responsibility for much of his emotional decline, concluding in hindsight that he was more disturbed than they had realized.[4] Concerning the decision to cut off John financially, John's father testified that "In looking back on that, I'm sure it was the greatest mistake in my life. We forced him out at a time when he just couldn't cope. I am the cause of John's tragedy. I wish to God I could trade places with him right now."[1]

Dr. Hopper, the psychiatrist who had treated John and encouraged his parents to emotionally and financially separate from them, testified about his belief that he had misdiagnosed John, whom he now believed was seriously mentally ill.

After showing the jury the video testimony of Jodie Foster, the defense presented expert testimony from their two psychiatrists and a psychologist, all of whom agreed that Hinckley was both psychotic and met criteria for the insanity defense at the time of the crime.

The lead defense expert was William Carpenter, M.D., an expert in schizophrenia from the University of Maryland.[20] Carpenter testified for three days, concluding that John may have had an intellectual understanding of the wrongfulness of the shootings, but due to his mental illness could not emotionally appreciate the acts. Carpenter believed that Hinckley had symptoms consistent with schizophrenia, including poor social interactions, a retreat from reality, suicidally depressed thoughts, and an identity disturbance that caused him to adapt characteristics of fictional individuals such as Robert DeNiro's character Travis Bickle in *Taxi Driver*, and even aspects of John Lennon. One key symptom Carpenter believed John suffered from was delusions. According to Carpenter:

I use the term "delusion" because it will be important to understand that as a technical judgment that I have made that relates to this withdrawal from reality and the development of the relationship, for example, with Jodie Foster, [which] as it developed over time, took on a quality of a delusion and became delusional. So it was not that it was only a fantasy and a fantasy that became an obsession. It was both of things. (Ref. 1, p. 31)

Another symptom of schizophrenia that Carpenter believed Hinckley experienced were ideas of reference, believing that nonspecific events referred specifically to him. An example of this was John's reported belief that Reagan was waving specifically at him shortly before the shooting.

A second psychiatrist, Dr. David Bear, testified that "It is a psychiatric fact that Mr. Hinckley was psychotic."[21] Dr. Bear further testified that Hinckley's obsession with Jodie Foster was a sign of "disordered thought." Bear was critical of Hinckley's psychiatric treatment by fellow defense witness Dr. Hopper, which he described as an "absolute calamity," and he speculated that Hinckley's violence might have been triggered by his prescribed Valium.[22]

In one of the most controversial incidents of the trial, Dr. Bear insisted that he be allowed to testify about the result of the computerized tomography (CAT) scan of Hinckley's brain.[23] This incident was one of the first uses of neuroimaging in an American criminal trial, and the prosecution vigorously opposed the admission of such testimony. After some debate about its admissibility, Dr. Bear testified that Hinckley's CAT scan of the brain was abnormal, showing widened sulci, which he believed was significant because one-third of patients with schizophrenia also have this finding. This opinion was further supported by defense radiologist Marjorie LeMay, who testified that the findings were suggestive of permanent "organic brain disease," but did not make any conclusions on the impact of this finding on his behavior.[24] The impact of the CAT scan was perhaps reduced by defense expert Dr. Daniel R. Weinberger, who admitted that while results like Hinckley's were seen in a lower percentage of normal individuals his age than in those with schizophrenia, most people with such a finding would not be diagnosed with schizophrenia.[25] In contrast to the defense case, the prosecution provided three experts to refute the claim that Hinckley's abnormal CAT scan was significant or diagnostic.[26]

Defense psychologist Ernest Prelinger discussed test results that showed that Hinckley's scores on psychological testing measures were abnormal. Although Hinckley had a measured IQ of 113, the results of his testing on the Rorschach Ink Blot test were consistent with the responses seen in patients with schizophrenia.[27] Prelinger diagnosed Hinckley with major depressive disorder, paranoid personality disorder, and "borderline schizophrenia."[28]

In contrast to the defense case, Dr. Park Dietz, the lead of four prosecution psychiatrists, was of the opinion that Hinckley did not have schizophrenia and did not meet criteria for the insanity defense.[29] Dietz testified that Hinckley did have a personality disorder, but challenged the conclusions of the defense experts with alternative interpretations of the symptoms that they felt were evidence of schizophrenia. Dr. Dietz closely adhered to the strict DSM-III (the American Psychiatric Association's *Diagnostic and Statistical Manual of Mental Disorders*, 3rd edition) criteria for schizophrenia in saying that Hinckley did not have that diagnosis, in contrast to the defense experts, who, although they agreed on the diagnosis "schizophrenia," appeared to approach the term in different ways, using different criteria than those of the DSM-III. Although Dietz's precise use of DSM criteria was in contrast to the looser approach of the defense experts, the relevant issue was whether Hinckley's mental illness was eligible for the insanity defense. The *Brawner* decision affirmed that the relevant definition of a "mental disease or defect" included "any abnormal condition of the mind which substantially affects mental or emotional processes and substantially affects behavior controls."[16]

Although much of the defense testimony focused on Hinckley's psychiatric diagnosis, prosecution testimony heavily focused on the specific evidence of Hinckley's knowledge of the criminality of his actions leading up to and on the day of the crime.[1] The prosecution's approach to this arm of the insanity test looked at the *Brawner* language that the defendant "appreciated the wrongfulness" in the most straightforward way and argued that evidence that Hinckley was aware that his acts were illegal was sufficient. In contrast to the prosecution's approach, the defense interpreted the word "appreciated" to require "not only cognitive awareness" but also "emotional understanding of the consequences of his actions."[18]

Dietz noted that the letter Hinckley wrote Jodie Foster and left in his hotel room "indicated he was going to attempt to get Reagan and he indicates his knowledge that he could be killed by the Secret Service in the attempt. That is an indication that he understood and appreciated the wrongfulness of his plans because the Secret Service might well shoot someone who attempted to kill the President." Dietz opined that further evidence of Hinckley's knowledge of wrongfulness stemmed from his long history of deception of his family and of Dr. Hopper with respect to his stalking of Jodie Foster, his acquisition of guns and ammunition, and of his travel plans.[1]

Dietz also addressed evidence that Hinckley could conform his conduct to the requirements of the law. Dietz noted that despite following President Carter to Dayton and Nashville, Hinckley either chose not to carry a gun or chose not to use one he carried. Dietz noted that Hinckley "thought to himself on those occasions that he could do it another time" and that Hinckley's "ability to control his conduct on those dates to conform to the requirements of the law is part of the background for how it is that we know that he had that ability on March 30th." Hinckley told Dietz that he never experienced "a compulsion or a drive to assassinate or to commit other crimes." Dietz further testified that on the on the day of the attempted assassination, there was abundant evidence of Hinckley's ability to legally conform his conduct to the requirements of the law:

He concealed the weapon ... from people in the hotel lobby, from taxi drivers, from people at the scene at the Hilton, until the moment he chose to draw his weapon. That ability to conceal his weapon is further evidence of his conforming his conduct, that is, he recognized that [w]aving a gun would be behavior likely to attract attention, and did not wave the gun. He concealed it. His ability to wait, when he did not have a clear shot of the President on the President's way into the Hilton is further evidence of his ability to conform his behavior. A man driven, a man out of control, would not have the capacity to wait at that moment for the best shot. (Ref. 1, p. 84)

Another prosecution expert, Dr. Sally Johnson, testified to her opinions developed after fifty-seven separate interviews with Hinckley over a four-month period after the crime.[30] Like Dietz (and in contrast to the defense experts), her testimony focused not only on diagnostic issues but also how Hinckley's thinking and behavior affected his appreciation of the criminality of his actions and his capacity to conform his conduct to the requirements of the law using the specific criteria outlined in *Brawner*.[31]

As the trial concluded, trial Judge Barrington Parker gave the jury very specific instructions for nearly two hours with respect to how to decide the ultimate issue.[32] In his instructions to the Hinckley jurors, Judge Parker stated:

The burden is on the Government to prove beyond a reasonable doubt either that the defendant was not suffering from a mental disease or defect on March 30, 1981, or else that he nevertheless had substantial capacity on that date both to conform his conduct to the requirements of the law and to appreciate the wrongfulness of his conduct. If the Government has not established this to your satisfaction, beyond a reasonable doubt, then you shall bring a verdict of not guilty by reason of insanity. (Ref. 1, p. 114)

After 24 hours of deliberation spread over four days, Hinckley was found not guilty by reason of insanity on June 21, 1982.[33]

Where Are They Now?

After his acquittal, Hinckley was committed to John Howard Pavilion, the maximum-security forensic unit at St. Elizabeth's Hospital in the District of Columbia. In the early years of his hospitalization, he proved to be a challenging patient. His preoccupations with Jodie Foster continued, and he made a number of inappropriate contacts with the media.[34,35] He secretly communicated with *Penthouse* magazine, where he sarcastically noted that he ate "lousy food" and took "delicious medication."[36]

He attempted suicide by overdose in 1983, and due to his inappropriate interactions had restrictions placed on his telephone use and access to the media. He eventually adapted to life at St. Elizabeth's, developing a romantic relationship with Leslie deVeau, a fellow insanity acquittee.[37] By 1984, he unsuccessfully requested to Judge Parker that he be considered for a release hearing.[35] During the 1986 Christmas holiday, the hospital allowed him to leave the facility for a day visit with his family (and the recently released deVeau) at their home.[37] In 1987, the hospital believed that Hinckley had substantially improved, only to discover after Judge Parker ordered a search of his room that he possessed photos of Jodie Foster.[38] The court also learned that Hinckley had written letters to serial killer Ted Bundy and another failed assassin, Charles Manson follower Lynette 'Squeaky' Fromme.[39] More disturbingly, a private journal was found in which Hinckley mocked his psychiatrists. Saying that they knew no more about him than someone reading the newspaper, he called psychiatry a "guessing game" in which he did his "best to keep the fools guessing" about him. Despite this development, the hospital notified the court of a plan to take John on a supervised local outing. The hospital then withdrew the request after they discovered he had attempted to commission a nude drawing of Jodie Foster.[40]

By 1997, Hinckley had improved to the point that he had gone on numerous local excursion outings with recreational therapy and filed a motion for monthly 12-hour unsupervised passes with family. By this time, Hinckley was no longer diagnosed with schizophrenia, instead carrying a diagnosis of "narcissistic personality disorder," as well as diagnoses of "psychotic disorder not otherwise specified, in remission," and "major depressive disorder, in remission."[41] Although the hospital felt he was at low risk under supervision, the government experts were concerned about a period where Hinckley had allegedly become preoccupied with a hospital pharmacist. The court denied the request, ultimately leading to Hinckley appealing the rejection of family passes.[42]

In 1999, the United States Court of Appeals, D.C. Circuit, ruled in favor of Hinckley's challenge to the district court's denial of his extended excursion passes.[42] Over the next 10 years, Hinckley went on an increasing number of family passes without major problems. During this period, Hinckley was started on a low dose of risperidone, an antipsychotic. At a hearing in November 2004, Hinckley's doctors testified that he had been started on this medication to prevent a relapse, despite the fact that his psychotic disorder had reportedly been in remission since 1983 and he had been off of antipsychotics for 12 years prior to the resumption of his medications.[41]

By 2005, Hinckley had been granted overnight passes with his family. Since that time, despite ongoing and consistent opposition by the U.S. Attorney's office, Hinckley's passes gradually increased in length and frequency. Although hospitalized for over thirty years, Hinckley continued to get sensational media attention during release hearings. At a 2008 hearing, a discussion of Hinckley's past and present romantic interests was referred to in a *New York Post* headline as "Nut's Lurid Harem."[43] By 2012, decades of financial support of his legal case by Hinckley's family ended, and his private lawyers of over two decades filed a motion to withdraw as his legal counsel due to unpaid bills.[44]

Hinckley's passes to Williamsburg were closely monitored by the Secret Service and, although he sometimes tested the limits of his pass requirements, he was allowed to continue to have increasingly longer passes. He was noted to have girlfriends, sometimes several at once, but no longer had incidents of inappropriate interactions with hospital staff or celebrities. After the death of his father in 2008, the government raised concerns about the ultimate viability of a plan that increasingly relied on the involvement of Hinckley's elderly mother.[45]

James Brady died in 2014, and the surprising classification of his death as a homicide over three decades after his brain injury raised the possibility that Hinckley would be charged with the murder of James Brady.[46] Ultimately, the new charges were not filed against Hinckley, and his gradual deinstitutionalization plan continued.[47]

Hinckley was finally approved for conditional release from the hospital in 2016 to live with his elderly mother in a gated community in Williamsburg, Virginia.[45] He was discharged from St. Elizabeth's Hospital on September 10, 2016, 35½ years after his arrest for the assassination attempt.[48]

Impact on Practice

Even before the Hinckley verdict there was a national movement to restrict or eliminate the insanity defense in some manner, but the three years following the verdict led to a dramatic increase in laws to change the defense.[49] Like the public reaction to the 1843 acquittal of Daniel M'Naghten, acquitted by reason of insanity for the killing of the private secretary of the British Prime Minister, the Hinckley verdict was met with a huge public and media outcry, leading to intense criticism of the insanity defense and the field of psychiatry.[3,50,51] As noted by attorney Bruce Berner, "Nothing escaped completely unsullied – the jury, psychiatry, the criminal process in general, and, above all, the insanity defense."[52] Hinckley's trial occurred during a period of elevated consciousness of high-profile murders and assassinations, including the assassinations of San Francisco Mayor George Moscone and Supervisor Harvey Milk in November 1978, the attempted assassination of Pope John Paul II in May 1981, the assassination of Egyptian President Anwar Sadat in October 1981, and the shooting of John Lennon in December 1981.[53-56] The publicity surrounding John Lennon shooter Mark Chapman in 1981 involved extensive descriptions of mental illness, although he ultimately chose to plead guilty. The San Francisco "White Night Riots" in May 1979 resulted from an outcry over the successful use of a diminished-capacity defense by San Francisco Supervisor Dan White, who assassinated Mayor George Moscone and fellow Supervisor Harvey Milk in 1978.[57]

Part of the outcry over Hinckley's verdict was driven by the public's incorrect perception about the frequency of the use and success of the insanity defense. According to Steadman, "The public's perceptions appear to be heavily influenced by selective news reports which are limited to a small atypical segment of cases involving psychiatric testimony for bizarre or mass murders and assassinations."[58] Many of the cases that led to these perceptions involved defendants with whom the insanity defense was neither considered nor warranted.

Misconceptions about the insanity defense were clearly present in many people's opinions about the Hinckley verdict, and a majority of respondents in one survey reported they had a belief that Hinckley was not insane (despite not knowing the legal standard for insanity), a lack of trust of the psychiatric testimony (despite at least some experts agreeing with the view that Hinckley was criminally responsible), and a belief that an insanity acquittal was a "loophole."[59] Further, some of the outrage was driven by the belief that Hinckley's acquittal meant that he would escape any consequences for his actions and be quickly released. The headline of the *New York Post* following the verdict was "Hinckley Beats Rap," and other news sources perpetuated the idea that an insanity acquittal was an escape from significant consequences.[3] Although the testimony of the prosecution experts was not inconsistent with the public sentiment, psychiatrists as a group took much of the blame for the verdict. Columnist George Will made one of the harshest attacks on the field, saying "psychiatry as practiced by some of today's itinerant experts-for-hire is this century's alchemy ... Some of today's rent-a-psychiatry is charlatanism laced with cynicism," and he hoped that "the verdict will serve the social good only if it generates disgust with the incompatible marriage of psychiatry and law."[60]

As discussed above, Hinckley was tried under what was the most common insanity standard at the time, referred to in federal courts as the Brawner Rule, from the 1972 case *United States v. Brawner*.[16] Because the Brawner Rule itself was a variant of the model insanity definition developed in the 1962 Model Penal Code by the American Law Institute, the rule is more commonly known as the ALI Standard.[61] Following the Hinckley verdict, several changes were made that affected the laws regarding insanity in the federal court as well as in multiple states.

Federal Law Changes

The outcry over the Hinckley verdict led to rapid action by the U.S. Congress. This was not a new issue: just days before Reagan's shooting, Senator Orrin Hatch introduced a bill to eliminate the insanity defense in the Federal Criminal Code.[62] This bill (along with six others) were the subject of posttrial Senate hearings that started three days after Hinckley's acquittal, entitled "Limiting the Insanity Defense."[2] Ultimately, Congress passed the Insanity Defense Reform Act of 1984

(IDRA), which narrowed the federal standard to a stricter definition, more in line with the traditional M'Naghten approach.[63] The act had several elements intended to make it more difficult to succeed with an insanity defense. The new law eliminated the volitional prong of the insanity test, placing it philosophically more in line with the landmark 1843 English M'Naghten case in that it continued to allow the verdict only if the defendant "was unable to appreciate the nature and quality or the wrongfulness of his acts."[17] In addition, the Reform Act added the term "severe" to the requirement of the defendant having a "mental disease or defect." Although the use of the word "severe" would suggest a desire to exclude certain psychiatric disorders from consideration, the act did not elaborate further, leaving it to the discretion of courts to determine if a specific disorder was "severe" and thus eligible for the defense.

Another element of the IDRA prohibited "ultimate issue testimony" by expert witnesses, an issue previously allowed to some degree under the Brawner Rule.[64] This language addressed the perception that the opinions of experts usurped the authority of the judge or jurors to be the ultimate deciders on how to apply the legal language to the defendant's case. By restricting ultimate issue testimony, the psychiatrist would not be allowed to conclude if the defendant met the legal criteria for insanity, instead being limited to a discussion of the psychiatric condition of the defendant.[65]

Finally, the IRDA ensured that (as with the majority of state jurisdictions), the burden to prove that the defendant was insane was on the defense, rather than allowing the philosophically more challenging requirement that the prosecution prove that the defendant was not insane. In addition to changing the burden of proof, the law also raised the level of certainty required to convince the trier of fact that the defendant was insane. By the standard under which Hinckley was tried, the prosecution was required to prove sanity to the same level as any other element of a criminal case: beyond a reasonable doubt. A beyond-a-reasonable-doubt standard requires the prosecution to prove the elements of a case sufficiently strong enough to convince a reasonable person to a degree of very high certainty. A second standard of proof is called "preponderance of the evidence." This standard, used in most cases of civil litigation, only requires that the issue being argued is more likely than not to be true. While some insanity standards only require that a defendant proves insanity by this standard, Congress opted for the stricter "clear and convincing evidence" standard, which required a greater level of certainty than "preponderance" but less than the "beyond a reasonable doubt" standard. Thus, by both shifting the burden of proof (to the defendant) and changing the standard of proof, the IDRA made it substantially more difficult for defendants to prove that they meet the criteria for insanity.[2]

Although much of the debate about the insanity defense focused on the standard used to define insanity, the change in the burden of proof was the issue more likely to have impacted the insanity verdict in the Hinckley case. In the congressional hearings held following the verdict, Congress called five jurors from the Hinckley trial to testify.[66] With little outcry over the potential implications on the justice system by demanding congressional testimony by jurors who made a lawful but unpopular verdict, the jurors testified that their verdict was strongly affected by the judge's instructions, despite the impression of some senators that the jurors simply did not understand the complex legal issues they were required to address. As Judge Parker instructed the jury that the prosecution bore the burden of proving Hinckley's sanity "beyond a reasonable doubt," the jury was forced to consider whether the unquestionably aberrant behavior of Hinckley and his prior history of psychiatric treatment were sufficient evidence to doubt his sanity, even if he did not clearly meet the Brawner Rule standard. Had the defense been required to prove Hinckley's insanity, the outcome might well have been different, and many analysts consider this issue to be the true deciding factor with respect to the acquittal.[1]

Like many laws written in response to an infamous criminal case, much of the intent of the IDRA would presumably be to have prevented the Hinckley acquittal if the law had existed prior to the case. Although the shift of the burden of proof away from the prosecution might have altered the outcome of the case, it is less clear how adding the word "serious" to "mental disease or defect" would have affected the outcome. The prosecution experts certainly articulated a depiction of Hinckley's illness as one primarily explained by a narcissistic personality and social ineptitude, but the defense's position that Hinckley suffered from schizophrenia and that his preoccupation with Jodie Foster was evidence of a delusional system would likely satisfy most observers' conception of a "severe" mental illness.

State Law Changes

The Insanity Defense Reform Act was restricted to insanity pleas in federal district courts; it did not even apply to the bulk of criminal cases tried in the District of Columbia, under the jurisdiction of its own court system for nonfederal cases since the early 1970s. Within the first few years, many state legislatures acted to initiate reforms in the wake of the Hinckley verdict. Common changes included creating an additional alternative verdict called "guilty but mentally ill," shifting the burden of proof to the defense, and in the case of Utah, eliminating the defense completely.[49]

Ironically, one of the places least affected by the Reform Act was the city in which the crime took place. The majority of criminal cases in the District of Columbia are tried in D.C. Superior Court, the equivalent of a state court system. At the time of Hinckley's trial, D.C. Superior Court used a modified form of the Brawner Rule, but unlike the federal courts, it specifically placed the burden of proof in insanity cases on the defense by a preponderance of the evidence. Despite the fact that Congress retains veto power over laws passed by the Council of the District of Columbia, there were no legislative changes to the nonfederal insanity standard in the District of Columbia in reaction to the Hinckley verdict.

Despite the attempt to restrict the insanity defense, many of the reforms were of limited effectiveness. States that eliminated the insanity defense often simply offset the loss of that option by having more defendants found incompetent to stand trial or other strategies that ultimately diverted them into the mental health system.[49,67] Elimination of the volitional prong in the Insanity Defense Reform Act and a number of state laws proved to be less relevant than initially perceived.[63] Elimination of the ability of psychiatrists to testify on the "ultimate issue" was also criticized. Slovenko described this rule by saying it was "unduly restrictive, difficult to apply and generally served only to deprive the trier of fact of useful information."[68] As Buchanan noted, restrictions to ultimate issue testimony have proven a challenge to many courts, as "its spirit runs contrary to the principle whereby helpfulness is the first criterion determining the admissibility of expert evidence."[69]

REFERENCES

1. Bonnie RJ, Jeffries JC, Low PW: *A Case Study in the Insanity Defense: The Trial of John W. Hinckley, Jr.* New York/St. Paul, MN: Foundation Press; Thomson/West, 2000
2. U.S. Congress. Senate. Committee on the Judiciary. *Limiting the Insanity Defense: Hearings before the Subcommittee on Criminal Law of the Committee on the Judiciary.* 97th Cong., 2nd sess., Washington, D.C.: U.S. G.P.O, 1982
3. Bloom JD, Dick DW: Commentary: 1982 was AAPL's year of living dangerously. *J Am Acad Psych Law.* 36: 175, 2008
4. Hinckley J, Hinckley JA, Sherrill E: *Breaking Points.* Grand Rapids, MI: Chosen Books, 1985
5. Caplan L: *The Insanity Defense and the Trial of John W. Hinckley, Jr.* Boston: Godine, 1984
6. Taylor S: Witness says Hinckley trailed actress with gun. *New York Times,* May 26, 1982, p. 19

7. Thompson R: Screen writer: *Taxi Driver*'s Paul Schrader. *Film Comment.* 12: 6–19, 1976

8. Schrader P: *Collected Screenplays*. London: Faber, 2002

9. Prosecutive Report: John Warnock Hinckley, Jr. Attempted Assassination of Ronald Reagan, President of the United States March 30, 1981, 1981, pp. 1–91. Available at: https://vault.fbi.gov/president-ronald-reagan-assassination-attempt. Accessed Jan. 29, 2018

10. Ranney A: *The American Elections of 1980*. Washington, D.C.: American Enterprise Institute Press, 1981

11. Montgomery PL: Suspect in Lennon's slaying put under suicide watch. *New York Times*, Dec. 11, 1980, p. 40

12. Hasson J: John W. Hinckley Jr. rushed out of the courtroom. UPI. May 12, 1982. Available at: www.upi.com/Archives/1982/05/12/John-W-Hinckley-Jr-rushed-out-of-the-courtroom/8690390024000/. Accessed Jan. 29, 2018

13. Taubman P: Suspect got idea some time ago, investigators say. *New York Times*, Apr. 2, 1982, p. 1

14. Pasewark RA: Insanity plea: A review of the research literature. *J Psychiatry & L* 9:357, 1981

15. Banks CP: *Judicial Politics in the D.C. Circuit Court*. Baltimore: JHU Press, 1999

16. *United States v. Brawner*, 471 F.2d 969 (D.C. Cir. 1972)

17. M'Naghten's Case. Eng Rep 8:718, 1843

18. Fuller VJ: United States v. John W. Hinckley Jr. (1982). *Loy L A L Rev.* 33: 699 (2000)

19. Hevesi D: Vincent Fuller, 75, lawyer who won Hinckley case. *New York Times*, Jul. 29, 2006. Available at: www.nytimes.com/2006/07/29/us/29fuller.html. Accessed Jan. 30, 2018

20. Pear R: Prosecutors hire 3 psychiatrists to study Hinckley. *New York Times*, Jun. 22, 1981, p. 16

21. Taylor S: Psychiatrists worry over image in Hinckley trial. *New York Times*, May 24, 1982, p. 27

22. Taylor S: Hinckley treatments termed 'absolute calamity.' *New York Times*, May 19, 1982, p. 22

23. Taylor S: Judge rebukes Hinckley witness over CAT Scan. *New York Times*, May 20, 1982, p. 45

24. Taylor S: CAT scans said to show shrunken Hinckley brain. *New York Times*, Jun. 2, 1982, p. 95

25. Altman LK: Limits of CAT scans cited by physician. *New York Times*, May 20, 1982, p. 45

26. Taylor S: Hinckley's brain is termed normal. *New York Times*, Jun. 4, 1982, p. 21

27. Kiernan LA: Psychologist says Hinckley's tests similar to those of the severely ill. *Washington Post*, May 21, 1982. Available at: www.washingtonpost.com/archive/politics/1982/05/21/psychologist-says-hinckleys-tests-similar-to-those-of-the-severely-ill/86c0da1a-74f1-4d2e-929d-08ba85dd8f19/?utm_term=.8de222c6621d. Accessed Jan. 30, 2018

28. Taylor S: Psychologist sees split in Hinckley mind and emotions in shootings. *New York Times*, May 22, 1982, p. 16

29. Taylor S: Hinckley described as sane when he shot Reagan. *New York Times*, Jun. 5, 1982, p. 9

30. Psychiatrist says Hinckley had a sense of reality. *New York Times*, Jun. 13, 1982, p. 32 Available at: https://timesmachine.nytimes.com/timesmachine/1982/06/13/issue.html

31. Closing Arguments, United States of America v. John W. Hinckley, Jr. (1982). Available at: http://rawhidedown.com/wordpress/wp-content/themes/Rawhide Down/PDFs/ClosingArguments.pdf Accessed Jan. 29, 2018

32. Taylor S: Hinckley jury weighs verdict in shooting of Reagan and 3. *New York Times*, Jun. 19, 1982, p. 21

33. Taylor S: Hinckley is cleared but is held insane in Reagan attack. *New York Times*, Jun. 22, 1982, p.1

34. Associated Press: Hinckley says Reagan 'Is the Best President.' *New York Times*, Oct. 5, 1981. Available at: www.nytimes.com/1981/10/05/us/hinckley-says-reagan-is-the-best-president.html. Accessed Jan. 30, 2018.

35. Taylor S: Hinckley tells court 'I Am Ready Now' to press for release. *New York Times*, Jul. 28, 1984, p. 1

36. Penthouse Interview: [of] John W. Hinckley, Jr., in *Penthouse*, v. 14, March 1983

37. Walsh E: Strange love, *New Yorker*, Apr. 5, 1999

38. Glaberson W: Hospital reverses itself on Hinckley visits. *New York Times*, Jun. 29, 2000, p. 18

39. Noble KB: Hinckley is told to surrender all correspondence. *New York Times*, Apr. 15, 1987, p. 19

40. Denial of Hinckley outing linked to Foster sketch. *New York Times*, Aug. 21, 1988, p. 22

41. *U.S. v. Hinckley*, United States District Court, District of Columbia, 346 F. Supp.2d 155 (2004)

42. *U.S. v. Hinckley*, United States Court of Appeals, District of Columbia Circuit, 163 F.3d 647 (1999)

43. Gittens H: Nut's lurid harem. *New York Post*, Jun. 19, 2008. Available at http://nyp.st/1coL3xf. Accessed Jan. 30, 2018

44. Associated Press: Hinckley's lawyers, unpaid, want off case. *New York Times*, Aug. 24, 2012, p. 13

45. *U.S. v. Hinckley*, United States District Court, District of Columbia, 200 F. Supp.3d 1(2016)

46. Corasaniti N: Coroner is said to rule James Brady's death a homicide, 33 years after a shooting. *New York Times*, Aug. 8, 2014, p. 11

47. Hermann P: John Hinckley won't face murder charge in death of James Brady, prosecutors say. *Washington Post*, Jan. 2, 2015. Available at: www.washingtonpost.com/local/crime/prosecutors-will-not-charge-hinckley-with-murder-in-death-of-james-brady/2015/01/02/67de0024-929a-11e4-a900-9960214d4cd7_story.html?utm_term=.5f714f22cbc1. Accessed Jan. 30, 2018

48. Boburg S: Would-be Reagan assassin John Hinckley Jr. is freed after 35 years. *Washington Post*, Sep. 10, 2016. Available at: http://wapo.st/2c09FWb?tid=ss_tw-bottom&utm_term=.fd496ab53983. Accessed Jan. 30, 2018

49. Steadman HJ: *Before and after Hinckley: Evaluating Insanity Defense Reform*. New York: Guilford Press, 1993

50. Clarke JW: *On Being Mad or Merely Angry: John W. Hinckley, Jr., and Other Dangerous People.* Princeton, NJ: Princeton University Press, 1990
51. Sharf BF: Send in the clowns: The image of psychiatry during the Hinckley trial. *J Commun.* 36: 80–93, 1986
52. Berner B: The insanity defense: Guilty by reason of Hinckley?, *The Cresset,* Sept. 1982, p.7
53. Arraignment delayed in slaying of Mayor Moscone. *New York Times,* Nov 30, 1978, p. 20
54. Montgomery PL: Lennon murder suspect preparing insanity defense. *New York Times,* 1981, p. 12
55. Apple RW: Pope is shot in car in Vatican Square; surgeons term condition; Turk, an escaped murderer, is seized 'guarded'; made threat in '79. *New York Times,* May 14, 1981, p. 1
56. Kifner J: Sadat assassinated at army parade as men amid ranks fire into stands; Vice president affirms "all treaties." *New York Times,* Oct 07, 1981, p. 1
57. Lindsey R: Dan White, killer of San Francisco mayor, a suicide. *New York Times,* Oct 22, 1985, p. 18
58. Steadman HJ, Cocozza JJ: Selective reporting and the public's misconceptions of the criminally insane. *Public Opinion Quarterly* 41:523–33, 1977
59. Hans VP, Slater D: John Hinckley, Jr. and the insanity defense: The public's verdict. *Public Opinion Quarterly* 47:202, 1983
60. Will G: Insanity and success. *Washington Post,* Jun 23, 1982. Available at www.washingtonpost.com/archive/politics/1982/06/23/insanity-and-success/17aa333d-02c3-4a02-8241-cc9fd9645580/?tid=ss_mail&utm_term=.89865647fed5. Accessed Jan. 30, 2018
61. The American Law Institute's insanity test. *Duke Law Journal* 1959: 317–23, 1959
62. S.818 A bill to amend title 18 to limit the insanity defense, in Congressional Record, 1981, pp. 1–4
63. Finkel NJ: The insanity defense reform act of 1984: Much ado about nothing. *Behav Sci Law* 7:403–19, 1989
64. Diamond BL: From Durham to Brawner, a futile journey. *Wash ULQ:* 109, 1973
65. Slovenko R: Commentary: Deceptions to the rule on ultimate issue testimony. *J Am Acad Psychiatry Law* 34:22–5, 2006
66. Taylor S: 5 Hinckley jurors testify in senate. *New York Times,* Jun 25, 1982, p. 10
67. Buitendorp RD: Statutory lesson from Big Sky country on abolishing the insanity defense, *A. Val UL Rev* 30:965, 1995
68. Slovenko R: Insanity defense in the wake of the Hinckley trial, *The. Rutgers LJ* 14:373, 1982
69. Buchanan A: Psychiatric evidence on the ultimate issue. *J Am Acad Psychiatry Law* 34:14–21, 2006

13   Conclusion

Peter Ash

Litigation in mental health cases from 1970 to the turn of the millennium markedly changed how psychiatry is practiced. Psychiatric inpatients in 1970 lacked many of the protections we take for granted today. They had far less ability to control their treatments than they were to have by 2000, due in large part to the changes wrought by the legal cases discussed in this book. Back in 1970, psychiatric patients were yet to obtain the clinical information needed to give informed consent (*Canterbury v. Spence*, 1972); minimum standards for humane inpatient treatment (*Wyatt v. Stickney*, 1972); right to liberty that would block long-term involuntary commitment justified by a vague need for treatment (*O'Connor v. Donaldson*, 1975); a clear right to refuse treatment (*Rogers v. Commissioner of Department of Mental Health*, 1983; *Cruzan v. Director, Missouri Department of Health*, 1990); a guarantee of confidentiality of their statements in therapy (*Jaffee v. Redmond*, 1996); or a right to be released to an appropriate community setting when they no longer required inpatient services (*Olmstead v. L. C.*, 1999). The extent to which children shared these benefits was unclear (*Parham, v. J. R.*, 1979). Outpatients also benefited from these added protections, and gained further protection from exploitation by their treaters (*Roy v. Hartogs*, 1976). Some of these key benefits, such as informed consent and the right to refuse treatment were not limited to mental health patients, but extended to all medical patients. Members of the public gained additional protections from that small minority of patients with mental illness who were potentially dangerous (*Tarasoff v. Regents of the University of California*, 1976), and the insanity defense was reexamined (*U.S. v. Hinckley*, 1982).

Why did all these changes happen when they did? Appelbaum[1] points out that three requirements for legal changes all came together in the 1960s: a public perception that change is required, a legal theory to justify the change, and a group of legal actors interested in taking on these issues in the courts. In the 1960s, psychiatric practice came

158

under increasing criticism from both within the profession and from outside. By the late 1960s, law journal articles on mental illness tended to be anti-psychiatry and opposed to psychiatric medications.[2] Public concerns about inpatient psychiatry were highlighted by the success of Ken Kesey's *One Flew Over the Cuckoo's Nest*,[3] first published in 1962, and later adapted into a Broadway play (1963) and an Oscar-winning movie (1975). Interest in greater civil rights can be traced to the civil rights movement for rights of African Americans in the 1950s and 1960s, which was followed by a focus on the civil rights of other groups, such as persons with disabilities and even criminal defendants. The courts were instrumental in expanding the rights of criminal defendants through a number of decisions, which included finding a right to an attorney for indigent defendants (1963),[4] requiring defendants to be advised of their *Miranda* rights at the time of arrest (1966),[5] and increasing due-process protections for juvenile delinquents (1967).[6] The civil rights cases led to increased publications about civil rights issues in the legal literature and were the training ground for young, idealistic attorneys interested in these issues. In the early 1960s, the federally funded Legal Services Program (see Chapter 4) established legal services for the poor and led to civil rights attorneys looking for clients. Legal groups were formed to focus on mental health issues: the Mental Health Law Project in Washington, D.C, in 1968,[1] and the Bazelon Center for Mental Health Law in 1972. Within the mental health professions, forensic psychiatry and psychology became more organized disciplines with the establishment of both the American Academy of Psychiatry and the Law and the American Psychology-Law Society in 1969.

The problems of the litigants whose stories comprise this book became focal points for these forces for change. All their cases were decided in the 30 years between 1970 and 2000. Since 2000, although there have been landmark cases of relevance to forensic psychiatrists in such areas as sexual harassment, disability, the death penalty, civil commitment of sexual offenders, and mental health treatment of prisoners, few legal cases have had such a concentrated effect on how psychiatry and psychology are practiced. This is not to say that all the problems identified in the cases in this book have been solved. In inpatient practice, the question of how to treat civilly committed patients who are not an immediate danger to others but who refuse medication remains unresolved in many jurisdictions. Although procedures for medicating patients who refuse treatment have been developed in some states[7] and for patients in prison,[8] in many states patients who refuse medication go untreated.[9]

Although state courts have continued to work through many of the issues discussed in this book, the legal changes affecting medicine since the mid-1990s have mostly resulted from legislative action at the national level. The Health Insurance Portability and Accountability Act (HIPAA) of 1996 provides federal minimum standards for the confidentiality of medical and mental health records. In the early 21st century, the focus shifted to questions about the distribution of healthcare benefits. The Mental Health Parity and Addiction Equity Act of 2008 requires most group health plans to provide mental health benefits commensurate with physical benefits, a long-sought goal of the mental health professions but one that has yet to be fully implemented. The Affordable Care Act, passed in 2010, extended insurance benefits to many who were previously uninsured and helped fuel a national debate over how healthcare should be financed. The outcome of that debate will likely affect the structure and quality of mental health services for years to come. As the debate unfolds, practices will be further refined through newly emerging case law revolving around stories as yet untold.

REFERENCES

1. Appelbaum PS: *Almost a Revolution: Mental Health Law and the Limits of Change*. New York: Oxford University Press, 1994
2. Brakel SJ, Davis JM: Taking harms seriously: Involuntary mental patients and the right to refuse treatment. *Indiana Law Review* 25:429–73, 1991
3. Kesey K: *One Flew over the Cuckoo's Nest*. New York: Viking Press & Signet Books, 1962
4. *Gideon v. Wainwright*, 372 U.S. 335, 83 S. Ct. 792 (1963)
5. *Miranda v. Arizona*, 384 U.S. 436, 86 S. Ct. 1602 (1966)
6. *In re Gault*, 387 U.S. 1 (1967)
7. *Rennie v. Klein*, 720 F.2d 266, 653 F.2d (3rd Cir. 1983)
8. *Washington v. Harper*, 494 U.S. 210, 110 S. Ct. 1028 (1990)
9. *Hargrave v. Vermont*, 340 F.3d 27 (2003)

Index

161